Upon
the Mercy
of
Government

by KIERAN SHEEDY

*The story of the surrender, transportation and imprisonment of
Michael Dwyer and his Wicklow comrades,
and their subsequent lives in New South Wales*

Radio Telefís Éireann
1988

To the memory of my grandfather Patrick Sheedy who,
following the eviction of his father and family from their farm
in Co Clare, made his way to Australia and joined in the rush for gold
before returning to his native parish where he entertained (bored?) the
locals with tales of the Australian bush,
earning himself, in the process, the nickname of
Wagga.

FOREWORD

The genesis of this book began for me with a mild curiosity which developed, over a period of time, into an increasing interest and, finally, into near obsession. In common with many generations of schoolchildren, I had learned T.D. Sullivan's poem about Michael Dwyer's escape from the cottage in Derrynamuck and I was also aware that following his surrender he had been transported to Botany Bay where he had ironically become a policeman and died there. With this rather simplistic (but often quoted) resume of Michael Dwyer's later life, I began my research, but having read Charles Dickson's admirable book on Dwyer, which was published in 1943 but which deals mainly with his early life and his Wicklow campaign. I decided to concentrate on the period of Dwyer's life from his surrender onwards and the trail, both hot and cold, led me from Wicklow to Dublin, London and Herefordshire, and in New South Wales from the Mitchell Library and City Archives in Sydney to the cemetery in Bungendore. The positive response to a three-part Bi-Centennial documentary series which was broadcast on RTE Radio 1 in January 1988 gave me the necessary spur to develop the material into book form which, although my lines of communication with Australia were finally stretched to the limit, will, I trust, make a contribution to a greater understanding of the history of both Ireland and Australia during the early part of the nineteenth century.

Kieran Sheedy
June 1988.

LIST OF ILLUSTRATIONS

Page

Front cover illustration: This fanciful picture of Michael Dwyer appeared in 'Walker's Hibernian Magazine' in 1803 before his surrender.

Back cover illustration: View of the entrance to Cork Harbour from an etching made in 1809.

PART ONE

1

Despite rumours that it might be further delayed, the East India fleet of the British navy received orders to sail from Cork Harbour on the 28th of August 1805. The imposing fleet was already in place; at its head were the ships of the line the Terrible (74 guns), the Diadem (64 guns), and the flagship of the convoy the Bellequia (64 guns). Moored at the entrance to the harbour, they were further reinforced by the frigates Leda and Narcissus; behind them were positioned the main bulk of the convoy consisting of thirty eight transport ships and nineteen East Indiaman and tagging along for protection, for part of the journey at least, were two convict ships bound for the penal colony of New South Wales - the William Pitt carrying female prisoners from London and the Tellicherry with its human cargo of Irish prisoners, one hundred and thirty men and thirty six women. In addition there were on board five Wicklow men, veterans of the 1798 Rising who, having finally surrendered, had been imprisoned in Kilmainham Jail in Dublin for the previous eighteen months. They had not been brought to trial but had, under some duress, finally agreed terms with the Government of Ireland in Dublin Castle which resulted in their exile to New South Wales, not however as convicts, but with the entitlements of free men.

These Wicklow men were Michael Dwyer, their leader, his first cousin Hugh Vesty Byrne, Martin Burke, John Mernagh and Arthur Devlin. Accompanying them also on board the Tellicherry were Michael Dwyer's wife Mary and Hugh Byrne's pregnant wife Sarah with two of their young children. Martin Burke's wife Rachel did not accompany her husband and both John Mernagh and Arthur Devlin were single. But despite having, finally, negotiated favourable terms of exile, there was double disappointment for Dwyer because he and his wife Mary had decided to leave behind in Ireland their four young children on the understanding that they would be sent out to join them at an unspecified future date. But Micheal Dwyer had been secretly promised also, at the time of his surrender, that he with his wife and children, would be exiled to the United States of America. He had clung to this belief resolutely during his term of imprisonment in Kilmainham jail and still felt betrayed at what he considered a flagrant breach of his surrender terms.

The prospect of starting a new life, even as a free person, in the dreaded colony of New South Wales had the hallmarks of a life sentence about it; there was always a ring of finality attached to transportation to Botany Bay as it was highly unlikely that they would ever be allowed to return to Ireland again nor could they be even certain that the promise to send out their children would be honoured. For the four other Wicklow men, however, the terms of exile were far better than they could have reasonably hoped for. Hugh and Sarah Byrne had decided to leave their eldest son Philip, aged eight, behind, but had brought with them their second son Michael, aged five and their two year old daughter Rose, and for the pregnant Sarah Byrne there was still the added hazard of having to give birth during the voyage. But at least they were still alive, they were together; they did not have to wear the convicts chains or have their heads shaved; they would not be confined like cattle to the hold of the ship; there was unconfirmed talk that the colony in New South Wales was fast developing in terms of its economy and agriculture and it was now even publishing its own newspaper; their status as freemen would entitle them to grants of land on their arrival; there was every prospect that they could settle down to a normal life in the colony and give their families security and an opportunity of future prosperity which would be denied them in their own native land.

Michael Dwyer and his comrades were born into the final quarter of the eighteenth centry in Ireland when there were signs, at last, that the stultifying and repressive period of the Penal Laws against the majority Catholic population and Northern Dissenters was waning. The economic sanctions imposed on the Protestant merchant classes by Britain were finally being opposed and hopes of a better way of life for the dispossessed began to permeate even into the fastnesses of the Wicklow mountains. The writing of the expatriate Englishman Thomas Pâine, incorporated into the American Constitution, had led indirectly to limited demands; initially among the Protestant business classes, for greater economic freedom. The Irish Volunteers were formed and Grattan's Parliament soon held out the prospect of, at least, minor reforms. But, as the last decade of the eighteenth century progressed, the euphoria, which at one stage briefly seemed to unite the whole country, quickly evaporated. The issue of Catholic Emancipation revealed the impotence of Grattan's Parliament and, as the awesome power of the masses let loose in the excesses of the French Revolution became apparent, and as copies of Thomas Paine's latest pamphlet 'The Rights of Man' began to flood the country, the frightened ruling classes hastened to batten down their traditional power bases. The Society of United Irishmen, which Michael Dwyer and his comrades joined in their native Wicklow, came under suspicion; help was sought from France but the French fleet was unable to land at Bantry Bay and in 1798 the local populace, goaded into rebellion by a savage and undisciplined military operation, following some initial successes was finally crushed at Vinegar Hill in Co. Wexford.

Michael Dwyer, who had gained the rank of Captain in his local unit of the United Irishmen, impatient for action in

Billy Byrne pictured beside the ruins of John Mernagh's house in Glenmalure, Co. Wicklow. His grandfather gave the house to the Mernaghs following their eviction from The Glen of Imaal.

The granite stone monument in Glenmalure, Co. Wicklow commemorating Michael Dwyer and Fiach Mac Hugh O'Byrne.

Wicklow, set off on his own, joined in the Wexford campaign and fought in several battles and skirmishes including the defeat at Vinegar Hill. Martin Burke also fought in Wexford, Arthur Devlin and John Mernagh were both active in Wicklow and a wounded Hugh Byrne was captured and sentenced to death but managed to escape from prison as did Martin Burke. They would all have availed of a general amnesty later that year but for the opposition of some of the fanatical members of local yeomanry who threatened and often carried out the murders of those who had returned to their homes having supposedly been granted immunity by the amnesty. Arthur Devlin, in the company of his brother, left the country and joined up with an army regiment in England but Dwyer, Burke, Byrne and Mernagh set up a guerilla band in the mountains. Following the surrender of the resourceful Protestant leader Joseph Holt, who was transported to New South Wales in 1800, Michael Dwyer took command of the remaining forces and with skill, imagination and daring, led his small guerilla band which harried both militia and yeomanry forces and became the sole defenders of the local population matching each reprisal raid and house burning.

But, as the years passed, and a more stable situation developed again in Wicklow, by the year 1803 they had spent five years in the mountains and while they still retained the respect of the local population they were now becoming somewhat of an anachronism and had to resort to occasional robberies and to the levying of protection money on local mills and businesses to provide for themselves and their families. This is how Dwyer himself recounted his way of life in these latter years:

"The way I avoided being captured was this; I never slept in a house always either in a hiding place or in the open air, and by wrapping myself in such covering as I carried I was always able to do so even in the severest weather. I always had a store of bacon and such of provisions in some concealment to which I never ventured but in the case of absolute necessity. If it snowed I made my way to this place of concealment while the snow was falling still defacing the marks of my feet as I went. While the snow lay on the ground I never moved. At other times I was accustomed to go to any cottage always without any previous notice, with a cocked pistol in my hand I made the owner to give me full intelligence of all that was passing in the country and to give me such provisions as the house could afford and as I chose to demand. Having done so I went off first saying to the owner of the house, for his own safety and give immediate information of what he had done. Before any pursuit could be made and by then I would be seven or so miles off. I would live in this manner for many years. For firearms I prefer to use a musket by day and a blunderbuss by night".

By 1803 their numbers had now dwindled to a mere handful but the Government in Dublin, with the prospect of a renewed war with France looming, could not afford to take the chance of Dwyer linking up with the French in such a contingency and continued to send troops down to Wicklow to try and capture him. Moreover, new roads were cut through the mountains, and near Dwyer's birthplace at the top of the Glen of Imail a new barracks was built at Leitrim which would have a commanding view of the valley and was strategically positioned to hamper his movements. In addition the local corps of Yeomanry from Saunders Grove and Talbotstown still made occasional forays in search of him but these searches tended to be half-hearted to say the least, and seemed to be chiefly motivated by the expenses which they received for their efforts. Attempting the capture of Dwyer had become a growth industry with them and his actual capture would have brought a valuable source of income to an end.

Michael Dwyer's own position was further complicated by the fact that he had married a local girl, Mary Doyle, in the Autumn of 1798. Three children had also been born to them despite their long periods of separation and Mary Dwyer was expecting a fourth child. As for the others Hugh Byrne had married Sarah before 1798 when he was working in a local brewery in Rathdrum and three children had been born to them.

Martin Burke was a member of one of the best known families in Imail and one Government informer at the time claimed that Dwyer would not have remained free for five years but for the help of the Burkes. It was also reputed that, in 1802, Martin Burke had offered to leave the country and join a regiment abroad but without success. John Mernagh from Glenmalure was a giant of a man six feet two inches tall and weighing sixteen stone, described as the finest man in the country although his face was slightly disfigured from an attack of the 'cow pocks'. His family had been evicted from their farm in Imail and were taken in by a Charles Byrne in the townland of Bolenaskea in Glenmalure who gave the Mernaghs the use of his old house.

Over the years many overtures had been made to Dwyer in particular to persuade him to surrender but Dwyer, not being willing to leave behind either his young wife and family or even to go into exile taking them with him, never gave serious consideration to these offers. He still retained the somewhat unreal hope that one day the authorities would forget about him and that, eventually, he would be able to resume normal life as a mountain tenant farmer. In the meantime, he felt confident that he would continue to evade capture and remain hidden in the mountains which he knew so well. But in July 1803 an event was to take place in Dublin which, although he took no active part in it, was to become the catalyst which, in its aftermath, would spell disaster for Dwyer and his followers. That event was the rebellion of Robert Emmet.

2

Alexander Marsden, the Under Secretary of the Irish administration based in Dublin Castle, was in a mellow mood as he sat down to write to his immediate superior, the Chief Secretary William Wickham, on March 16th 1803. The St. Patrick's Day celebrations were already under way in the city and Marsden had enjoyed a goodish dinner accompanied no doubt, by the best of wines, claret and Irish whiskey. He was, therefore, in a somewhat expansive mood as he wrote what was virtually a daily report to Wickham: 'Many of my letters to you are written after dinner, and you know that in Ireland makes a serious difference'. The Chief Secretary William Wickham knew, only too well, that affairs were carried out differently in Ireland. Although he had spent many years on the Continent, mainly based in Geneva, during the previous decade, ostensibly as a diplomat but in reality as Britain's chief spy, all of this expertise had still left him unprepared for the vagaries of Irish politics. In exasperation, he had written to the Prime Minister Addington in London claiming 'that the system of jobbing and supplanting and calumniating each other is so deeply rooted that I am bound constantly to mistrust the very best'.

The relationship between Wickham and his Under Secretary Marsden was a relatively cordial one. The Dublin-born

Alexander Marsden was the son of one of the city's most prosperous merchants and a founder member of the National Bank of Ireland. He had been educated in Trinity College, Dublin and had practised as barrister for fourteen years before succeeding Cooke as Under Secretary, following the recent passing of the Act of Union between Ireland and Great Britain which resulted in the dissolution of the Irish Parliament in Dublin. Marsden's immediate task was to administer the various promises, emoluments and financial bribes which had been scattered around like confetti to help persuade the members of the Irish Parliament to vote themselves out of existence. But Marsden was also responsible for security in the country and he inherited a large network of spies which had been built up during the period of the 1798 Rising. There was never a shortage of individuals of all classes and religious persuasions who were more than willing to help themselves to some of the generous secret service funds by giving a variety of largely useless information to Dublin Castle.

But, by March 1803, although the fragile peace between Great Britain and France negotiated the year before at Amiens now seemed to be threatened, there were few reports of disturbances in Ireland and, on St. Patrick's Day, Marsden was able to reassure Wickham that 'a drunken holiday has passed off without incident even in Dublin'; but he then added, in a more serious note, that 'the newspapers are in good training, the Dublin Journal and Evening Post do us I think credit'. Marsden was very proud of the fact that, through means of secret payments, he had managed to buy off the newspapers and intrepid journalists such as Cody went directly to Dublin Castle to check out the current Government thinking.

So, as another St. Patrick's Day passed by uneventfully in Dublin, Marsden had every reason to be pleased with himself; he had successfully concluded most of the secret Union deals; the country, meanwhile, had settled down again to a sullen acceptance of the status quo. The odd agrarian outrage still occured in country areas but when Wickham went down personally to visit Limerick he discovered that the troubles were greatly exaggerated by the local gentry anxious that their local corps of Yeomanry should be placed on permanent pay. There were some remaining rebels still active in the Wicklow mountains, led by Dwyer who continued to be a source of embarrassment but Marsden whose family had a country home, Verval in County Wicklow, was almost alone among the administration in Dublin Castle in believing that Dwyer posed no real threat.

Marsden was much more interested in the activities of the emigre 1798 leaders who were now in exile in France at this time and on March 29th he reported some current news to Wickham in a letter which he would take a long time to live down. 'Emmet is in Ireland. I did not before suppose, and but for the authority would still doubt it, but we must expect that a game will be played here and that some of the ex-Irish will be ordered to return. Emmet, however, is not likely to be one of them'. The Emmet family, of course, would have been well known to Marsden as they had lived for a long period in St. Stephen's Green and Dr. Robert Emmet Senior had been State Physician of Ireland. One of his sons, Christopher, a brilliant young lawyer and a gifted orator, was a contemporary of Marsden's but died at a young age in 1789. Now, although he had reported the news of Robert Emmet's return from France, Marsden seemed to pay little or no attention to his movements in Dublin. He could not convince himself that the youngest member of the Emmet family, still only twenty four, would actually be trusted with the organisation of a rebellion. But Robert Emmet was already going one step further. He was in the process of organising his own rebellion and Marsden would be almost the last person to find out.

3

Less than two months later, on a late Sunday evening in May 1803, a young Wicklow girl, Ann Devlin, whose family had moved up from Wicklow to Rathfarnham outside Dublin, watched with heightened curiosity as a group of four men in single file on horseback, approached the house in Butterfield Lane where she was acting as an unpaid housekeeper to a Mr. Ellis who, in fact was Robert Emmet. Ann Devlin was a first cousin of Michael Dwyer and Hugh Byrne and Arthur Devlin. Her mother Winifred was one of the three daughters of Charles Byrne of Cullentra who had married into the Dwyer, Byrne and Devlin families. They had all been active in the 1798 Rising and Bryan, Ann Devlin's father, had been imprisoned in Wicklow Jail for over two years. The women of the family then showed a steely resolve in attending public executions of local men, in shielding their bodies from further mutilation by the yeomanry and in giving them proper burials. Ann Devlin with two of Michael Dwyer's sisters at night disinterred the bodies of the Ulstermen Sam McAllister and Adam Magee and succeeded in transferring them to Kilranalagh Cemetery. When Bryan Devlin was released from Wicklow Jail he surrendered the leases on his farm and rented a farm in Rathfarnham where he set up a small dairy and hired his three horses out to local farmers. The family soon prospered but they were soon set on a course of disaster when Arthur Devlin, a cousin on their father's side of the family, suddenly arrived back in Dublin in the spring of 1803.

Arthur Devlin had first deserted from the British army but, having failed to get to the Continent, joined the British navy under an assumed name and was acting as a recruiting sergeant in the south of England when he met up with some of Robert Emmet's supporters on their way back to Ireland from France. Devlin now deserted again and, bringing with him almost fifty other disaffected Irish, arrived back in Dublin still wearing his sailors dress and soon became one of Emmet's chief organisers, responsible for setting up various other secret arms depots around the city.

Emmet was anxious to make contact with any remaining pockets of resistance in the country and so Arthur Devlin was given the task of approaching Dwyer in Wicklow. Dwyer, whose natural caution had stood him well over the years, was suspicious of Arthur Devlin's sudden reappearance in Wicklow and it took a second visit by Devlin and a visit also from the Northern weaver Jemmy Hope who brought some guns to Dwyer, before he would commit himself to even paying a visit to Emmet in Dublin. Even then Dwyer would not specify any particular date but, suddenly, arrived on horseback at Butterfield Lane in the company of Burke, Byrne and Mernagh. There they met with Robert Emmet and Thomas Russell, the ex-army officer who had been jailed for years following the 1798 rebellion and was one of its main political strategists; his nephew William Hamilton was also present as was Jemmy Hope and his wife Rose. For three days both the brandy and talk flowed freely as wild schemes for the overthrow of the Government were made and wildly optimistic numbers concerning the rebels who would join them were also bandied about. Hamilton looked for a guarantee from Dwyer that when the revolution had succeeded the dispossessed would not take away their lands from the settlers and Dwyer, joining in the spirit of the occasion, promised strong support from Wicklow which he knew, only too well, he could not deliver. A second meeting was arranged but on this occasion Dwyer was less specific about his support, privately committing himself to coming into Dublin only when it had been in Emmet's hands for forty eight hours. As for Emmet, Dwyer thought that he was a fine young man if only he had a bit of sense! Dwyer would not be lured from his Wicklow mountains without almost a cast iron guarantee of success. When they were leaving Butterfield Avenue Ann Devlin asked them, almost prophetically, who was going to look after her; they replied that Arthur Devlin would, but in the final analysis, no one would look after Ann Devlin or her unfortunate family.

4

Alexander Marsden was in no hurry to reach his office in Dublin Castle on the morning of July 23rd. William Wickham was in London attending a session of Parliament and the Lord Lieutenant, the Earl of Hardwicke, was at his residence in the Vice Regal Lodge in Phoenix Park. It was Saturday, the end of another week and there was no great pressure of work. It was finally about eleven thirty when Marsden arrived at his office and was immediately bombarded with reports from various spies and Government supporters that a rebellion was being planned in Dublin that night. Marsden, used to receiving such reports, was not unduly alarmed. Some of the information received was that a number of rebels from County Kildare were planning to come into the city but General Sir Charles Asgill, who was in charge of the Dublin district, had recently returned from Kildare and had reported to Marsden that there were no signs of any disturbances there. From an informer called McGucken he had heard, earlier that week, that both Dublin and the North were supposed to rise this very day and that Robert Emmet was to be the leader of the rebellion. Even now Marsden could not contemplate a rebellion led by the young Emmet, and continued to downplay even a gunpowder explosion which had occurred in

Patrick St. just a week before. The town major, Henry Sirr, now also received information about a rising that night but it was not until two o'clock in the afternoon, with a flood of new information beginning to come in, that Marsden finally decided to inform the Lord Lieutenant. Coincidentally the Commander-in-Chief of the army forces, General Fox, was at the time conferring with the Lord Lieutenant in the Vice Regal lodge in the Phoenix Park and Marsden, hurriedly, sent them a note asking them to come down to the Castle immediately. It was four o'clock when they arrived and, having heard Marsden's evidence, they agreed to take preventative action but without causing any undue alarm. General Fox was asked to send reinforcements to guard the principal buildings of the city, including Dublin Castle, but he was also asked to wait until dusk before doing so. The Lord Lieutenant left the Castle soon afterwards and, obviously not overconcerned about the rumours, returned to the Phoenix Park. General Fox went to the army headquarters at the Royal Hospital Kilmainham where he sent out various instructions to his army commanders and asked Sir Charles Asgill, the officer in charge of the Dublin district, to meet him at the Royal Hospital at nine o'clock that evening. Sir Charles had been invited out to dinner that night and was already in his dress uniform but he immediately set off by coach hoping, no doubt, that the evening's entertainment might yet be salvaged. When he arrived there he was sent by Fox to the Castle to check on the developing situation.

In the meantime, several members of the various Corps of Dublin Yeomenry had arrived at the Castle offering their services as rumours of the rebellion continued to sweep through Dublin but Marsden refused their help relying, naturally, on the regular army forces to attend to the situation. Marsden and General Asgill had supper together at the Castle and the General then returned to his home and, resigned no doubt to the fact that there would be no dining out that night, changed from dress suit into mufti! It was nearly nine o'clock when he returned to the Royal Hospital for the conference and there met with General Fox, Brigadier Gen. Dunne, Colonel Cotten, the officer of the Day and Lieut. Colonel Vassal of the Royal Hospital. The consensus at the meeting was that there was no immediate cause for alarm although Sir Charles Asgill did venture the opinion that extraordinary things could happen in Ireland. And he was very right, for at that very moment one of the most unlikely rebellions in Irish history had already begun and fighting was taking place in Thomas St., less than a mile away and quite close to Dublin Castle itself.

5

The streets and hostelries of Thomas Street in Dublin were crowded on the evening of July 23rd. It was the eve of the feast of St. James and was celebrated in true fashion by the inhabitants of the nearby parish; Saturday was also pay day and, in that most disaffected of areas at the edge of the city where town and country intermingled, spirits were high.

In a quiet laneway running up from the Marshalsea Prison to Thomas Street, Robert Emmet, in a busy workshop, prepared for the moment he had long since been waiting for, namely the donning of his splendid green and gold military uniform with breeches of creamy white cashmere, and then the supreme moment of leading his men into battle. "Who's the general?" a somewhat unwilling helper called Pat Farrell asked Emmet. "How bad you are for knowledge" came the reply. But Emmet's military plans had already gone disastrously wrong that day. Several of his Kildare and Wexford followers, dismayed by what they considered the lack of preparedness, had already pulled out and there was now strong pressure on him to postpone the rising. But there was even worse news as the hackney coaches which were to be used for an attack on Dublin Castle had been stopped by a cavalry officer and the coachmen had driven off with them in panic. One of his principal men,

Chief Justice, Lord Kilwarden who was killed in Thomas Street, Dublin, during the Emmet Rebellion, on the night of 22 July 1803.

Michael Quigley, now rushed in erroneously claiming that the army was already on the offensive and coming their way.

Emmet at first wavered but then persevered. He put on his uniform and picked up a copy of his proclamation stating that 'our object is to establish a free and independent republic in Ireland ... we war not againt past opinions or prejudices, we war against English dominion.' At nine o'clock, as the bell rang out on the Quays, a single rocket was fired over the roof-tops and Robert Emmet, drawing his sword and, accompanied by Quigey and Stafford in uniform and a group of followers, marched out from Marshalsea Lane on to Thomas Street to call upon some astonished passers-by to join in his revolution. For Emmet, the great idealist but the hopelessly inadequate military strategist, his revolution began and ended the same moment that he stepped out onto the street. Within half an hour, the attack had turned into a disorganised riot. As Emmet marched into Patrick Street he continued to call out 'Turn out my boys, turn out, now is the time for liberty. Liberty my boys, turn out, turn out!'. With that he fired his pistol in the air, possibly his only violent action on that night, and marched off towards Kevin Street. While General Fox was still procrastinating in the Royal Hospital, other military units stationed in the city quickly got the upper hand and, as a drunken crowd emerged from the hostelries ready to fight with or against anyone or anything, Emmet, with his rebellion already out of control, tried to cry a halt and announce that they should all try and retreat to Wicklow and join up with Michael Dwyer and fight another day. But there were more determined characters in his ranks like Henry Howley who, with the memories of 1798 atrocities fresh in their minds, were still determined to get in a blow of defiance and the fighting continued. It was at this time that the carriage bearing the Chief Justice Lord Kilwarden made its way up Thomas Street heading in the direction of the Castle. In the carriage also were his nephew Rev. Richard Wolfe and his daughter Elizabeth Wolfe. Ironically they had come in from their home in Rathcoole to seek the safety of the Castle when the mob descended on the carriage. Kilwarden was pulled out and piked to death as was his nephew; his daughter was not harmed but allowed to run screaming to the Castle with the shouts of the crowd 'God bless you miss!' ringing in her ears. The fighting was all over in a few hours; Emmet and his principal followers managed to escape but the Lord Chief Justice was dead and when the hysterical Elizabeth Wolfe arrived screaming into Dublin Castle Alexander Marsden's worst fears had been realised.

6

The embarrassment felt by the Irish Government in the weeks following Emmet's rebellion was acute. But for the killing of Lord Kilwarden and his nephew they might have muddled through but now all the previous warnings of the Lord Limerick's and other leaders of the Orange faction in the country seemed to have been justified and the conciliatory policies of the Lord Lieutenant were in shreds. The Chief Secretary William Wickham arrived back hurriedly from England letting it be known to the waiting newspapermen that he had brought his family back with him and the danger was over. The Habeas Corpus Act was immediately suspended in Ireland, the Martial Law Bill was enacted and soon Wickham was reassuring London, who had become even more alarmed when a copy of Emmet's proclamation reached them, that everything was under control: "We must give the enemy no breathing time; the fugitives must be pursued into every corner, insurrection wherever it shows itself must be instantly put down and punished by military execution and, above all, those who harboured traitors and facilitated their escape must be severely punished". Major Henry Sirr had redeemed himself, in the eyes of the Government, by arresting Emmet and many of his followers, fourteen of whom were executed in September as was Emmet himself. At first it seemed as if Marsden would be made the scapegoat for his failure to detect the rebellion in advance but Wickham, on his return, declared himself satisfied with Marsden's handling of the events of July 23rd and soon it was the Commander- in-Chief of the Army, General Fox, who was made to shoulder the blame. It was not until one o'clock in the morning that troops from the Royal Hospital had finally been sent into the streets and, by that time, the rebellion had been put down by other individual units. When the Lord Lieutenant heard of this delay he confronted General Fox and, following some heated exchanges, Fox agreed, at Hardwicke's request, to give up his command and return to London where, to Hardwicke's annoyance, he was immediately put in charge of the London district. The fact that General Fox seemed to have been made the lone scapegoat was viewed with disfavour in many quarters both in Dublin and London and, as he was the brother of the Whig leader James Charles Fox, this helped to heighten the tension. Fox was succeeded as army chief by Lord Cathcart but his orders seemed to indicate that he should report directly to the Duke of York in London rather than to the Lord Lieutenant, a decision which both Wickham and Hardwicke vigorously opposed on the grounds that it diminished both their offices.

Meanwhile, in Ireland, pressure from the Orange faction was building up to remove Marsden from office or to have him, at least, examined by a secret committee to defend his actions leading up to the day of the rebellion. William Wickham was now promising the members of the Privy Council that he would 'clear the country forever' of at least two hundred of the subordinate leaders of the counties of Dublin, Kildare and Wicklow and by the end of October Thomas Russell, the last of the leaders to be convicted, was hanged in Downpatrick Jail. The Government now were able to turn their attention to Wicklow. Arthur Devlin, who had been sent by Emmet in the direction of Kildare on the morning of the rebellion, was not involved in the fighting in Thomas Street and soon escaped to

Wicklow where he joined up with Dwyer again. Michael Dwyer had remained in Wicklow and had taken no part in the fighting but the administration in Dublin, and in particular both Wickham and Hardwicke, were convinved that he had played an active role in at least encocuraging it. Hardwicke, desperately needing some kind of propaganda victory to reverse the adverse publicity his administration had received, now sent a letter to Dwyer offering him terms of surrender and a 'safe retreat' from the Kingdom with all his family and several of his relations. The letter was given to Ann Devlin's mother Winifred, who was Dwyer's aunt, and she was specially released from Kilmainham Jail where all of Bryan Devlin's family had been imprisoned since the rebellion. Dwyer, quite separately, had been offered similar terms a short time before by William Hoare Hume, a local landlord and member of Parliament for Wicklow, but he rejected both offers out of hand and was still holding out for a free pardon which would enable him to continue to live in Wicklow. He foolishly believed also that the Government, preoccupied with the rebellion in Dublin, would now leave him alone. But he was very wrong and his reading of the current situation in Dublin was, for him as far off the mark as their understanding of his military strength in Wicklow.

The Throne Room in Dublin Castle, where the Privy Council
held their meetings.

Brigadier General W. C. Beresford who led the military
campaign in Wicklow against Dwyer.

7

On Tuesday November 7th Alexander Marsden watched impassively as the carriages belonging to the various members of the Privy Council clattered into the Castle Yard. It was a typical November day in Ireland, cold and showery but, for once, the rain was welcome as it marked the end of a drought which was so long and severe that the Privy Council had felt it necessary, a few weeks before, to highlight the fact that there was a deficiency in potato stocks which formed so large a part in the food of the country, and prohibited also the use of oats and oatmeal for the purposes of distilling so that they might be preserved for the 'sustenance of people'.

The business of the Privy Council was usually of a routine nature and not very well attended but a full attendance was expected on this day as the Government, still reeling from the effects of Emmet's rebellion, was planning to reveal details of a major offensive against, what they believed, were a large number of rebels still hiding in the Wicklow mountains under the leadership of Michael Dwyer. The draft of a proclamation offering a reward of five hundred pounds for the capture of Dwyer had already been circulated, in advance of the meeting.

Marsden watched with wry amusement as the various members of the Council made their way into the Castle. He had dealt with most of them in the recent past in the context of the Union bribes; Lord Ely, for example, had been handsomely rewarded but was still badgering the Lord Lieutenant about one still unfulfilled promise namely that his younger son, Lord Tottenham Loftus, be granted a bishopric. Other members of the Council included the impecunious Henry Langrishe, Lord Limerick, one of the chief protagonists of the Orange faction whom Marsden knew to be one of his fiercest critics, Charles Agar the Archbishop of Dublin whose promotion to the See of Dublin ensured his vote for the Union, the Attorney General Standish O'Grady and Lord Norbury, the Chief Justice of the Common Pleas, both of whom had been involved in the recent trial of Robert Emmet; Isaac Curry, who had fought a duel with Henry Grattan, but would live to repent the Union and the newly appointed Chancellor Lord Redesdale, a fanatical English Protestant and a former speaker of the House of Commons who was convinced that Emmet's rebellion was the beginning of a religious war whose declared aim was to exterminate the Protestants in Ireland!

The meeting was chaired by the Lord Lieutenant Hardwicke who knew that he would have to rely heavily on the support of his Chief Secretary William Wickham. But, before the meeting could get under way, a new member of the Privy Council, Lord Cathcart, now the commander of the army forces in Ireland, had to be sworn in. Hardwicke was only too well aware that many of the members present had been very vocal recently, accusing his administration of laxity and neglect and that pressure was being kept up in London in anticipation of the new session of Parliament which was to meet within three weeks. They had been frustrated so far in their attempts to get rid of Marsden mainly, as Wickham had noted, that "Marsden was the person who conducted the secret part of the Union... Ergo the price of each Unionist, as well as their respective conduct and character, is well known to him. Those who vapour away and vapour in so great a style in London are well known to him. They live in hourly dread of being unmasked!"

The Earl of Hardwicke, Lord Lieutenant of Ireland 1801-1806.

William Wickham, Chief Secretary of Ireland 1801-1804.

But, for the Lord Lieutenant himself also, Emmet's rebellion had been a severe setback. A moderate by nature, religious and moral if somewhat plodding and uninspired, Philip Charles Yorke, The Earl of Hardwicke, like so many liberally minded Englishmen before and after him, had come over to Ireland determined to create a mood of reconciliation in the country and to unite the various factions within the framework of the newly created Union between Ireland and Great Britain. He realised, on his arrival, that he would have to put aside his commitment to Catholic Emancipation but he also made sure that loyal Catholics in the country would not be disadvantaged, a policy which did not endear him to the Orange faction. He still believed that this policy of his had been justified and indeed, following Emmet's rebellion, the loyal Catholics of Waterford and Roscommon had publicly condemned it while Dr. Troy, the Catholic Archbishop of Dublin, had also issued an address of loyalty which was read out at all Masses in the Archdiocese, an address which was principally aimed at what were termed 'the lower orders of our communion'.

So, it was a tense and disunited Privy Council which met on November the 8th but there was little disagreement about the issuing of the proclamation against Michael Dwyer which was read out: "Michael Dwyer, late of Imeal in the county of Wicklow stands charged with repeated acts of High Treason and with furthering the rebellion that lately broke out in Ireland". It went on to state that a sum of 500 pounds was being offered for his capture and a further five hundred to anyone giving information leading to his arrest. All officers of the law and yeomen in Wicklow were urged to redouble their efforts and an instruction was given to the officers commanding the military forces 'to punish according to martial law not only Dwyer himself but anyone assisting or sheltering him'.

The use of court martials was something, in fact, which both Hardwicke and Wickham had been anxious to limit believing that prisoners should be tried by the Court of Law and not even the recent enactment of the Martial Law Bill had caused then to change their minds. They were now also reluctant to hand over the initiative in such cases to the new army chief Lord Cathcart. Wickham had been careful to point out to him that, while he had the right to hold a court martial himself, he had not the right to delegate this authority, adding that the discretionary powers for granting the authority to assemble court martials was vested solely in the office of the Lord Lieutenant. As for Lord Cathcart, he seemed to be anxious to avoid becoming entangled in any procedural squabbles between the Governments of Dublin and London and he readily agreed to their suggestion that Brigadier General Beresford should lead the forthcoming offensive in the Wicklow mountains against Dwyer with Gen. Sir Charles Asgill, commander of the district, having the overall responsibility.

Hardwicke, at the time, continued to rely heavily on William Wickham for support but, quite unknown to him, Wickham, despite his outer calm and air of assurance, was undergoing an extraordinary crisis of conscience which had been brought about by an incident which happened on the day of Robert Emmet's execution. Shortly after his arrest, Emmet had written to Wickham asking that the lives of others might be spared but that he should have access to his friends while awaiting trial. Wickham did not reply to this letter but was aware of the growing interest being shown in Emmet's trial in the city. On the morning of his execution, when Emmet was being taken from Kilmainham Jail to the place of execution in Thomas Street, he asked the sheriff for permission to return to his cell and there he wrote a final letter to Wickham which he then handed to the Superintendent of Kilmainham Jail, Edward Trevor, for delivery. Wickham receieved the letter that afternoon after Emmet had been executed and he became so affected, not only by its contents but by the fact that it was the last letter that Emmet had written, that, in the intervening seven weeks, William Wickham had changed his whole philosophy and was rethinking his perception of the political problems of Ireland in the context of its relationship with Great Britain. His mind, in fact, had become so troubled by this that he was actively considering, not only resigning from his post as Chief Secretary in Ireland, but of leaving public life altogether. Emmet's letter, of itself, had contained no great revelations but was rather a vindication of his actions and a plea to be given the time not allowed him in court to explain his actions.

But all this hidden turmoil which Wickham was experiencing remained hidden as the Privy Council meeting drew to a close and the proclamation against Dwyer was now sent to the Government printer John Grierson and then to the newspapers for publication.

In the following weeks, with the new session of the Houses of Parliament looming, Hardwicke now decided to send Marsden over to London to brief various members of Parliament and to supply them with the Irish Government's version of the events surrounding Emmet's rebellion. He felt sure that the Whigs, under the leadership of James Charles Fox, would bring up the issue of the dismissal of General Fox in Parliament and would also be critical of the Government's handling of the whole affair. Hardwicke himself had, at least, one advantage because his half- brother Charles Yorke had recently been transferred from the War Ministry in Addington's Cabinet to take charge of the Home Office. Marsden was also asked to furnish a detailed account of the events of July 23rd and this document was forwarded to Charles Yorke who would be defending the Government of Ireland in the upcoming debates in Parliament.

But above all, Hardwicke badly need a morale booster to counter the adverse publicity he had received on the home front and he was looking for the forthcoming military offensive against Dwyer in the Wicklow mountains to provide for him and quickly.

8

Winter had set in early in Wicklow and, by the beginning of December, the snow lay several feet deep on the higher slopes of the mountains. Michael Dwyer, with less than a dozen of his remaining followers, was taking shelter in an abandoned miner's digging near the Wicklow Gap in the townland of Oakwood above Glendalough. With him were Hugh Byrne, Martin Burke, John Mernagh, Lawrence O'Keefe, a deserter from the North Cork Militia, a force composed largely of Catholic peasants who had fought against the rebel forces in Wexford. Also present were three soldiers who had deserted from the Royal Barracks in Dublin, during Emmet's rebellion.

Michael Dwyer was already shaken by the events of the previous few weeks because, as news of the new proclamation against him was reaching Wicklow, an army detachment suddenly arrived at his parents' home in Eadestown on November 13th and arrested his sister Etty and also his married sister Mary Neale, whose husband was on the wanted list for supporting Emmet. His mother was arrested also but was released a short time later and his father John was still imprisoned in the New Geneva Jail in Waterford. On the same day, soldiers also visited his wife's family home and arrested his two sisters-in-law, Catherine and Eily Doyle, on a charge of harbouring him; Dwyer's wife Mary managed to avoid arrest but, over the next few days, several men relatives and friends were also arrested as was Martin Burke's wife Rachel. They were taken, initially, to Baltinglass Jail in Wicklow from where the women were transferred to Kilmainham and the men to a prison tender, the Hieram, which was anchored under the guns of the Pigeon House in Dublin Bay. To add further pressure to the local inhabitants who supported Dwyer, additional soldiers were quartered in selected houses where it was thought he used to frequent and the owners were followed when they left their cottages. The new military barracks which had just been completed in Leitrim at the top of the Glen of Imail was now billeted with soldiers and, as the military preparations got under way, the entrances and exits to all of the valleys were manned by the army.

This increased military activity and, in particular, the additional quartering of soldiers was placing a heavy burden on the local population and, for the first time, even some of Dwyer's most trusted supporters were asking him to consider surrender. The local parish priest had written a letter to him also in the same vein and it was in these worsening circumstances that Dwyer and his followers managed to arrange a meeting in the cave at Oakwood. It was here, for the first time, that Dwyer proposed to his comrades that they should consider the possibility of surrender on condition that they should be pardoned and sent to the United States of America. Dwyer's proposal was readily agreed to by Hugh Byrne and Martin Burke. Arthur Devlin was not present at the meeting but the thought of surrender was anathema to John Mernagh and he opposed it. As for the three deserters they realised that any surrender terms offered would not apply to them. The meeting ended inconclusively and, because of the growing military presence, they went their separate ways. Dwyer had mentioned also the possibility of approaching the local landlord William Hume but, because of John Mernagh's stance at the meeting, he delayed and before any approach would be made to William Hume, Dwyer's own hand was soon forced by the activity of Beresford's troops and very soon his surrender, and that of his comrades, would be a very close run thing indeed.

9

On November 22nd the new session began in London but King George III, in his opening speech, only briefly referred to Emmet's rebellion. The Marquis of Sligo, proposing the address in the House of Lords, said that if there was ever a moment for peculiar pride in the name of Britain it was surely now and the Earl of Limerick, seconding the address, refuted Napoleon's recent contention that Britain was a nation of shopkeepers, contending that, when it came to war, Britain was more than a match for France. It was Friday December the 2nd when Hardwicke's half-brother Charles Yorke rose in the House of Commons, with Marsden watching from the gallery, to move for a continuation of the Irish Habeas Corpus Suspension Act and the re-enactment of the Martial Law Bill. He attempted in his speech to be as low key as possible, putting much of the blame for Emmet's rebellion on French agents but adding, somewhat paradoxically, that the number of traitors in Ireland had very much diminished. Colonel Hutchinson, a member from Cork, praised Hardwicke's administration in Ireland but added that not enough attention was now being paid to Irish affairs in the united Parliament.

It was not until the following Monday, December 5th, when both bills were read for a second time, that the real debate began as Mr Eliot declared that he found it difficult to believe that the Government in Ireland claimed not to have been taken by surprise because, if they had any advance information about the rebellion, it was a pity they had not told Chief Justice Kilwarden who had lost his life for want of such information. William Windham, one of the great Whig political figures of the time, was even more scathing when he asked that the Government should make up their minds as sometimes they were dismissing the rebellion as a contemptible riot and, at other times, when it suited their purpose, it was of such formidable magnitude that it required no less a measure than martial law to put it down. He also pinpointed the fact that the Lord Lieutenant had remained in his lodge in the Phoenix Park. Surely, Windham asked, he would not have quitted the capital if he had knowledge of the rebellion in advance. These comments of Windham's were quite damaging to Hardwicke, and Marsden in the gallery must have winced as the Prime Minister Addington, who followed Windham, scarcely helped matters by lamely suggesting that Hardwicke had returned to the Vice Regal Lodge in the Phoenix Park to prevent any public alarm.

The opposition were to have the best of the debate and, when the bills got a third reading, Admiral Berkeley gave notice that, on a further date, he would move for papers to exonerate General Fox. Both bills were then duly passed but, on December 9th, during a debate on the Army Estimates, James Charles Fox, the Whig leader, made his first intervention on behalf of his brother, stating categorically that on the day of Emmet's Rebellion the Lord Lieutenant had told his brother that he did not believe that there would be any rising at all and he added ominously that he trusted that other opportunities would arise for "sifting the matter to the bottom". The events of July 23rd were discussed again in great detail until one member, losing patience, ventured an opinion that "the Orangemen and Catholics are so full of inveteracy and uncharitableness that an angel from heaven could not settle unfortunate differences of opinion which agitate, inflame and separate them". Finally, the

Home Secretary Charles Yorke rose again and, under a great deal of pressure, said that the question of blame should be investigated by the production of documents and by the examination of witnesses at the bar. The Government of Ireland's attempts to put a brave face on their shortcomings had backfired badly and it was decided that Marsden should remain in London until January. In Dublin Hardwicke was still worrying about the reporting orders of Lord Cathcart, even going so far as threatening to resign his office. He wrote a long letter to his brother in the Home Office in this vein but received a blunt reply implying that if he felt that badly about the matter he should indeed resign. A chastened Hardwicke quietly let the matter drop and waited anxiously for news from Wicklow.

10

On Saturday December 10th, the military offensive in Wicklow, under the command of Beresford, finally got under way when a general search of the county began in very adverse weather conditions. A few days before, some soldiers had reported sighting in the distance what they took to be a large number of men. At first they thought it might be a group coming from a wake or maybe a hurling party, but there was embarrassment all round as it proved to be only reflections in the mist. But now the major search had begun and, on that very first day, the military achieved an early breakthrough. Martin Burke had called in at the home of a local man, Patrick O'Brien, in the Glen of Imail, not realising that some of the local Corps of Yeomanry were inside drying themselves at the fire. When he saw them Burke pretended that he had come to the house looking for a piece of harness, excused himself and left, but their suspicions were aroused and they followed him outside. Burke tried to escape and some members of the Monaghan Militia, who were nearby, joined in the chase. The River Slaney was then in winter flood and Burke crossed and recrossed it in a vain attempt to shake off his pursuers. He was finally surrounded in mid-stream but, in a curious example of family loyalties at the time, he refused to surrender until a maternal relation of his called Allen, who was a barrackmaster in nearby Davidstown, was sent for. When Allen arrived Martin Burke surrendered, was put in irons and sent under escort to Baltinglass Jail where the Allen family ensured that he was not abused in any way.

The capture of Martin Burke on the first day of the military operation was regarded by the army as an event of the greatest importance because he was regarded as being one of Dwyer's principal followers and soon a flurry of letters were being exchanged between Wicklow and Dublin. Beresford assured his commander General Asgill that the reward money would be paid promptly to the soldiers concerned as an encouragement to further exertions and he asked whether Burke was to be sent to Dublin or tried by court martial in Wicklow adding that, whatever the sentence of law was, it should be executed in the Glen of Imail.

Lord Cathcart was quickly informed of the arrest and he, in turn, wrote to the Lord Lieutenant seeking instructions as to what should be done with Martin Burke. Hardwicke was no doubt pleased that Cathcart had contacted him about a possible court martial and had not acted independently and on the next day he sent a note to William Wickham seeking his opinion as to the advisability of court martialling Burke whom he described as Dwyer's Lieutenant-General. Hardwicke was at his lodge in the Phoenix Park at the time still recovering from the shock that he, his wife and two daughters had received when they were coming into Dublin to attend Sunday service in their coach two days before. The first four horses had taken fright in the Phoenix Park and tried to leap over a wooden railing, but the horses broke loose from their harness and no-one was seriously injured. The postillon was thrown off as was the coachman, and a footman had a narrow escape when he fell under the horses while attempting to bring them to a halt.

William Wickham, having received the note, consulted with Hardwicke and they came to the conclusion not to hold a court martial in Wicklow. Wickham informed Cathcart of the decision and he, in turn, confirmed this to General Asgill.

In the meantime, Beresford had written again to Asgill having, apparently, mellowed somewhat in his attitude to Martin Burke, local representations having been made on Burke's behalf: "Of all the gang, if mercy was, or could be extended to any man he was the most proper object because, never by any account, from the Gentlemen of the County was there a charge of him being concerned in any murder and, having more than once, prevented the murder of loyal men". But the possibility of court martialling Michael Dwyer, if he were captured, was not being ruled out and Beresford wondered if, in that circumstance, Burke would also be included adding: "if however, as I have reason to believe will be the case, Dwyer should throw himself upon the mercy of Government it will supersede the necessity of any immediate determination relative to Burke as I shall send them all immediately to Dublin, conceiving that Government would not wish to have brought to punishment any of the inferior agents 'till it had been decided relative to the principals. If however, Dwyer does not immediately surrender and that Burke will not give such information as enables me immediately to take him I am convinced that an instantaneous example will have the most salutary effect upon those who have been his adherents or shelterers and upon the lower orders of the country in general".

So it seemed that the fate of Martin Burke might still depend on what Michael Dwyer would do in the next few days and Beresford's declared confidence that Dwyer would soon surrender was, in fact, well founded. The news of Burke's capture and possible court martial must have spread like wildfire in the mountains and Dwyer would have been one of the first to know, as Martin Burke and his family were on very close terms with him. There would have been direct pressure now from the Burke family to try and save his life and Dwyer also would have felt a personal obligationtowards his closest companion but he had to move quickly. On the day following Burke's

The restored cottage at Derrynamuck, Co. Wicklow, from
where Michael Dwyer escaped in 1799.

The back gate of Humewood Estate in Co. Wicklow where
Michael Dwyer surrendered in December 1803.

arrest Dwyer sent a message to a Captain Tennison, a local magistrate and a leading member of the Glen of Imail Corps of Yeomen, offering to surrender without any other conditions than that his own life and that of Martin Burke be spared and that they should be sentenced to transportation. Captain Tennison, having consulted with his superiors, perhaps even with General Beresford, sent a message back to Dwyer saying that the only terms now acceptable were that he should throw himself upon the mercy of Government. Dwyer was unwilling to accept terms which, de facto, meant agreeing to unconditional surrender and now, with the military pressure ever increasing, he turned to his last hope, William Hume, the local landlord and member of Parliament, whose terms he had turned down with disdain just a few weeks before.

On the following morning, December 13th, just three days after the capture of Martin Burke, Dwyer's wife Mary arrived at Humewood and according to an official report "surrendered herself to Captain Hume". She had come making a very straightforward offer on behalf of her husband, namely that he would surrender to the Government on the sole condition that his life would be spared. William Hume was naturally aware of the military search now taking place and he felt it was necessary to consult with General Beresford at his headquarters in nearby Saunders Wood but Beresford, still believing that Dwyer would be captured anyway within a very short time, would still only agree that Dwyer should surrender himself "upon the mercy of Government". Hume, despite hearing this however, now went one step further and, on his own initiative, gave Mary Dwyer an assurance that if her husband surrendered he would use his influence as a prominent landowner and local member of Parliament to persuade the Government to spare his life. That was the extent of the terms negotiated at this time and a fearful, but obviously relieved, Mary Dwyer left Humewood to inform her husband. Michael Dwyer at this time was probably sheltering in the nearby home of a Protestant friend called Billy 'The Rock' Jackson. There was little time now for protracted negotiations or delaying, and, persuaded no doubt by his wife and by Billy Jackson and shaken by recent events, Michael Dwyer agreed to the surrender terms.

So on the following evening, Wednesday December 14th, William Hume, taking with him for his personal safety one of the members of his Corps of Yeomen, walked out through the back gate of his Humewood estate and waited at the nearby area of the Three Bridges where Michael Dwyer, who was hiding nearby, soon joined them. The surrender terms having been confirmed he walked back with William Hume into Humewood and into captivity.

11

On the night of Michael Dwyer's surrender a tremendous storm of wind and rain swept the country from the south-east which continued throughout Thursday causing severe damage in particular to shipping along the east coast. Two coal ships were badly damaged in Dublin and a sloop of war that lay at the Poolbeg was dragged from its moorings and finally came to rest at Carlisle Bridge. In Humewood that Wednesday night, while the storm raged outside, Michael Dwyer and his wife were being treated very well; food and drink was liberally served and the conversation lasted long into the night, with William Hume asking Dwyer to relive some of the major engagements of the past five years. Hume specifically asked about a military uniform which Robert Emmet had sent to Dwyer before the rebellion but Dwyer never seriously considered wearing it and the uniform had remained hidden in a local house from where it was later retrieved by Hume.

It was during the course of this night that additional terms of surrender were worked out between them. One of Dwyer's priorities, and that of his wife, was the release of their own relatives and friends who had been arrested a few weeks before. Mary Dwyer, in speaking to Hume, would also have referred to her own desperate plight as the mother of three young children with no means of supporting them and with her husband possibly facing a long prison sentence or even transportation for life. The additional terms now worked out, and agreed by Hume, were that he would seek the approval of the Government that all their relatives would be set free and that Mary Dwyer and her children would be allowed to live with her husband while he remained in prison, something that was not too unusual in those days particularly in the case of debtors.

But, most important of all, Dwyer, with his wife and family were to be given a free passage out of the Kingdom. But their final destination was to become a matter of controversy as Michael Dwyer was in no doubt that Hume, on that night, promised that he and his family would be sent to America but that he was also advised by William Hume not to tell anyone about these secret terms. For William Hume's part, he made no mention of these new terms to the military forces in Wicklow in the days following the surrender although he later claimed to Marsden that he had informed William Wickham about them, stipulating only that Dwyer should be sent outside the Kingdom. There is no evidence to suggest, however, that Hume, at any stage, ever mentioned the specific destination of America in his later discussions with the Government.

One can only speculate whether Hume, on that night, mentioned America to the Dwyers as being a possible destination or something that he would attempt to arrange. But he must have known that it was highly unlikely that either the British- or indeed the American Governments-would agree to such a move as Michael Dwyer was so well known as a prominent Irish rebel leader. On the other hand Dwyer, while in prison, clung resolutely to the belief that America was to be his final destination and obeyed Hume's strictures not to tell anyone about his terms and tried to make absolutely sure that while he was in prison that he did nothing to jeopardise this agreement.

Strangely enough, Dwyer at this time did not feel any need to negotiate terms for Martin Burke although William Hume intimated that Dwyer's original surrender terms would be available to his other comrades who were still in hiding.

Because of the adverse weather conditions it seems likely that Hume did not inform Beresford about the surrender until the following morning and Mary Dwyer was allowed to leave Humewood to reassure both her own and his family about their safety and to arrange to send word to his remaining comrades about Hume's offer of surrender.

Brigadier General Beresford, having heard the news of Dwyer's surrender, which he had been confidently expecting, rode over to Humewood and, having congratulated Hume, immediately questioned Dwyer about the extent of his operation in Wicklow and as to whether he was planning a further rebellion with the help of the French. The Irish Government, apart from Marsden, had grossly overrated Dwyer's importance, being still convinced that he was a prime mover in Emmet's rebellion and that he had anything up to twenty five thousand men on call in Wicklow awaiting a French invasion. Beresford was relieved to hear from Dwyer that this was far from being the case although he must have been somewhat incredulous to discover how pitifully small Dwyer's following now was.

Beresford also discussed the surrender terms with William Hume who seemed to fudge the issue completely and their main discussion then centred on how Dwyer was to be sent to Dublin. Beresford presumed that Hume would hand him over to his charge but Hume was anxious to retain responsibility for the safety of Dwyer who had surrendered to him and requested that his own Corps of Yeomen should escort him to Dublin. It is not likely, given the status of Hume in the county, that Beresford had any serious objections to this. He had already forecast the early surrender of Dwyer when writing to Dublin, and he now realised that he would get most of the credit for it anyway. That same night he wrote to General Asgill making some highly interesting comments about what he believed were Dwyer's surrender terms: "I have reason to believe that the assurances given to Dwyer that his life shall be spared have been somewhat stronger than there has been warrant, for the fellow does not appear to have any doubt or anxiety on that head. Captain Hume however, tells me that he has thrown himself unconditionally on the mercy of the Government he promising to use his personal interest with the Government to save his life. I cannot omit saying that if his solicitations on this head can or will be listened to no-one more deserves to be attended to than those of Captain Hume; his zeal, activity and exertion have been unremitted and undefatigable. The account which Dwyer gives of the disposition of the people is to us very satisfactory and the more so is corroborated by every person with whom I have of late conversed on the subject as well as by the unasked-for declarations of the people themselves".

Dwyer remained in the guardhouse at Humewood during Thursday and Friday and Beresford wrote again to Dublin saying that he would delay sending Dwyer to Dublin no longer than it was necessary "to procure the necessary information from him to guide us in the pursuit of any other still at large".

A strong oral tradition, rarely aired in public, has survived in the Wicklow mountains, namely that in the days following Dwyer's arrest, several of the houses where he had received shelter over the years, were burnt to the ground. There has been speculation that Dwyer might have given the authorities information about them. In the written records of the military there is no direct evidence to support this claim although it might be argued that Beresford's statement that they wished to 'procure the necessary informatiom from him to guide us in the pursuit of any others still at large', could be construed in the above context. But this was a highly disciplined military operation and the burning of houses would not have been allowed by Beresford. It is far more likely that any such burnings were caused by individual groups of militia or yeomen who were frustrated at having been denied any portion of the huge reward money which had been offered for Dwyer's capture. In fact, it is on record that at least one yeoman was disciplined for offences committed during the Wicklow operation.

With regard to the suspicion of Dwyer giving information about the movements of his comrades, the reality was that, since their meeting in the cave at Oakwood, they had all gone their separate ways and had very little contact with each other, although Dwyer seemingly met with John Mernagh the day before he surrendered and did not dare mention to him that he was about to surrender. The military search for his remaining followers now continued with disappointment being felt among the troops that the reward money for Dwyer had been denied to them. But letters of mutual congratulations were again circulating in Government circles and Hardwicke summed it all up when writing: "It would be a great object at any time but is particularly important at the present moment".

Hugh Byrne was the next of Dwyer's comrades to surrender to William Hume. Having heard of Dwyer's surrender he quickly sent a message to Humewood on the following day but he was unwilling to risk going there directly and sent a message instead that he was ready to surrender at a certain house in the locality. So, on Friday December 16th William Hume, accompanied by a Sergeant Perry of his Corps of Yeomen, went to the named house and Hugh Byrne surrendered to him there. Byrne was not kept at Humewood, however, but was sent to Baltinglass Jail where he joined Martin Burke. Following Byrne's surrender, it was decided to send Dwyer to Dublin on Saturday morning. General Asgill had suggested that he should be sent directly to the New Provost Prison but the Government decided instead that he should be brought first to the Castle, to satisfy their curiosity if nothing else, and then to be sent to Kilmainham Jail to await an official examination at a later date.

The propaganda value of his surrender was now being exploited in full and the Dublin newspapers needed very little prompting in this regard from the Government. Already Martin

Burke's capture had been reported in detail and in that Saturday's edition of the Freeman's Journal two separate stories appeared, the first contradicting another item that he had already surrendered and on another page there was the up-to-date news of his actual surrender. In the next issue the leading article was simply headed DWYER and while it may have lacked a factual basis it certainly did not fall short on cliches:

"The surrender of the rebel robber Dwyer and his gang, is almost corroborating proof of the desperate ebb to which disaffection is reduced in this country. Nothing can be more certain than this daring marauder held constant correspondence with the United Traitors; it was by persons of that description that he was so long protected in the mountains and enabled him to elude the vigilant search which was made after him. It is also certain that the chiefs of the late conspiracy held correspondence with him, and that Emmet and his associates after the defeat of their projects on the 23rd of July intended to have joined him in the fastnesses. He would not, therefore, have surrendered had he the most remote hope of renewed rebellion; and although the exertions of the Government might have rendered it impracticable for him and his gang to continue unbroken, he would have availed himself of the facility of evading justice as an individual until he could again join the public tumult. But it is clear that he could no longer gain protection from the sympathy of treason, and chose rather to throw himself upon the humanity of Government than trust to the warring attachments of his fellow ruffians and fellow traitors. In ordinary times no importance would attach to such an offender against the laws; his only distinction would be his crime and punishment but when political reformers claim allegiance with a foreign despot and his slaves and with every domestic profligate and violator of the laws we receive the surrender of the Mountain-Robber with additional satisfaction when we consider him an adherent of the Dirty-Lane [Emmet] conspiracy".

Most of the information for this article obviously came from the Government and the specific details of Emmet's plans to join Dwyer in Wicklow after the Rebellion had failed had come to light only a short time before when Michael Quigley, one of Emmet's principal conspirators, following his arrest had secretly agreed to become an informer. In the following weeks all of the provincial newspapers in the country, as was the custom, copied the story although the further one got to Dublin the less hysterical the reports tended to be, with the exception of Belfast; even the London Times regarded his surrender as being of sufficient importance to devote a leading article to it forecasting that the "desperate ruffian's gang were now expected to surrender". One wonders if Marsden, who was still in London, was the source of their information.

All of this coverage heartened the Lord Lieutenant greatly as during that same week the Dublin Evening Post, displaying a small modicum of independence at last, was reporting in detail the recent House of Commons debates on the Emmet rising which, from a Government point of view, made for rather dismal reading.

For his journey to Dublin on Saturday December 17th, Michael Dwyer was given one of William Hume's best horses and, for his escort of Yeomen, it was a profitable and enjoyable day out as their leader William Murray later collected the sum of thirty two pounds to cover their expenses. They took the usual road to Dublin through Donard and then on to Blessington where they stopped for refreshments. The whole affair began to take on the air of a victory march as people along the way came out to shout words of encouragement and when they stopped at a hostelry in Blessington, no doubt, everyone wanted to buy him a drink. The majority of his escort would have known both Dwyer and his family well and Dwyer's surrender, in fact, represented a valuable loss of income for them. William Hume, attending to the surrender of Hugh Byrne and awaiting news of Arthur Devlin and John Mernagh, remained behind at Humewood.

His attitude to Dwyer, of course, would have been completely different; his own father had been killed locally in 1798 when, in an incident which did not involve Dwyer, he tried, single handedly and foolishly, to arrest one of the rebels and, in a struggle, was shot by his own gun. William Hume himself was regarded as being liberal in his views and had the reputation of being a humane landlord but he would, nevertheless, have regarded Michael Dwyer as, at best, a nuisance and, at worst, a potentially dangerous enemy. There always lurked at the back of Hume's mind the very real possibility that, if any outrage occurred within his jurisdiction, or if any of his tenants had a major grievance, Dwyer had the capability of seeking redress by burning down his house. Indeed many of his tenants would have actively supported and protected Dwyer as also would many of the workers of his estate and Hume, recognising this, had recently written to the Government saying that, as long as the people protected Dwyer, he would not be able to take him. So it was to his own advantage to be in a position, at last, of getting rid of Dwyer, but it was equally important that he should be regarded as having acted generously towards him apart from any humane considerations of his own. By offering him good surrender terms he, undoubtedly, saved Dwyer and his comrades from a harsher sentence of the law, but by holding out to Dwyer and his wife, even secretly, the prospect of a free passage to America, he was leaving himself open to a later charge of breaking his word. Perhaps he genuinely believed, in the case of Dwyer and his wife, that he could persuade the Government although there is not a single shred of evidence to support this. And he also must have realised that the Government would be the final arbiters and, in the final analysis, that they would ultimately shoulder the blame.

Despite the break for refreshments at Blessington, Dwyer's escort made good time and reached Dublin by mid-afternoon where a newspaper reporter was on hand near the Castle to witness the scene: "Dwyer the noted insurgent was brought into town on Saturday evening last between four and five o'clock escorted by a party of Captain Hume's cavalry Corps of

Wicklow. He was dressed in country style, in a white frize jockey and appeared to be somewhat inebriated. The noble Captain was much displeased at the mob gazing at him and used some ruffianly expressions (no doubt having received some as well). He has been lodged in Kilmainham Jail". Owing to his condition it was not possible for even a preliminary examination to be conducted with him at the Castle, and he was transferred that same night to Kilmainham Jail where many of the female relatives were imprisoned. There one of the many turnkeys-cum-informers who inhabited Kilmainham Jail reported that: "Michael Dwyer is just arrived. He is very drunk and by much ado we have got him to bed. He appears to be a most complete villain in his liquor but I got out of him that he saw his Aunt, Mrs Devlin when we sent her to him". Mary Dwyer seemingly did not travel with her husband to Dublin but arrived at the Jail a few days later and was allowed to stay with him. But, as he spent his first night in Kilmainham Jail, Michael Dwyer was quite insensible to the cares of the world.

12

On the following Wednesday, December 21st, Martin Burke and Hugh Byrne were also transferred from Baltinglass to Kilmainham Jail; for Hugh Byrne it was his second visit to Kilmainham having been imprisoned there briefly in 1799; he had been arrested in the house of a relative in Dublin and charged with the burning of Yeomens' houses in Wicklow and robbing them of arms. He was courtmartialled in Wicklow and sentenced to death but with another prisoner managed to escape from Jail and rejoined Dwyer in the mountains. One of his brothers had been hanged in 1798 and his father also spent some time in prison.

Martin Burke had fought at the battle of Stratford during the rebellion in Wexford in May 1798, but was captured in Wicklow later that year and brought to Baltinglass Jail from where he also managed to escape with one arm still fastened to his side with an iron bolt. By the time he arrived in Kilmainham Jail he may have still been unaware that his wife Rachel had been freed on the previous Saturday in similar circumstances to Winifred Devlin. The Superintendent of Kilmainham Jail at the time was Dr Edward Trevor who was also paid by the Government to eke out information from prisoners while in custody and he recently had been mainly responsible for persuading Michael Quigley to become a secret informer. When Trevor heard of Dwyer's surrender he decided to try and persuade Arthur Devlin to surrender, not to William Hume, but rather to himself. Devlin had been actively engaged with Robert Emmet in his rebellion, and Trevor, who had been concentrating on getting as much information as he could from Emmet's followers, knew that Arthur Devlin was now the most important of those still evading arrest. Trevor wrote a letter to Devlin offering him terms of surrender and he released Martin Burke's wife, Rachel, to deliver the letter to him in Wicklow, promising her terms also for her husband if Devlin surrendered to him.

As Christmas approached the military search in Wicklow for John Mernagh and Arthur Devlin was still continuing. A man by the name of James Kehoe was now arrested on the charge of harbouring Mernagh and he was tried before a Court Martial which was held in Wicklow - the military at last had got their Court Martial. Hardwicke sent down a well-known Dublin barrister called Prendergast to act as Judge Advocate and Kehoe was found guilty and sentenced to five years transportation. Prendergast, while in Wicklow, wrote to William Wickham saying how peacable the county now was adding that it was Dwyer alone who kept that part of the island in a state of disturbance. "The inhabitants rejoice now at his being in the hands of the Government as they are no longer subject to the contributions which he was in the habit of levying previous to his surrender". Prendergast was referring mainly to the sentiments of the loyal inhabitants of the county although, of course, in the recent past, because of the increased hardships which were imposed on them, a large number of Dwyer's supporters had been advising him to surrender.

It is difficult to assess how widespread the practice of 'levying of contributions' was. Some firms such as a local woollen mill seemed to pay up cheerfully enough but for others it was quite simply regarded as extortion. Dwyer and his comrades could also behave in a boorish manner as happened on the occasion when when he and Martin Burke arrived at a local christening party and proceeded to polish off the drink before the other guests arrived. They were also involved in a number of highway robberies and were ruthless in dealing with informers who tried to infiltrate their ranks. But this type of activity must be judged in the light of the atrocities committed on the local inhabitants particularly in the year following the 1798 Rebellion when, in fact, Dwyer and his followers represented the only safeguard or insurance that the local people had when confronted by such unlawful acts of savagery.

It was no coincidence that Hugh Byrne had been charged with burning the Yeomens' houses in 1799 which were in fact nothing other than reprisal raids. Dwyer, by 1803, might have been outliving his usefulness in this respect, but, to the great mass of tenant farmers and labourers in the area, he was already regarded as a folk hero. When Mary Dwyer appeared at a local fair a short time before his surrender, she was received with great devotion "to which she did not seem insensible". Already the exploits of Michael Dwyer were becoming part of the local tradition of the area. He had already become a symbol of freedom and his name, from now on, would always be linked with Fiach Mc Hugh O'Byrne as two great defenders of the rights of the people in the county of Wicklow and were so recalled both in song and story.

Christmas was now approaching but Chief Secretary William Wickham would not be taking part in the festivities. He had injured his knee some time previously, while attending a shooting party, and now it had become swollen again forcing him to remain in bed over the holiday period. He was now thoroughly disillusioned with public life; the short- comings of Irish political figures had always irritated him; he was still mulling over the orders of Lord Cathcart to report directly to London and on December 23rd he received a cautious and inconclusive legal judgement from the Solicitor General Plunkett who pointed out to him that the military establishments of the two countries were no longer distinct, which effectively meant that the objections of Wickham and Hardwicke might not hold up. The erosion of the power of Irish Lord Lieutenants was already beginning.

But, above all, Wickham was still deeply troubled by Emmet's letter, so much so that he was now on the point of submitting his resignation, and as he spent the period of Christmas in bed he must have taken up Emmet's letter and again mulled over its contents:

Sir,

Had I been permitted to proceed with my vindication it was my intention not only to have acknowledged the delicacy with which I feel with gratitude that I had been personally treated but also to have done the most public justice to the mildness of the present administration of the country and at the same time to have acquitted them as far as rested with me, of a charge of remissness in not having previously detected a conspiracy which from its closeness, I know it was impossible for it to be done. I confess that I should have preferred this mode had it been permitted as it would thereby have enabled me to clear myself of an imputation under which I might in consequence lie, and have stated any such an administration did not prevent, but under the peculiar situation of this country, perhaps either accelerated my determination to make an effort in the overthrow of a Government of which I don't think equally high. However, as I have been deprived of that opportunity I think it right now to make an acknowledgement which justice requires of me as a man and which I don't feel in the least derogatory from my principles as an Irishman.

I am etc. etc.

ROBERT EMMET.

Wickham had also in his possession a copy of Emmet's speech from the dock which already had been published in pamphlet form and his main preoccupation was of attempting vainly to comprehend why this young Protestant Irishman, with an upper class background, not yet twenty four years old, in love with a beautiful young girl, Sarah Curran, would, almost deliberatly, set out to sacrifice his life for the cause of establishing the separate and independent nation of Ireland.

Wickham had now become convinced that the first priority in Ireland should be the disestablishment of the Protestant Church and the consequent abolition of the controversial system of gathering tithes. He could not, of course, approach Hardwicke with these radical policies; indeed Hardwicke had regarded Emmet's speech in the dock as being "of a rather mischievous tendency". Wickham had come to the conclusion that he could not reconcile his position as Chief Secretary with his new beliefs and he began now to write several drafts of a document which he planned to circulate privately among friends of his in England. But, on Christmas Day, he wrote to his friend Charles Abbott in England about more topical matters: "I write to you from my bed where I am keeping a merry Christmas. The surrender of Dwyer is an object of the very first importance together with the capture of Quigley and his associates and has set my mind at rest as the immediate neighbourhood of the Capital and if the French would keep away I would vouch for the rest. I cannot doubt that Ireland is the principal object of their preparations". Wickham was fully convinced that a French invasion of Ireland would occur soon and, indeed, it was an option that Napoleon was seriously considering at the time. The newspapers, during that winter, were filled with such rumours and with anti-French invective, but readers were also assured concerning Napoleon that "the wooden walls of England are an impregnable barrier to his ambition". On Christmas Eve a number of Dublin printers were arrested for having published The Memoirs of Bonaparte and a carpenter by the name of Kavanagh, who lodged in Beresford Street, was arrested on a charge of treasonable practices because in his desk was found several seditious papers and a history of Bonaparte; even the boatmen on the Canal did not escape censure and a topical visual joke of theirs was not considered to be particularly funny, readers being warned that "there is a party of ruffians of these turf and dung luggers on the Grand Canal who call their filthy crafts the Brest Fleet!"

William Wickham believed also that Michael Dwyer was in close contact, at the time, with French agents, and when he received letters from some former contacts of his on the Continent who were predicting the imminent invasion of Ireland, he wrote again to Abbott on the following day: "It was a most fortunate thing that Dwyer should have surrendered before any of the late communications from France have reached him. This will make the difference of an army to us. Had his men remained in Wicklow at the time of the landing of the enemy there is no doubt that the most formidable insurrection would have broken out there". Wickham went on to speculate that the most likely landing place for the French in Ireland would be near Dublin and that they would land either in Killiney Bay or create a diversion there and land their main force somewhere to the north of the capital. He probably based this assertion of his on a report prepared in 1795 for the Government by the Duke of Carhampton, which came to the same conclusion. Because of this perceived danger to Dublin, it was now decided to build a string of Martello or Corsican towers along the Dublin coast from Bray to Ireland's Eye mainly for cosmetic purposes to give the appearance to France, at least, of being prepared although Wickham still mused if the French land "then God help us all".

Christmas in Kilmainham for Michael Dwyer was almost an occasion of happy reunion. His wife had been given permission to join him there; he was given a clean and reasonably well-furnished cell; his food was satisfactory and he was supplied with plenty of spirits to drink. He was allowed access to all of his recently imprisoned female relatives whom he expected would be released within a short time. He had negotiated what he considered to be very satisfactory terms with William Hume. After, what he hoped would be a short time in prison, he would be able to start a new life with his family in America. For the first time in over five years he was able to relax.

Out on the Wicklow mountains, Arthur Devlin spent the period of Christmas trying to make up his mind whether or not he should surrender to William Hume. He recognised that his situation was more precarious than the others as he had taken an active part in Emmet's rebellion or at least in the planning of it. He hadn't been present in the cave at Oakwood when Dwyer discussed the possibility of surrender and it was said that he was on the Wicklow coast at the time trying to make separate plans to escape from the country. But news obviously reached him about William Hume's terms of surrender and, two days after Christmas, he arrived at Humewood where he also surrendered to Hume. While he was there he received the letter from Dr Trevor which was delivered by Martin Burke's wife Rachel offering terms for both himself and Burke if he were to surrender to Trevor and, prompted by it, he asked William Hume that Martin Burke now be included in his surrender terms and Hume agreed. Because of his links with Emmet, Arthur Devlin was brought immediately to Dublin and imprisoned in the Tower of Dublin Castle to await an official examination.

On December 30th Lord Hardwicke wrote a long letter to his brother in the Home Office in London in which he set out a detailed account of the military operation in Wicklow to date. In it he stated confidently "that the dissolution of this gang would not only restore tranquility and confidence in every part of the county of Wicklow, but would tend to discourage and intimidate the disaffected in other places". But perhaps the most significant part of his letter was the reference to Dwyer's surrender: "Though it is certainly to be regretted, on account of the murders and other crimes which Dwyer had committed in the course of the last five years that any such expectation should have been held out to him that his life should be spared, yet considering the great importance of breaking up this gang which has so long disturbed that part of the county of Wicklow, that their exploits and importance have been greatly exaggerated at a distance as well as the indefatigable exertions of Mr

Hume, I apprehend it will not be possible to bring them to trial, but we must content outselves with transporting him for life as a felon and a convict".

So on December 30th at least, Hardwicke was still not aware of any secret or additional terms negotiated by William Hume. He had decided that Dwyer would be transported as a felon and a convict and that meant only one place, namely New South Wales. The newspapers were now also forecasting that Dwyer would soon join his fellow Wicklowman Joseph Holt in Botany Bay, but Michael Dwyer was still secure in his belief that a far different fate awaited him and his family.

13

J ohn Mernagh was now the only remaining member of
Dwyer's main comrades still at large. He had opposed the
idea of surrender at the Oakwood meeting but he had
always held independent views. At one period he had led
his own small band of followers in Glenmalure and there were
rumours of friction between Dwyer and himself with regard to
the issue of overall leadership. But, despite this, they still managed to work closely together and Mernagh had accompanied
Dwyer and the others to Dublin for the discussions with
Emmet. When the meeting had ended on that bitterly cold day
in the cave at Oakwood John Mernagh, in a reaction perhaps to
the mood of the meeting, gathered together a small band of followers determined to fight on but he too had underestimated
the intensity of the military operation and now, following the
capture of Martin Burke and the surrender of Dwyer, Byrne
and Devlin, all of the military resources in the area were concentrated against him in an attempt to bring the military campaign quickly to an end.

On January 9th 1804, one of his followers, Jack Byrne, surrendered and informed Beresford that Mernagh, now in a desperate situation, and obviously recognising the hopelessness of

Michael Dwyer from the portrait drawn and engraved by George Petrie, in Kilmainham Jail, 1804.

Kilmainham Jail, Dublin.

prisoners who had just been released from Fort George in Scotland. Dwyer next went into some detail as to how Devlin and Jemmy Hope had arranged his meeting with Emmet at Butterfield Avenue. He went on to describe what happened at the meeting but that he had dismissed Emmet and his plans and had taken no part in the rebellion. One could argue, at this stage, that Devlin would not have thanked Dwyer for going into such detail but Dwyer, for his part was careful to point out that Devlin had taken no part in the actual fighting on the night of July 23rd. When asked to give the names of the various leaders who had been involved with Emmet he replied that he did not know because Emmet and Russell had boasted of the secrecy with which they had acted. He also rejected the possibility of a rising in Wicklow and claimed that in the event of a French invasion the people would not join in. This must have been music to the ears of Wickham or perhaps he was disappointed that one of his pet theories had been so firmly disproven. Dwyer admitted that he had killed soldiers in Wicklow but did not expand on that particular theme and there was no mention of reprisals, house-burnings, robberies or the levying of contributions on businesses. He went on to regale them with his account of how he survived in the mountains and the examination ended with a curious piece of non information, namely that the "key of the letter which Emmet got from France was in Dowdall's trunk which Major Sirr opened", obviously a piece of useless gossip that he had picked up somewhere in the prison as Dowdall, by this time, had escaped to America.

But perhaps Dwyer's most interesting observation came when he was asked to give the reasons for the breaking out of fighting in Wicklow. "In 1798 the people were told that the Orangemen intended to murder them, the loyal were assured that they were to be massacred by the people - troops were sent into the country, on their approach the people fled, the houses were found empty, and thus both parties were confirmed in their belief - but they have since discovered the truth and Protestants and Catholics are now as good friends as ever".

The only official reaction to Dwyer's examination came from Marsden who, when sending a copy of it to the Home Office in London, laconically dismissed it as having nothing but curiosity value. The Government, however, was again careful to exploit its propaganda in full and the Dublin newspapers and the London Times all reported that he had been examined at length and, while no details were divulged, readers were more than compensated by a detailed and, predictably, exaggerated description of him which contrasts unfavourably with the drawing made by the artist George Petrie who was granted permission to visit him in Kilmainham about this time. On the same day, Arthur Devlin refused to allow himself be examined at all, and it is not certain if he was actually brought before the examiners. Since he had been placed in Dublin Castle Devlin, because of his close links with Emmet, had been receiving very different treatment. According to another prisoner, Thomas Cloney of Wexford, "Devlin was ordered to walk around the Castle yard for several days with some well trained agents of infamy there, in order that I might see him, and another gentleman who was confined in a room on the second floor (Emmet's first cousin John St John Mason) should also be appraised of his arrival. The man, whose name was Arthur Devlin, was there made to appear to us in the character of an informer against state prisoners. After keeping Devlin, who proved to be a firm and decided character among a gang of unprincipled vagabonds for several days to no purpose, they sent him to Kilmainham Jail".

The object of this particular exercise was to make St John Mason and Cloney think that Devlin had turned informer thereby putting additional pressure on them to admit to their involvement with Emmet. But Devlin, apart from not wishing to incriminate anyone connected with the Rebellion also realised that he would have to conceal the fact that he was a deserter from both the British army and Navy and was in no position or mood to answer questions from any quarter. Following his refusal to be examined no further action was taken against Devlin and he was transferred to Kilmainham Jail.

Although Devlin officially had been given the rank of a second class priosner, by the end of March he was complaining that "we are treated worse than hounds in a kennel" and he demanded his proper allowance from Trevor: "I have been given terms sir with the Government on my surrender to them and although you seem well inclined to do so, you cannot alter them".

But Devlin was legally in a difficult position still as some of the state prisoners who were experts on law and knew about his past career informed him that the colonel from whose regiment he had deserted in England had still the right to claim him from the civil authorities and in that event Devlin would face a court martial and certain death.

14

The sudden resignation of William Wickham came as quite a severe blow to the Lord Lieutenant, who had come to rely on him for advice and support and with another House of Commons debate in London on the handling of the Emmet rebellion in prospect, the resignation could not have come at a more inopportune time for him. Hardwicke believed, like the others, that the resignation was a result of ill health but Wickham was still preoccupied with putting the final touches to his paper which would outline his new and radical proposals regarding the future relationship between Ireland and Great Britain. It was finally completed and he headed it as follows: "Three reasons for resigning the Office of Chief Secretary to the Lord Lieutenant of Ireland submitted to private friends in the month of January 1804".

Wickham argued in his paper that the principal reason why differences had arisen between Catholics, Protestants and Dissenters in Ireland was due to the mistaken policy of making the Protestant Church in Ireland an established church. With regard to his own position, he continued: "the only question for present consideration is whether any advantage can arise from my openly avowing opinions which in the present state and temper of public feeling, the alarming state of the King's health, closely connected with the Irish question, and the many other circumstances of difficulty in which the Government of England is placed would be almost universally rejected." He then proceeded, at great length, in stating that in the aftermath of Emmett's rebellion he had traced the conspiracy to its source and had brought everyone who had been charged to court rather than relying on the use of court martials. He then quoted in full Emmet's letter to him recounting that Emmet had written the letter "without blot, erasure or interlineation in a firm and steady hand saying that when he closed sealed and directed it 'I am now quite prepared'". The extent of Wickham's feeling of guilt can be judged by the fact that in one of his drafts he added underneath the famous quotation from the Gospel of St Matthew 'But I say to you love your enemies, bless them that curse you, do good to them that hate you, and pray for them that despitefully use you and persecute you.'

William Wickham then emotionally summed up again, in a quite fortright manner, his reasons for resigning: "I hereby repeat that no consideration on earth could induce me to remain after having maturely reflected the contents of this letter, for in what honours or other earthly advantages could I find compensation for what I must suffer were I again compelled by an official duty to persecute to death men capable of thinking and acting like Emmet has done in the last moments for making an effort to liberate their country from grievances the existence of many of which none can deny one and which I myself acknowledge to be unjust, oppressive and unchristian. I will know that the manner in which I have suffered myself to be affected by this letter will be attributed to a sort of morbid sensibility rather than to its real cause but no one can be capable of forming a right judgement on my motives who has not, like myself, been condemned by his official duty to dip his hands in the blood of his fellow countrymen, in execution of a portion of the laws and institutions of his country of which his conscience cannot approve.'

By any standards it was an extraordinary document coming from such a high ranking Government official and, in some respects, the sentiments expressed matched Emmet's own sense of idealism. But, on February 20th, William Wickham quietly left Ireland on board the yacht Dorset and retired from public life, ostensibly on health grounds with a pension of eighteen hundred pounds. Apart from a brief period, when he was a member of the Treasury board, he never sought public office again. His friends, on receiving his paper, no doubt put it down to mental exhaustion, although significantly, he was asked to renew his secret service oath on his retirement. And, for William Wickham, there would be no mental respite as Emmet's letter would continue to haunt him for the rest of his life.

His successor, as Chief Secretary, was Sir Evan Nepean who, for the previous nine years, had been Secretary to the Admiralty and was succeeded in that post by Marsden's brother William, the famous orientalist and numismatist. Evan Nepean had the reputation of being a hard working official and a man of moderate opinions who had in 1778 supervised the setting up of the new penal colony in Botany Bay, but during the single year in which he remained in the post he, too, had to struggle both to comprehend and come to terms with the Irish political situation.

One of his first official duties was to report to the Home Office that John Mernagh had at last been captured on February 19th. Following his unsuccessful attempts to get to Humewood, John Mernagh had, for a short period, returned to the Glen of Imaal although, according to a letter written by Sir Charles Asgill at the end of January, the military search for him was actually halted in order that he might be given an opportunity of surrendering. Mernagh failed to oblige and the search was resumed because 'it was very evident he had no intention of surrendering'. Information was then received that Mernagh was trying to reach a man by the name of Doyle in the area of Rathcoole, Co. Dublin and on the night of February 19th a group of the Newcastle Yeomanry, headed by a Captain Clinch of Peamount, surrounded a house in the area owned by a James

Doyle where Mernagh was hiding. Mernagh rushed out of the house and tried to escape in the dark but Captain Clinch followed him on horseback and, when Mernagh stumbled into a sandpit, he proceeded to jump his horse on Mernagh as he lay on the ground. But Mernagh, though he did not have a firearm, still did not surrender and continued to throw stones at his pursuers until he was overpowered and taken to the County Jail of Naas in Kildare. From there he was then brought to Kilmainham Jail to join the others and he was due to be examined in Dublin Castle on March 2nd. But Mernagh now emulated the performance of Arthur Devlin and refused to be examined as Nepean reported: 'Mernagh would not say a word. He is a very fine young man but hanged he must be. There is no shirking the business like the present.' But, despite this crisp and ominous statement by the new Chief Secretary, John Mernagh was returned to Kilmainham Jail and would be included in the surrender terms granted to the others.

In Wicklow the ten week long military campaign was now called off and another round of mutual congratulations took place, among them, the consensus being that they had rid the country at last of a highly dangerous gang. Michael Dwyer's female relatives had already been set free and the imprisoned men were due to be released from the prison tenders in Poolbeg at the end of the month. Dwyer's father had also been released from the New Geneva prison and so the first part of William Hume's terms were realised. But, quite unexpectedly, Martin Burke and Hugh Byrne were transferred back to Wicklow Jail on a warrant to stand trial for offences alleged to have been committed there, possibly dating back to 1799 when they both escaped from prison. But their trial was postponed until the Autumn and they were back in Kilmainham within a week. The charges were subsequently dropped when it was realised that they had agreed surrender terms with the Government.

Officially, however, Michael Dwyer had been committed to Kilmainham by Wickham on a charge of high treason and the others had been committed on the lesser charge of being involved in treasonable practises. These charges were, however, mainly for public reassurance, and William Hume had confirmed their surrender terms with William Wickham before Christmas without however mentioning the United States of America as a possible destination for the Dwyer family. It seems that this particular option was never considered at any time by the Government, and even if William Hume had been able to persuade Hardwicke, neither the Home Office in London or indeed the American Government would have allowed it. As far back as 1790, Jeremiah Fitzpatrick, the progressive Inspector General of Irish Prisons, had referred to the practise of the American Government shipping back to Ireland every convict they found except those who were tradesmen. But, on their return, the convicts were liable to be executed on the charge of returning from transportation without permission. As recently as 1798, President Adams had instructed his ministers in London to inform the British Government that he was determined to make use of the recent powers granted to him by an Act of Congress not 'to allow any traitors from Ireland to land in America'. As a result of these instructions Rufus King, the American envoy in London, had effectively stopped the intended shipping over of some United Irishmen prisoners at that time. It might be argued that if Dwyer had been pardoned and not brought to trial he could have been sent to America as a freeman but he was such a well known rebel and his surrender had been given so much newspaper publicity both in Dublin and London that there is little doubt but that the American Government would have prevented it. There was an American consul, James Wilson, in Dublin at the time and he, no doubt, would have informed the American Government about such a proposed move.

But the intentions of the Irish Government concerning Dwyer and his companions were, in fact, quite clear and, soon after his arrival in Ireland, Evan Nepean was instructed to write to the Home Office making a request for the provision of a ship to transport one hundred and forty men and thirty women to New South Wales. It was over a year and a half since the last convict ship, the Rolla, had left Cork Harbour bound for New South Wales and the number of prisoners given sentences of transportation in the various court sessions throughout the country was building up again. It was Hardwicke's intention that Dwyer and his comrades would be on board that ship and that he would be rid of them by the middle of summer at the latest.

On March the 7th 1804, the motion for investigating the cause of Emmet's rebellion was finally introduced by Sir John Wrottesley, the member from Lichfield, in the House of Commons in London. He put two clear options to the House; if the Government of Ireland had not been taken by surprise but were well informed of it in advance now was the time to remove any remaining doubts but, on the other hand, if it were proved that they had no advance knowledge, it would then "be incumbent to address His Majesty to dismiss those persons from the Government of Ireland". This was a thinly disguised call not only for the dismissal of Marsden but also for Hardwicke's removal from office. Sir John Wrottesley now showed that he had done his homework in trying to prove Government negligence by shrewdly taking as examples the two events to which the Government were most vulnerable, namely the Patricks St. gunpowder explosion which occurred a week before the rebellion and which had been publicly downplayed by Marsden and also the fact that Hardwicke had returned to the Vice Regal Lodge in the Phoenix Park on the afternoon of July 23rd and had remained there guarded only by a dozen soldiers. Lord Castlereagh opposing the motion for the Government attempted to distance himself from the dismissal of General Fox adding, rather unfortunately, that "Lord Hardwicke was not so uninformed as some gentlemen supposed". It was, at best, a half-hearted attempt by Castlereagh who probably believed that the Irish Government had been at fault but he was now also preoccupied with, and indeed even secretly advocating, the return of William Pitt to office as Prime Minister while still remaining a member of Addington's tottering Government. James Charles Fox again took the floor on behalf of his brother and castigated the Dublin Journal for what he termed its 'scurrilous and defamatory paragraphs' but, when the House divided, the motion for an official enquiry was defeated by a margin of two to one. Hardwicke's administration was spared any further embarrassment because, with the war effort against Napoleon faltering, it was now widely believed that it was only a matter of time before Addington would be replaced by Pitt as Prime Minister. So, to the exasperation of his opponents, Marsden retained his post as Under Secretary but Hardwicke's administration, despite his conciliatory policies would still, in the coming years, continue to be the subject of investigation by committees of the House of Commons. No sooner had the issue of Emmet's Rebellion ended than a new campaign began alleging that serious abuses were taking place in Kilmainham Jail. These allegations while presented to the Government were directed at its superintendent, Dr. Edward Trevor, the Inquisitor of Kilmainham, from whose brutality neither Dwyer, his companions nor the Devlin family, in particular, would escape.

15

A new Jail to serve the County of Dublin had been built at
Kilmainham in 1795 at the cost of sixteen thousand
pounds. It was situated near army headquarters at the
Royal Hospital about one mile from Dublin Castle and the old
jail, a few hundred yards away, was now mainly used as a laun-
dry. Kilmainham Jail was built like a fortress and consisted of two
quadrangles in which there were cells for sixty prisoners. There
were apartments for the Keeper, a common room, a workroom,
an infirmary, a chapel, ten exercise yards and even a treadmill.

Even though it was now only ten years old many well
known rebels had already been imprisoned there including
Napper Tandy, Wolfe Tone, The Sheares brothers, Thomas
Addis Emmet, Henry Joy McCracken and, in the recent past,
Thomas Russell and Robert Emmet. In the weeks following
Emmet's rebellion the Government had panicked and, availing
of the suspension of the Habeas Corpus Act in Ireland, had
indiscriminately arrested anyone thought to have been even
remotely involved. The suspects came from all classes in society and the jails and prison tenders in Dublin were soon filled.
The most important of these prisoners were sent to
Kilmainham and the debtors who were housed there were
transferred to the Marshalsea Prison off Thomas St.

By the middle of 1804, some of these prisoners had been held without trial for almost a year; in some cases there wasn't sufficient evidence available, in other cases where the Government had evidence it would have meant revealing the names of secret informers which they were unwilling to do but there was also an overall reluctance by the Government to bring to public notice, by means of a trial, any further embarrassing details about the Rebellion which might rebound on themselves. Some of these prisoners were Protestant friends and acquaintances of Robert Emmet, professional people who were experiencing prison life for the first time. The very rigid class structures which then existed extended into the prison system and the various prisoners were classified according to their status in society. At the top of this pecking order were the first class or state prisoners who naturally belonged to the upper or professional classes; in the next division were the second class prisoners who were largely equated with the middle classes and the third category was filled by 'the lower orders' who formed the main bulk of the prison population.

Michael Dwyer, because of his status of a rebel chief given to him by the military, was put among the first class prisoners on his commital to Kilmainham; Arthur Devlin was given the status of a second class prisoner, but Hugh Byrne, Martin Burke and John Mernagh, although initially having being placed in the second class division, were quickly transferred to the felons' side of the prison which in the case of Hugh Byrne was a breach of his surrender terms.

Both the living conditions and food allowances of these three categories were strictly defined and costed. The first class prisoners were usually given a cell of their own which was reasonably furnished and they were entitled to a generous daily food allowance to the value of three shillings and three pence. This allowance meant that they were entitled to receive each day one pound of bread, a half ounce of tea, three ounces of sugar, a half naggin of milk and one and a half pounds of either beef, mutton or pork, a quart of small beer and, on occasions, a half naggin of whiskey. For Dwyer, after spending five years on the run in the Wicklow mountains, it was like moving into a luxury hotel! The allowances of the second class prisoners were proportionately less but still generous, but for the majority of prisoners on the felons' side of the prison their allowance consisted of two loaves per week, a pint of milk a day and a supply of water. In addition they had to live in the most primitive of conditions and their empty cells were either covered with straw which was usually wet or had no covering at all.

Within that overall framework, however, there was plenty of room for manoeuvre by the prison authorities and, for the majority of the prisoners of all classes held in Kilmainham at that period, it had become little more than a hell hole owing to the conduct of its superintendent of whom the prisoners were soon to testify that "there is not so cruel a monster in human shape than Dr. Trevor".

Edward Trevor was born in the North of Ireland and, having served in the army, came to Dublin to seek his fortune and trained as an apothecary. He returned to the North again where he became involved in the cut and thrust of electioneering in County Down. In time he drifted back to Dublin, now calling himself a doctor, and in 1798 was appointed as both medical attendant and superintendent of Kilmainham Jail. Within a few years he had broadened his official portfolio to become the medical attendant for the Royal Hospital and the Hibernian School. In addition he was appointed the agent for Transports as well as becoming the principal recruiting agent in Dublin for both army and navy and in this capacity he regularly visited all of the prisons and tender ships in the city persuading prisoners to enlist in exchange for free pardons.

Trevor was also used by both Wickham and Marsden as their chief spy in Kilmainham Jail and Wickham, despite all his qualms of conscience, had no hesitation in granting Trevor the sum of two hundred pounds before leaving office. At a time when few would have taken on the position of superintendent of a jail with any great enthusiasm Trevor absolutely revelled in his job and daily strode along the corridors of the jail twirling his cane, dispensing favours and issuing edicts in the manner of a feudal monarch. The attendants and turnkeys were his slaves, the prisoners dependent on his every whim; this was his empire, his small stepping stone into society and while he danced to the Government's tune "the reptile crawled to the Castle and was found by the Government to be a supple syco- phant, crafty and unprincipled", this was never done at the expense of his own personal interests. He had a razor sharp mind, he could be utterly charming or utterly ruthless, he pos- sessed a gallows-type sense of humour with an underlying streak of vindictiveness and cruelty and a complete absence of any kind of morality, which in particular made the carrying out of his medical duties a ghastly joke.

He was especially valuable to the Government in the weeks following Emmet's rebellion when, by appearing to be sympathetic towards them, obtained valuable information from both Emmet and Russell and he was instrumental also in persuading Michael Quigley to agreeing to become a secret informer. He also tried, unsuccessfully to bribe Bryan Devlin, the father of Ann Devlin: "Dr Trevor often wanted me to turn informer and he offered me money for that purpose; he had taken out of his pocket great quantities of bank notes and offered them saying that he would be a friend to me and to my family all our lives and, when I refused him, he was grin- ning at the same time, 'well you case hardened old villain you shall be hanged"!

James Tandy and John St. John Mason were the two state prisoners in Kilmainham who were mainly responsible for organising the prisoners into making official complaints against Trevor. Both had been arrested and imprisoned soon after Emmet's rebellion, mainly because of their family backgrounds, although neither of them were involved in any way with Emmet's plans. John St. John Mason was a first cousin of Emmet's whose mother's family name was Mason from County Kerry. He had just started practising as a barrister and was arrested on his way to attend a court sitting in Limerick. He was sent to Kilmainham where he was put into a cell measuring only ten feet by six. He was involved at the time also in a personal equity suit upon which a great part of his property depended and immediately wrote a strong letter of protest to Wickham, but to no avail. He was to remain in solitary confinement until November although Trevor made sure that he had access to Robert Emmet and Mason in fact made a rather foolish attempt to try and free Emmet by bribing one of the guards, an action which confirmed the authorities in their belief that he had been involved in the Rebellion.

James Tandy was a prosperous wine merchant who, far from supporting Emmet, attached himself to the Lawyers Corps of Yeomen whose members had offered Marsden their services in Dublin Castle on the night of July 23rd. He had served for six years with the East India Company and was known to Lord Cornwallis, but he was the son of Napper Tandy, the 1798 leader, and became well known to the Government when, in 1802, he vociferously opposed Hardwicke's proposal to transport his father to New South Wales. Tandy was owed the sum of one hundred and fifty pounds by a Brabazon Morris and later he was to claim vigorously that Morris had given false information to the Government about him to avoid paying off his debt. When a warrant was issued for his arrest Tandy came into Dublin Castle bringing with him two friends including Sir Marcus Somerville, a magistrate from Drogheda. They were received by Marsden who was standing with his back to a fire, and a slighted Somerville whispered very loudly "Is this not a pretty thing that this fellow receives gentlemen, warming his backside at the fire; he deserves to be kicked and, for a farthing, I would kick him". Marsden, who could not avoid hearing these remarks, took the only immediate recourse open to a Government official of the early nineteenth century; he left the room and, having remained outside for some time, finally returned "with a struggle of composure", being careful however, to keep away from the fire. This intervention by Sir Marcus

Somerville would prove very costly for Tandy because, at a later meeting, Marsden told him bluntly that he could expect no favours from him. Having been examined Tandy was finally sent to Kilmainham and it seems likely that Marsden asked Trevor that Tandy should be given the full treatment while he was there. Trevor was only too willing to oblige and Tandy was put into the worst cell in the dungeons where he remained despite the fact that he had many influential friends in the city interceding for him and despite having received a promise of an early release from Wickham the week before he retired from office. The corridor outside Tandy's cell was flooded to a depth of eighteen inches by a mixture of water, human excrement and other filth which often seeped in under the door of the cell and, when his wife and daughter came to visit him, they had to be carried to his cell by an attendant. The window of the cell opened on to the corridor which, because of the stench, had to be kept closed. When he became ill his wife was refused permission to see him and later when he was put into a cell with three others they had to share a privy bucket which was not emptied for two or three days. Later it was moved to the corridor outside where the prisoners ate and when they wished to use it they had often to keep knocking for two and three hours before an attendant came to open the cell door.

In May 1804 the Government of Henry Addington finally collapsed and William Pitt was, once more, called upon to form a new administration; in France Napoleon had just given himself the title of Emperor of the French and, as Pitt attempted to rally the spirit of the British people to renew the war effort against France, it became known in Ireland that he was opposed to the idea of an early release for the state prisoners in Kilmainham. By the end of June, however, some of the prisoners, at the urging of St. John Mason, decided to take the initiative themselves; a commission of the Oyer and Terminer court was being held in the Sessions House in Green St. and, with some difficulty, the prisoners succeeded in getting a barrister to hand up a letter of theirs to the presiding Judges on the bench.

The letter stated that "a system of avaricious and malignant severity is practised in this prison which calls aloud for, and might be sufficiently demonstrated, by a fair and impartial investigation". Judges were obliged at that time, on receipt of such complaints, to visit the jail concerned and to interview both prisoners and jailers but, in the case of state prisoners, the Government had to be informed first and the Judge then awaited their instructions before proceeding.

The complaints of the prisoners were received by Justice George Daly who, having contacted the Government, was asked to visit Kilmainham on July 7th where he spoke to St. John Mason and was handed two separate memorials by him, the first having been signed by fourteen of the first class prisoners and the other by forty one prisoners of the second class. The signatures from the first class included, obviously, both Mason and Tandy and also two of Robert Emmet's friends, Philip Long the banker who had advanced him a sum of one thousand four hundred pounds, and John Patten, a Trinity College chemistry student and a brother in law of the poet Thomas Moore. Michael Dwyer did not sign the memorial at this stage as he had still no complaint to make about his treatment. Among the signatures in the second class petition were Bryan Devlin and Arthur Devlin and thirteen signatures were bracketed together at the end of the list with the explanation that they had been confined to the felons' side of the prison until a short time before. The last three names on this list were Hugh Byrne, Martin Burke and John Mernagh.

Justice George Daly reported back immediately to the Government stating that from his "imperfect investigations the grievances, if they exist at all are greatly exaggerated in the memorials". He then stated that it was the wish of the prisoners that the memorials be forwarded to Hardwicke who, on reading them, seemed to be genuinely shocked at the allegations which they contained. He would already have been aware of Tandy's complaints as would the Chief Secretary Evan Nepean because, when Nepean took up office, Tandy's wife applied to him seeking his release and Nepean, new to the job, quickly reassured her, "I am Madam a husband and father of a family and God forbid that I could possibly think of keeping a man in confinement without either bringing him to trial or to the bar". But an embarrassed Nepean was soon telling Tandy's wife that he had been overruled. Hardwicke on reading the memorials of the prisoners decided to hold a top level investigation and appointed Chief Justice William Downes to head it and he, in turn, asked Justices Osborne and Day to assist him. The investigation was to take place in Kilmainham over a period of three days from July 16th to 18th and it was decided not to inform the officers of the Jail in advance to ensure that they would be able to see conditions as they really were, an idle hope with someone as resourceful as Trevor in charge and given his close connections with Marsden in Dublin Castle.

But, before the investigation began, Michael Dwyer had, at last, fallen foul of Trevor. With the change of Government in London, the prospect of a convict ship for New South Wales being provided that summer was fading as the new administration was still settling in. Dwyer, in Trevor's eyes, was now obviously losing his potential value as a source of secret information and so on July 1st, without any warning, his allowance of tea, sugar and spirits were stopped and he was ordered out into the yard with the other prisoners. He immediately complained to Trevor asking him in particular not to deprive him of the spirits as he claimed "my health would suffer at being debarred of that to which I had been necessarily accustomed". Dwyer's children had also joined him in his cell as well as his wife and they were now also ordered to leave the prison during daytime hours. Mary Dwyer was then nine months pregnant and their fourth child Esther would be born by the end of the month. Trevor warned Dwyer that if he did not obey his orders he would have him transferred to the felons' side of the prison but Dwyer again asked him to restore his allowance of spirits saying that he did not deserve such treatment and that it was contrary to the terms pledged to him by William Hume. Trevor

then sent for John Dunn, the Keeper of the prison, and ordered him to take Dwyer to the felons' side.

Dwyer decided to go with him quietly but Mary Dwyer immediately left the prison and complained to John Hume, an uncle of William Hume's who lived at Synott Place in Dublin. Dwyer also had a letter written and delivered to Hume and, ten days later, John Hume visited Kilmainham where he spoke to Dwyer in the Jailers parlour. He questioned him about the incident with Trevor and spoke also to John Dunn who confirmed the fact that Dwyer had caused no trouble since his arrival and described him as 'a most quiet and peacable man' but added discreetly that Trevor was 'a most passionate man'. John Hume's solution for resolving the situation was a surprisingly simple one: he suggested that Dwyer should go and apologise to Trevor. Dwyer naturally objected, making the obvious remark that he had nothing to apologise about but, at the insistence of Hume, and still wishing to protect his secret terms, he had to swallow what was left of his pride, and agreed to go and apologise to Trevor asking him to be reinstated as a first class prisoner and also to be reunited with his wife and children. Trevor accepted the apology, asking him if he believed if it was Hume's intervention that caused him to accept it. When Dwyer replied that it was his belief, Trevor replied that he had punished him only as an example to the other prisoners. So, just one week before the official enquiry began Dwyer was allowed back to his cell, although his allowance was reduced to second class status and he now began to interest himself in the state prisoners' complaints.

16

On the morning of Monday July 16th - in what must have been the worst kept secret of the year - Chief Justice William Downes, accompanied by Justices Osborne and Day, arrived at Kilmainham Jail. They were also accompanied by John Pollock, Clerk of the Crown and registrar for the Court of the Chief Justice who would act as note-taker. The state prisoners were, naturally, delighted with this development although it was not completely unexpected; their treatment had improved dramatically over the previous few days and they had overheard a midnight conference on the night before during which the Keeper John Dunn told the staff in the kitchens to go out and bring back to the prison immediately the very best of provisions at any price!

Chief Justice Downes had decided to interview, separately and under oath, a number of the prisoners who had signed their names to the memorials; he would also visit the kitchens, some of the cells, and would finally interview some of the prison staff including John Dunn and finally Trevor himself. A room next to the Sherrif's execution room was assigned by Trevor for the interviews, a gesture that was not lost on the prisoners, and although the interviews were supposed to be confidential Trevor strategically placed himself in a corridor above the room from where he could hear everything that was being discussed.

In all thirty prisoners were interviewed including all of the first class prisoners who had signed the memorial and Michael Dwyer, still smarting over the bad treatment he had received, now decided to add his name to the list of complainants and asked to be interviewed also. Eight prisoners were chosen to represent the second class and they all now gave their testimony under the general headings of food and the service of food by the attendants, the reductions and deprivation of their state allowance by Trevor, their close confinement and the capricious distribution of prisoners, privy facilities, the poor treatment of visitors to the prison and finally, what they termed the overall malevolence of Trevor. What followed over the next three days was a repeated litany of complaints; the water supply was contaminated by excrement and, after meals, it was not uncommon for food utensils to be washed in the same emptied privy buckets. Many of the convicted prisoners in the felons' side were used as attendants having been promised a remission of their sentences and when they brought round the meat at meal times they tore off portions of it with their filthy hands, meat which in any case was often putrid. While the Keeper of the Jail John Dunn virtually escaped censure one of the attendants called George Dunn was singled out on account of his brutal behaviour. He had boasted that he first became a prison attendant in Mullingar Jail where he had been brought in to murder some prisoners and, following the execution of Felix O'Rourke, one of Emmet's supporters, he had gone round the prison brandishing a knife and shouting 'this is the knife that cut off the head of Felix O'Rourke!'

The prisoners complained also that, on a sudden whim, Trevor would transfer them to the felons' side where they were kept in solitary confinement and were loaded and bolted with up to four stone of irons. This was largely a mercenary move by Trevor as they were all entitled to a daily allowance of three shillings and three pence worth of food and transference to the

felons' side meant that the Keepers and ultimately Trevor bene-
fitted from the financial savings. In his capacity of medical
attendant also Trevor was in the habit of prescribing glauber
salts for all manner of complaints, including gout and, when
the prisoners were given this all-purpose medicine, they would
receive no provisions on that day, thereby adding a little more
to his overall profits.

When it was Michael Dwyer's turn to be questioned by the
Judges he recounted for them what had taken place between
Trevor and himself and, entering into the spirit of the proceedings and taking a lead from other first class prisoners, he went
on to complain of his not being able to eat the boiled fresh meat
because it was served offensively, adding that he would prefer
beef steak or mutton and a half pint of spirits daily! He then
asked that Trevor might be brought in so that he might be questioned about his recent treatment towards him. The Judges, surprisingly, agreed to this request and so, for the only time during
the investigations, Trevor was directly confronted by one of the
prisoners. Having been put on oath, Trevor, in his defence, said
that Dwyer had become 'pert' and so he transferred him to the
felons' side. He then turned the intervention of John Hume to
his own advantage by pointing out that Hume had insisted that
Dwyer should apologise to him, but the Judges instructed
Trevor not to tamper any more with Dwyer's conditions without good cause.

Hugh Byrne was interviewed also, having been chosen as
one of the eight prisoners who represented the second class. He
told the Judges that, on his arrival in Kilmainham, he had been
put into the second class for four days only and he was then
put on the 'jail allowance', namely two loaves of bread a week,
a pint of milk a day and water. Apart from his brief transfer to
Wicklow Jail he remained on the felons' side for fifteen weeks
having been recently upgraded again to the status of second
class. Both Martin Burke and John Mernagh had been treated in
exactly the same manner but Arthur Devlin had remained in
the second class since his transfer from Dublin Castle.

On the final day of the investigation it was Trevor's own turn to be interviewed and he was at his mercurial best, giving a brilliant performance of unashamed roguery. No one could have seemed to be so genuinely concerned about the welfare of the prisoners; there hadn't been a single day since July 23rd, he informed the Judges, that he hadn't visited the prison - he omitted to tell them that his chief concern during this time had been the collection of information for which he was well paid. He had always taken the utmost pains to see that the provisions supplied were of the highest quality and he strongly denied that he had made even the smallest profit out of anything that was supplied to the prison - the truth, of course, being the very opposite. With regard to specific complaints he would only admit that the supply of vegetables had been unsatisfactory but blamed the recent severe weather for this and he promised that the hangman Tom Galvin would not be used in future to bring food to the prisoners, thereby spoiling their appetites! He found St. John Mason to be both irritable and bad tempered and said that it was well known that no other prisoners would associate with him because of his temper and foulness of manner.

The Lordships finally interviewed the Keeper John Dunn. The prison butcher and baker gave evidence also and so, on Wednesday afternoon of July 18th, their Lordships took leave of Kilmainham Jail and everyone waited anxiously for their report to appear. The prisoners were confident that, given the weight of evidence, the abuses would cease and that, at least, Trevor would be replaced. Even better, they could look forward to an early release, but it would all depend on the official report of their lordships.

17

The report of Chief Justice Downes was written and submitted to Hardwicke with almost indecent haste. Judge
Osborne was able to be present in the Jail only on the first
day and so, having conferred with Justice Day and with the
help of his eponymous notetaker John Pollock, the report was
written on that same night by Downes's in his house at Merrion
Square as he was due to leave for country court sessions on the
following morning.

The report first noted the great irritation and resentment felt
about Trevor but concluded that "despite this evidence Dr.
Trevor, John Dunn and the turnkeys have conducted themselves with humanity towards the prisoners". There were only
minor criticisms made of prison conditions, some being quite
ludicrous such as adverting to the absence of table cloths and
towels in the prison and also to the indifferent manner of serving food and conducting prisoners to the water closets. Not
surprisingly they found the quality of the meat served to be
very good but the quality of the bread was criticised, a fact
which the baker himself had acknowledged. They made other
minor recommendations concerning exercise and the provision
of fires in the prison but the net result of the report was a complete vindication for Trevor. It was more remarkable because of

the fact that Justice Day had the reputation of being a humane man who would continue to interest himself in abuses, but it was obviously the report of the Chief Justice, who seems to have been unduly influenced by his clerk John Pollock who often had exceeded his role of note taker during the investigations by asking questions "which were intrusively and insidiously put". Pollock knew his fellow-Northerner Trevor well and obviously would have taken his side.

The report was sent to Hardwicke on the following morning who read it no doubt with a sense of relief. Evan Nepean must have been puzzled by it, given his knowledge of Tandy's treatment and Marsden surely was secretly delighted that Trevor had escaped so lightly. The content of the report was leaked to Trevor straight away but the prisoners were not informed of its recommendations although they sensed, from the jaunty behaviour of Trevor during the next week, that he did not seem to be worrying unduly about it.

A week passed by and the prisoners, still having been kept in ignorance about the contents of the report, organised a mass protest by walking together along the corridors of the prison. Trevor, for once, taken aback by this sudden and united show of strength, asked them to return to their cells and promised that he would have an answer from the Government by the following Monday. On that night, he arrived at the prison bringing with him a holding statement from the Government stating that no final decision on the report would be taken until the following Monday "when a matter relative to the state prisoners might take place in the intermediate time". Trevor, on being asked what these matters might be, in typical fashion answered that he did not know. He was then asked if the prisoners were to regard his message as being official and he replied that it had come from the highest authority "except the Lord Lieutenant". He asked them not to take part in any other actions until the week had elapsed.

If credence can be given to Trevor's statements it seems that some consideration was being given by Chief Secretary Nepean to release some of the prisoners who had now been held without trial for over a year. Many influential people such as Lord Charlemont were still petitioning for the release of James Tandy but, in advocating such releases, Nepean would have been opposed by both Marsden and Hardwicke who could ill afford to release any prisoner fearing that, in a short period, he might be again charged with plotting an invasion with the French.

On Monday August 6th, Trevor again met with the prisoners but now he gave an evasive answer saying that the Government was expecting a Court of Chancery to meet before any decision could be taken. If this was the case then it could be expected that both the Attorney General and Lord Redesdale, the Chancellor, could be relied on to adopt hardline attitudes and when Trevor was asked if a date had been set for such a meeting he replied in the negative.

This effectively ended the prisoners' hopes for an early release and Trevor, having been exonerated, was now free to indulge himself in Kilmainham Jail again and the instances of his cruelty and tyranny increased rather than diminished.

A week later, in an effort to dissuade the prisoners from holding any further mass protests inside the prison, the Sherrif of the County, Luke White, arrived without warning as a group of prisoners were taking exercise and, on the pretext of looking for proof of some vague plot, the soldiers, with fixed bayonets, forced them back into their apartments again. It was at this time also that the only musical instrument in the prison, a battered violin, was taken away and broken in pieces by a guard and when it was discovered that James Tandy had been feeding tame pigeons, they were all killed.

On August 13th the prisoners decided, however, to renew their action, and signed another letter which was handed to Hardwicke, as he and Marsden were riding together in a coach. Once again they pilloried Trevor and, for the first time, complained also about the shocking treatment which had been meted out to Ann Devlin who had been recently transferred to the Second Class. But this letter was ignored by Hardwicke and their only success came when, in the middle of September, James Tandy was released on the advice of Surgeon General Stewart. Ten months earlier Tandy had entered Kilmainham a healthy man but now he had to be carried out in the arms of two men with an abscess on his chest and looking like a skeleton. For the remainder of the prisoners, their treatment remained unchanged although John Patten was given what was considered the best cell in the jail which he shared with another prisoner and he was allowed to pursue his chemistry studies there.

Lord Hawkesbury had by now replaced Hardwicke's brother in the Home Office and, on September 10th, Evan Nepean wrote to him reminding him of the earlier request to provide a convict ship to New South Wales. Meanwhile in Kilmainham, John Dunn the Keeper had died, having been given a pint of castor oil by Trevor an hour before his death. A clerk, by the name of Kennedy, fared a little better when he was pensioned off to prevent him discovering irregularities in the prison's accounts. The new Keeper, handpicked by Trevor, was called Simpson, a drunken boor, who would soon make life even more miserable for the prisoners.

Hugh Byrne's wife Sarah had joined her husband in Kilmainham, but Hugh Byrne and Michael Dwyer incurred Trevor's displeasure again as another state prisoner, the engraver John Galland, recorded: "I have known Trevor to turn out Dwyer's wife and children and Hugh Byrne's wife who were in Kilmainham with the agreement of the Government out of jail, late in the evening without dinner, they not knowing where to put their heads; and all of this for the alleged offences of their husbands for which Dwyer and Byrne were previously punished". Galland himself had been out of favour since Trevor had asked him to engrave his family crest on the ivory handles of some knives and forks which he owned. When Galland, rather unwisely, insisted on charging Trevor six shillings a dozen for the job, Trevor demurred and shortly afterwards Galland found himself in solitary confinement living on wet straw from which he contracted lumbago. When his sister visited him she took away some of the straw and complained to Judge Day. Trevor then refused Galland's sister access to the prison and Nepean had to write officially to him and order him to allow her access to her brother in Kilmainham.

But, while the Government waited for news of the provision of a convict ship, Trevor now dreamed up a novel plan which would solve some of the Government's problems in this regard. He had employed two prisoners to act as attendants, sixteen-year-old Edward Doyle who had been sentenced to seven years transportation for stealing calico and Edward White who had been sentenced to death for robbery. According to the testimony of Patrick Doyle, another Wicklow man who was in Kilmainham, White and Doyle approached Dwyer and the others with an escape plan saying that they would lock up the Keeper and his attendants and then they could all escape together. But Patrick Doyle claimed that he climbed up onto a window ledge and saw outside the walls a large group of soldiers with fixed bayonets and reported this to the others. Another version of the story claims that Edward Doyle revealed the plot to Dwyer and was then transferred back to the felons' side. He would later join Dwyer and the others in New South Wales.

There was now further disappointment for the Government when news arrived from London that the provision of a convict ship was to be delayed again until the following Spring. A furious Hardwicke asked Nepean to write back and protest, in the strongest terms, to the Home Office, pointing out that the last convict ship, the Rolla, had left Cork as late as the month of November and that the convicts had arrived in New South Wales in perfect health. Already the jails throughout the country were crowded with prisoners sentenced to transportation and Hardwicke also wished to be rid at last of some of the troublesome prisoners in Kilmainham, including Dwyer.

But the Home Office in London did not change its mind and, with the chorus of complaints still coming from Kilmainham,

Nepean decided to pay a visit himself on December 15th. Advance notice was given on this occasion and the choicest meat which had been brought in on the day of the visit was immediately sent back after he had left. But the affable Dr. Edward Trevor was, naturally, on hand to give the Chief Secretary, his private secretary Col. Flint, and a visiting guest, the Receiver General of Excise, a warm welcome. The inspection took place a short time after Trevor had made James Byrne strip to humiliate him in front of other prisoners but, when he tried to speak to Nepean about it during the visit, Trevor suddenly took the Chief Secretary aside and whispered something to him and Nepean quickly turned away without speaking to him. But another prisoner, Edward Coyle, did manage to speak to Nepean although he was in a very agitated state of mind. Coyle had been kept in solitary confinement for long periods since his arrest, but Col. Flint, a man obviously of strict etiquette, was singularly unimpressed by Coyle's complaints as he later wrote in a letter to Trevor, "Coyle's behaviour towards you seemed to me most reprehensible as the violent language he used towards you was expressed in the presence of prisoners of the inferior class, upon whose minds it was natural that it should produce the very worst effects". Col. Flint would obviously not have been too concerned to learn that when the visit was over Coyle was immediately loaded with four stone of irons and when the new Keeper Simpson came to inspect them he ensured before leaving to drop the irons on Coyle's ankles, inflicting the maximum pain. As for James Byrne, his attempt to speak to Nepean had been rewarded by his being nearly starved and he was put into an unglazed cell in mid-winter in the company of four hardened criminals condemned for murder and rape where conditions were so bad that one of them was forced to drink his own urine.

And so Trevor survived, still protected in Dublin Castle by Marsden, whom it was alleged was an unnamed partner with Trevor in a bakery concern which supplied bread to Kilmainham Jail!

William Downes, Lord Chief Justice, 1810.

Justice Robert Day.

The new year of 1805 arrived and, with Dwyer's treatment at the hands of Trevor still deteriorating, he arranged for a long letter to be written to William Hume in Humewood which he both signed, in his own flowery handwriting, and also thumbprinted and Mary Dwyer set off for Wicklow to deliver it personally to William Hume. In this letter Dwyer recounted how he had been treated in Kilmainham since his arrival there thirteen months before. He accused Trevor of calling him a savage and a tyrant and that he had gone round the prison saying that Dwyer was unfit for any society. But when Dwyer had protested at what he considered were an abuse of his terms Trevor had exploded, saying "Your terms! Your terms! I know what your terms are better than yourself. You have no terms at all. There is no robber or highwayman could make better possible terms than saving his life and the Capital Offence is where you and such persons should be." This was the first intimation that Dwyer had received that America might not be his destination after all and he concluded his letter by asking Hume whether the sufferings that he and others had endured had happened with the knowledge of the Government because he believed they had not. He finally reminded Hume of the promises he had made to him on his surrender and that he should ensure they were carried out.

Mary Dwyer, who brought this letter to Humewood, naturally gave her own account also of how they had been treated in Kilmainham and an embarrassed Hume having received similar letters from Hugh Byrne and Arthur Devlin wrote to Marsden on February 19th. "There is scarcely a day passes when I am not tormented with letters or messages from these fellows in Kilmainham who surrendered themselves to me, viz. Dwyer, Arthur Devlin and Hugh Byrne complaining of ill treatment, of being almost naked with various other complaints, and yesterday Dwyer's wife came here to tell me that she and her children had been thrown out of the prison and that he was thrown into that part of the prison alloted for felons and put on the gaol allowance and she says without cause, which I am not certain of the fact. But, although I know of no punishment too severe for them, yet it places me in a very awkward and unpleasant situation in this country to have these complaints made, however unfounded, that the terms I promised them to induce them to surrender are not kept. At the time they surrendered I told Mr. Wickham that they should be sent out of the Kingdom as soon as possible and that, in the meantime, they should not be ill treated in person, that their relatives who were confined merely on their account, should be liberated and that Dwyer's wife and children should be allowed to remain with him while in prison and sent along with him. And I can assure you that it cannot be any service to the country to have her at large here now. I therefore request that she may be confined again with her husband in Kilmainham; that if something very particular has not occurred to prevent it that I know nothing of at the present".

When Hume forwarded this letter to Marsden he also enclosed the other letters sent to him in the same vein, by both Arthur Devlin and Hugh Byrne. The letters seem to have been ignored and, as Dwyer waited in vain for a reply from Hume, Evan Nepean now resigned his post as Chief Secretary and returned to the Admiralty in London,no doubt a sadder, if not wiser, man. On March 23rd Marsden, who was now deputising as Chief Secretary, at last acknowledged a letter received from the Home Office in London which confirmed the recent instructions of Lord Hawkesbury that a convict ship be immediately provided for Ireland. But Dwyer and his comrades were still not informed of the Government's intentions in their regard and soon another tragedy occurred in Kilmainham which resulted in Trevor being held responsible for the death of Ann Devlin's ten year old brother Jimmy, the young son of Bryan Devlin and first cousin of both Michael Dwyer and Arthur Devlin.

18

Of all those who had been involved with Emmet's rebellion the family of Bryan and Winifred Devlin suffered most. They had been arrested after the rebellion along with all of their three daughters and two sons including the eight year old Jimmy who had suffered from smallpox and they were all sent to Kilmainham Jail. Ann Devlin, then aged twenty two, had been singled out for special treatment as she had been acting as Emmet's housekeeper and strenuous attempts were made to persuade her to give evidence against Emmet in advance of his trial. She was first examined by Major Henry Sirr and Marsden and, when she resolutely opposed every attempt to persuade her to inform against Emmet, Marsden was reduced to calling her "an incorrigible girl, dead to all kindness and noble feelings that adorn the character of a woman". It was then left to Trevor to try and persuade her but his usual mixture of treacly charm, bribery and, finally, dark threats had no effect on the most single-minded of young women.

On the morning of Emmet's trial Trevor even had a coach waiting to take her to court but to no avail. It was a rare defeat for Trevor and, when the trial had ended, he came back to Kilmainham to taunt her, shaking his cane at her: "Bad luck to Ann Devlin you rebelly bitch; I hope you shall be hanged. I never saw but one woman hanged in my life and I hope you shall be hanged and if there was no one else to hang you I would hang you myself. And now for your comfort, your Pet will be hanged tomorrow and I will put you under the care of someone who will murder you". During the next three months, the Devlin family were kept in the felons' side of the prison and again Trevor told Ann Devlin that she would be hanged within five days as an example to all womanhood never to keep a secret.

When Michael Dwyer and Arthur Devlin first arrived in Kilmainham they both asked permission to see her but were refused. By this time, her mother Winifred had been released to bring Hardwicke's offer to surrender to Dwyer in Wicklow but Ann, by then, had been transferred to the old Kilmainham Jail where the female prisoners were now being held and where the notorious Kathy 'The Goose' Giles reigned supreme. While Ann Devlin was there one of the women prisoners tried to kill her with a knife but the wife of the Keeper, John Dunn, intervened and persuaded her husband to transfer her to another area, for which decision he was roundly abused by Trevor. This was the only occasion when Ann Devlin lost her nerve as she fell on her knees and begged Trevor not to send her back there. Her health now began to suffer and she contracted distemper and emphysema. But her resolve and strength of mind never faltered again and she proved more than a match for Trevor trading verbal insult for insult with him. She told him quite plainly that, if he ever had any honour, he had lost it and, on another occasion, compared him to a bald horse of her father's who, when bent on mischief, would give a sly side look, and then his eyes would have a red shade over them as Trevor's did when he came to tyrannise her. These remarks quickly spread all over the prison to Trevor's great discomfiture.

By March 1805 Ann Devlin and her father Bryan were the only two remaining members of the family still imprisoned in Kilmainham. But their once prosperous business in Rathfarnham was now gone and the eldest son of the family was trying to make a precarious living in the vicinity of Howth in Co. Dublin with their one remaining horse. Winifred Devlin and one of her daughters were living in dire poverty in lodgings and were so badly off that they had to send back the ten year old Jimmy to live with his father in the prison. The young boy became very popular with the prisoners and often went up to the old jail where his sister Ann was again being confined. At about ten o'clock, on a cold night in March, the brutish attendant George Dunn and Thomas Brown, a servant of Trevor's, came to Bryan Devlin's cell saying that the young boy had to go up to the old jail to join his sister there. Bryan Devlin objected because the boy had developed a fever a short time before and was only now beginning to recover from it and told them that he was fearful of the boy going out into the cold night air. But Dunn insisted, saying that his orders came directly from Trevor and had to be obeyed. The boy, who had neither shoes nor stockings, had to put on what little clothes he had and was taken away by the two attendants. Despite promises made to his father that he would be wrapped in a blanket and carried up to the old jail he was made to walk instead although he was so weakened by fever that he had to stop several times on the way.

When he arrived at the old jail, he told his sister Ann that he felt he was going to die and, his fever having worsened, he died there a few days later. Trevor, despite the protests of Ann Devlin, and in a cynical attempt to cover up the real reason for his death, ordered an apothecary who attended the prison called Vaughan to perform a crude autopsy on the boy's head. About the same time another state prisoner, James Camuskey, also died of medical neglect although the official cause of death, given after a rather doubtful inquest had been held, was 'death by visitation of God'.

As a result of these two deaths and, with reports circulating that members of the House of Commons in London had been approached, mainly by Tandy on his release, to investigate the continuing abuses in Kilmainham, Trevor, prompted by Marsden no doubt, decided on a complete reversal of policy with regard to some of the state prisoners. John St. John Mason and Edward Coyle, two of his most vocal critics, were now suddenly allowed to leave the prison under escort and to visit warm salt baths in the city; they were also allowed to take the sea air at Blackrock and Dun Laoghaire in the south of the city and, in what was the most cynical of exercises, Ann Devlin was now allowed to visit the Spa in Lucan to improve her health. She set off from the prison in a coach with one of her sisters, Mary Dwyer having been refused permission to accompany her, and she was guarded by a pair of dragoons and a prison attendant armed with a pair of pistols. Mary Dwyer was, subsequently, allowed to travel with her, but soon the trips were discontinued having served their propaganda value for Trevor.

Michael Dwyer, Hugh Byrne and the engraver John Galland now decided to write separate letters to Justice Day about their treatment and he duly contacted Dublin Castle indicating his readiness to act under the authority of government but, with news having come about the provision of the convict ship, Justice Day received no further instructions from the Government on the matter. At the beginning of April, another letter arrived from the Home Office confirming that a convict ship had been engaged and would be ready to sail from Deptford in England within a month or five weeks. Nicholas Vensiggart had been appointed as the new Chief Secretary but Marsden was given the task of making the necessary arrangement with regard to the convict ship and for liaising with the Home Office in London. All of the country's Sheriffs were now contacted and arrangements were made to have prisoners who had been sentenced to transportation transferred to Cork.

But there were now of, course, a sufficient number of such prisoners to fill at least two convict ships but the Government was not unduly worried about this as, with the war against France proceeding, there was an ongoing need for recruits in both army regiments and navy squadrons. In addition, it was common practice to pardon a number of prisoners as a result of representations or petitions made on their behalf following sentence. As for the women prisoners, in the final analysis, only thirty five of the youngest and healthiest would be transported.

The busiest man in Dublin of course was Trevor, who was now revelling in his dual capacity as transportation and recruiting officer. It was the practice for the Sheriffs from the southern counties to send their prisoners directly to Cork under military escort in carts and waggons but the prisoners from the northern part of the country were first brought to Dublin where they were shaved, bathed and given prison clothes before being shipped down to Cork. The journey from Dublin to Cork was often the most hazardous part for the prisoners as the vessels engaged were usually in very poor condition and were reeking with fever. As a result, it was not unusual for prisoners to die during the short voyage or even in the holds of the ships while they were still at port.

By the beginning of May, preparations throughout the country were at an advanced stage and on May 12th the Government finally decided to inform Dwyer and his comrades that they were being sent to the penal colony of New South Wales as convicts and without any members of their families being allowed to travel with them. The willing Trevor was entrusted with the task of passing on this information to them and a distraught Dwyer, his worst suspicions now realised, with his dream of America shattered and not having received any reply from William Hume to his earlier letters, immediately wrote to John Hume in Synott Place. "My solemn conditions are to be violated; the sacred honour of Mr Hume is set at naught, and my children are to be left without the smallest means of living or protection. This is such a terrible dereliction of everything which, even in uncivilised life, is held sacred that I know not what to do".

Dwyer requested John Hume to visit him as soon as possible warning that "any breach of faith with me will surely be published to the world" and went on to talk about the now besmirched honour of the Hume family name.

William Hume was, in fact, attending the House of Commons in London at the time because, over the following two days of May 13 and 14, the House was debating a petition presented by some of the Irish members seeking emancipation for Catholics. Henry Grattan, the old warhorse of the Irish Parliament, was making his maiden speech in presenting the petition but, without the backing of Pitt's administration, it was heavily defeated. As John Hume awaited his nephew's return from London, Trevor pressed ahead with his transportation arrangements and, having received point blank refusals from Dwyer and the others to agree to be transported to New South Wales, he resorted to his familiar form of friendly persuasion, as Patrick Lynch, another prisoner who was threatened with the same fate, recorded: "The Deputy Sheriff and Dr Trevor called on me and gave me orders to prepare for Botany Bay but I refused. In the night, being in bed, both John Mernagh and I were both compelled to get up and dress ourselves and were removed to the capital offence and put among the felons as before and, by their orders, we were both doubly-bolted with the heaviest irons they could procure and all this make us agree to be transported to Botany Bay as was done with Dwyer, Burke, Devlin and Mernagh which treatment induced them to consent to transportation".

Some of the other state prisoners were now also asked to agree to transportation but they also refused. Unlike Dwyer they had not surrendered to the Government and had not, as yet, been charged or brought to trial. Robert Carty of County Wexford gave an outright refusal and having done so his treatment naturally worsened, and two other prisoners, John Kelly and Patrick Doyle, who also refused, were likewise removed to the felons' side.

But now a House of Commons committee had ordered the publication of the Justice Downes report and the Government, although the Habeas Corpus Act still remained in suspension, were now trying to find a way to release most of the state prisoners with as little embarrassment to themselves as possible. It was doubly ironic for Dwyer to hear that John Galland, the engraver with whom he had become friendly, had been offered a free passage to America but had refused it as did William McDermott of Kildare. But, unlike Dwyer, they could have travelled there as free men without the stigma of charges being brought against them.

The Government now even resorted to an old trick of using the newspapers to help their cause and soon reports were appearing that "the offender who had been so long in Kilmainham Jail called Captain Dwyer of the Mountains had refused to go to Botany Bay. He requests to be sent to America, he and three of his myrmidons with their families and the expense of such a voyage to be defrayed for them, an audacious request with which the Government will not comply. He is, therefore, to be tried if he persists and three of his followers. Four of his gang had consented to go to Botany Bay rather than stand trial." This last sentence indicates that Dwyer may have held out longer than the others in his refusal.

On his return from the House of Commons debate, William Hume was faced with an embarrassing and potentially dangerous situation to himself in County Wicklow as news of his now supposed broken promise to Dwyer had become public and the prospect of Mary Dwyer and her children being left behind in Wicklow after her husband had been transported to New South Wales now galvanised him into immediate action. He was faced with the difficult problem of attempting to arrive at a compromise situation which would be acceptable not only to Dwyer and his comrades but also to the administration in Dublin Castle. Realising that the Government were in no position to allow them to go to America, he now travelled to Dublin and negotiated improved terms so that their proposed transportation to New South Wales would be acceptable to them. The Government, for their part, despite their threat of bringing Dwyer to trial, were more disposed to compromise owing to the united opposition of the state prisoners to the various proposals made to them in the recent past. The most important of Hume's new proposals was that Dwyer and the others would be sent to New South Wales, not as felons, but with the entitlements of freemen. They would not be granted pardons but would be allowed to exile themselves for life on the above terms. On arrival, they would then be entitled to receive grants of land which would enable them to begin new lives there. In the case of Dwyer and Byrne, their wives and families would also be allowed to travel with them; they would be given the sum of approximately one hundred pounds each, although Dwyer may have been granted two hundred, and Hume also promised Dwyer that he would be able to say goodbye his father before they left.

These new conditions were, no doubt, put to Dwyer and the others by the munificent Trevor, who probably took most of the credit for them himself, but for Dwyer and his wife Mary there was still disappointment as America now finally seemed to be ruled out. But, for the others, the new terms must have been much more acceptable; certainly neither Arthur Devlin nor John Mernagh would have agreed to enlisting in a British regiment overseas and, with the war with Napoleon still being waged, it was unlikely that they would be allowed to go to France. But there were major family problems to be worked out by both the Dwyers and Byrnes if they agreed to the new terms. They each had very young families and were only too aware of the risks attached to bringing them on a long voyage with the consequent danger of the outbreak of fever. The Dwyer children ranged from five years down to ten months and the Byrne children from eight years to two. To complicate matters Sarah Byrne was pregnant and if she travelled with her husband would have to give birth during the voyage to New South Wales. They were now pressed by the Government to give a speedy answer or to face the consequences and when the Dwyers finally agreed to the terms it was only with great reluctance. Trevor rushed off to Dublin Castle with the good news but for the Dwyers and Byrnes there were still very important family decisions to be taken.

19

By the beginning of June news duly arrived from London that the convict ship was already on its way from the Downs to Cork and it was confirmed by Marsden that provisions, clothing and medicine for the convicts had been provided and would be put on board when the ship arrived. Marsden, in writing to the Home Office, also added, somewhat prematurely, that the prisoners from the various county jails were already in Cork and that they were being housed in various jails there. The name of the ship was the Tellicherry, a vessel of four hundred and sixty eight tons and fourteen guns and with a crew of forty. It was built in London just a few years before, was owned by a shipping group called St. Barbe and Co., and its Captain was Thomas Cuzens. The ship was no stranger to Ireland having arrived previously in Cobh in January 1804 bringing with it all of the equipment needed to erect a series of signal posts all around the coast which were to provide an early warning system against the threatened invasion by Napoleon.

On arrival in Cork the first task of Captain Cuzens was to discharge the cargo he had brought from London for some navy transports at anchor in Cork harbour and at the same time, the Tellicherry was inspected by Dr Robert Harding, the official medical Inspector of Transports in Cork, who was also a part-time Government informer. The Tellicherry, according to regulations, had been specially adapted to take on its human cargo and, having completed his inspection, Harding reported that he found the space set aside for the male prisoners to be large enough but not sufficiently ventilated as the ship's scuttles were not well formed. He felt, however, that the space allocated to female prisoners was too small although he added nonchalantly that "as they generally sleep in different parts of the ship it is not of much moment".

By June 19, Marsden was again confidently assuring the Home Office that the convicts from the northern jails and from Dublin had now been sent to Cork, that all the southern prisoners were already there and that the full compliment of prisoners would soon be ready to board the Tellicherry when it was ready to receive them. This was only partly true and, in fact, the whole operation was now beginning to look distinctly ragged. The prisoners from the northern jails and some of the Dublin prisoners had already left for Cork in a wherry called the Renown but its enterprising master, Nyland, was in no hurry to reach his destination and sailed first across to Milford Haven, having obviously some unofficial business of his own to attend to; he then put in to Waterford for a few days before, finally, arriving at Cork where he failed even to report to the authorities there.

But he did not hold up the operation as there was now a long delay before the remainder of the Dublin prisoners were sent to Cork. This was due, in part, to the resolving of the Dwyer situation but the main problem stemmed from the fact that, with the huge excess in numbers, the Government had not yet decided which of the prisoners were to be shipped down to Cork. The Tellicherry had room for one hundred and thirty men and thirty-six women but the number of male prisoners already in Cork amounted to over a hundred and seventy and Harding also estimated that in the case of the women, there would be at least fifteen too many, excluding the convicted women from Cork itself. These numbers would be greatly increased when the second contingent from Dublin arrived and it seemed that the recruiting agents in both Dublin and Cork would still be kept busy. The number had been reduced by one when a prisoner by the name of James Neil who was being escorted by the Waterford City Jailer and two sailors along Faran's Quay in Cork suddenly broke away from them and managed to escape. He was however, recaptured and returned by the Sheriff of Waterford two weeks later.

The Tellicherry still was not ready to take any of the prisoners on board as provisions from the Victualling Office in Cork for the colony in New South Wales were still being loaded; in all a total of one hundred and thirty thousand pounds of salt beef and the same amount of salt pork was put on board to supplement the colony's depleted provision stores. The owners of the Tellicherry, as regulations demanded, had provided a surgeon on board but Marsden, solving another of his problems, wrote to Charles Hewitt, the resident agent for Transports at Cork, officially announcing that his Excellency the Lord Lieutenant had appointed John Connellan, on the recommendation of the Medical Board, to be an assistant surgeon on board. Connellan was a 1798 informer from the Dundalk area who was now being looked after by the Government for services rendered at the time. He was trained as an apothecary and as navy surgeons of the period needed very little qualifications it is likely that Connellan qualified at one of the many rather dubious private medical schools in Dublin at the time. One of the best known was the school run by John Kirby who set up a hospital called St Peter and St Bridget, a slightly misleading name as the hospital had only one bed!

By July 18th, the Tellicherry was now ready to take prisoners on board but, even now, the second ship due to bring the rest of the prisoners from Dublin had not yet sailed and Dwyer and his comrades were still in Kilmainham. The owners of the Tellicherry now officially complained about the delay but Marsden, in turn, blamed the delay on the fact that there was some fever aboard the Renown. But there was also some fever on board the Tellicherry as Harding reported on July 28th: "I saw a soldier who informed me that he was ill for two days lying in the berths with the other soldiers and women. If they are not more circumspect and cautious about contagion the consequences must be very bad".

Meanwhile in Kilmainham Jail Michael and Mary Dwyer had come to the painful decision not to risk bringing their four young children initially with them to New South Wales. But Hugh and Sarah Byrne had decided to leave behind only their eight year old eldest son Philip, but to bring with them their five year old son Michael and their two year old daughter Rose.

The Dwyers now found themselves again at the mercy of Edward Trevor as they tried to arrange for their children to be sent out to New South Wales at a later date. Trevor, as Agent of Transports, would be responsible for making these arrangements and, while it is easy to appreciate the reluctance of the Dwyers to expose their young family to the rigours of a long and potentially dangerous voyage, it is more difficult to understand why they were planning for the children to be sent out within a few years when the very same dangers would prevail and they could scarcely be sent out unaccompanied at that time.

But Trevor seemingly agreed to this arrangement as was shown when Dwyer wrote a letter to him in an uncharacteristically shaky hand on June 29th: "I beg you will accept my warm thanks in return for your kindness towards my children. Nothing lies in my power more than to thank you for your kind and humane assistance and be assured that I would sooner ask you for that favour than any of my fellow prisoners, though perhaps you wouldn't think so even if it lays in your power". Dwyer now seems to have been under severe mental pressure and when the matter was further discussed the magnanimous Trevor readily gave Dwyer and his wife every possible assurance with regard to the children and the hapless Dwyer had to eat humble pie again, and write another suitably grovelling letter.

Respected Sir,

With a heartfelt gratitude and fully sensible of how far I am from deserving any kindness from your honour I make bold to return my sincere thanks for your kindness to me, and the consolation you gave me by promising your interest to send my children after me to Botany Bay; and your own humane mind will tell you that there is nothing so distressing to the parents as parting of their children especially me who had the misfortune to forfeit them and their country and I declare to you that I never was sorry until now for offending the Government until I see their kindness in forgiving the injuries on them and considering the wants of those that were guilty of such offences, now I am sorry to the bottom of my heart for having offended so good a Government and shall ever exclaim against any man or men if I hear any of them speak or act against the Government, this I declare to be my real sentiments at this moment and will till the hour of my death for I never saw my error until now; as for my children I shall leave it to yourself for it would be too much boldness of me to ask for so great a favour and I so ill deserving of any, but I sincerely lament for it and still hope for your humanity that I may expect my children and shall find myself happy in earning them bread and they and I shall be forever bound to pray for your welfare.

and I remain
yours etc etc,
Michael Dwyer
July 20th 1805.

It might be presumptuous to suggest that Trevor himself dictated the content of this letter but it is very possible as he was then in the process of collecting material of this sort for future use. Equally the tone of the letter may have been the result of a deliberate attempt by Dwyer and the others to wring as many benefits as possible from him before leaving. Arthur Devlin had written to Trevor in a similar fashion also asking if help could

be given to his aged mother. "Pardon me, sir, for this application, nor think that if it is not granted, I will be less grateful.
No, I will be forever thankful. I am content with anything you
do; because we are all treated by you, beyond my expectation".
Taken at its face value it is difficult to accept that this letter was
written by the same man who, eighteen months before, refused
to be examined in Dublin Castle.

As the date of their departure approached, Mary Dwyer and
Sarah Byrne, no doubt, made their last tearful visits to their
families. Michael Dwyer's father is reported to have come up to
Dublin to see him and Dwyer is reputed to have given him a
hundred pounds, which he had received from the Government,
although some of this money must have gone to help in the
rearing of the children who remained behind. Martin Burke's
wife Rachel did not choose to accompany him to New South
Wales and there is no report of her having visited him in
Kilmainham following her release in December 1803. On
Thursday July 25th Michael and Mary Dwyer said their good-
byes to their children as did the Byrnes to their son Philip. It is
likely that the Dwyer children were cared for by Dwyer's sister
Mary Neale, while Philip Byrne was already being reared by
his mother's family who lived in Dublin.

So, on the evening of July 25th, having been imprisoned in
Kilmainham Jail for over eighteen months, Michael Dwyer and
his group stepped into waiting carriages which would take
them along the Circular Road and down to the Quays in Dublin
where a revenue cutter, the Camden, under the command of a
Captain Murphy, was ready to receive them. As the carriages
moved away from the prison no doubt the last person they saw
standing outside the front gates was Dr Edward Trevor and,
even then, Dwyer's heart must have sank as he wondered if
Trevor would keep his promise. The cutter Camden was a fast
sailing ship which was used by both revenue officers and
smugglers alike and, on the following morning they left for
Cork as did the Lees wherry which was carrying the remainder
of the Dublin prisoners. Soon they were making their way

down the East coast of Ireland and were catching a glimpse of their native Wicklow for the last time. The Camden is reputed to have stopped briefly in Wicklow Harbour but, from the Government's point of view, it was scarcely the ideal place to visit for fear of their escaping. By August the 1st they were entering Cork Harbour and as they sailed in they must have been astonished to see what appeared to be the entire fleet of the British navy spread across the harbour because, in addition to normal traffic, the East India fleet was at anchor there and, no doubt, Arthur Devlin, as the only sailor among them, was busy pointing out the various types of sailing vessels.

Cork Harbour, at the time, was of immense strategic importance to Britain, not only because of its location but owing to the fact that it was one of the safest and best protected harbours in the world. "The entrance is safe and the whole of the navy of Britain may ride in it secure from every wind that blows. It is evidently most convenient for the Western world and to what some may seem paradoxical, it lies more advantageously for the East Indies than any of the English ports, but the shipping that generally resort here to victual and take in lading are those borne from Britain to the West Indies and Carribee Islands".

The Lees wherry had made good time also but both Captain Cuzens and Lieutenant Sainthill, who was supervising the arrival of the convicts, received quite a shock when they discovered the terms which had been agreed with Dwyer's party. An agitated Sainthill wrote immediately to Dublin "they say that they shall not be put in irons or put with the convicts and that their wives and children are to go with them. I hope it is not true as I am sure the Master of the Tellicherry could not comply with as the ship is completely filled, he has not room to make such an accomodation, and in the next place, it would put the safety of the ship's crew in great danger to have such men at large. I shall request Captain Cuzens not to put them in irons at present. When he is at sea, of course, he will do what he conceives most proper". Dr Harding examined them on the following morning but unlike the other prisoners, they were not shaved. Harding was more than compensated by this small loss of earnings as he would charge the Government six and a half pence each for shaving one hundred and seventy convicts, a guinea a day for visiting a ship, another guinea for visiting a jail and one British crown for examining a convict.

On August 5th the assistant surgeon, John Connellan, arrived and was soon writing to Marsden seeking letters of introduction for use in New South Wales while adding that "Dwyer and his party are behaving themselves very well". They now had, no doubt, reassured Cuzens as to their peacable intentions during the voyage but a problem arose about their food allowances and there was still time for a last letter to be sent to their newly discovered benefactor in Dublin saying that no orders had been received in this regard and that they were only receiving a pound of bread and a pound of beef every day. The letter was again addressed to Trevor in terms of the most grotesque flattery and signed by all five although the final sentence of the letter gives the impression that it was written in half-jest rather than desperation: "We, therefore, conclude with every grateful thanks, wishing you and your progeny all happiness that this life and the next can afford".

By the middle of August, a list of all prisoners who were to be transported was finally drawn up and they were now put on board. The problem of accomodating 'Dwyer and his gang' had been solved when Captain Cuzens decided to make the ship's hospital available to them despite fears being expressed about the possibility of a major outbreak of fever on board during the voyage. To try and overcome this the Captain and Surgeon were already allowing the prisoners to remain up on deck as much as possible during the day as the weather was fine. It had been a particularly fine summer and so the prisoners were able to acclimatise themselves to conditions on board ship and to remain healthy before their long voyage was due to begin.

The excess number of prisoners were now disposed of when twenty three men enlisted in a Plymouth navy division and a further seventeen enlisted with a Captain Chilcott. Seventeen male prisoners still remained who were either too old to enlist or were suffering from the fever. At least twelve women were left behind in Cork Jail, the board of the Female House of Industry in the city having firmly turned down a request to take them in. Another convict ship, the William Pitt, carrying female prisoners from London, now arrived in Cork Harbour and both ships applied to the master of the Bellequia, the flagship of the East India Fleet, for permission to sail with them.

By the middle of August, Lieut. Sainthill had forwarded a list of the prisoners who would be transported to Marsden in Dublin but he was still complaining at, what he considered, the over-generous treatment being given to Dwyer adding that he had given the group the sum of three hundred and fifty pounds which had been sent down from Dublin. Mary Dwyer was now given permission to travel into the city to purchase essential goods such as clothes and farm implements which would be needed on their arrival in New South Wales. On August 23rd, Marsden returned the list of prisoners and letters also arrived for Connellan and Dwyer which were to be given on arrival to the Governor of New South Wales explaining their status. Finally, on August 28th, permission was given to the East Indies fleet to set sail. On that same day Hardwicke and Lord Cathcart were inspecting a major army exercise which was taking place under canvas at the Curragh in Co. Kildare. General Beresford was actually within sight, having recently inspected a newly arrived regiment on Haulbowline Island. Justice Day was also in Cork attending a court session and in Dublin it was just another busy day for Alexander Marsden and Edward Trevor.

But the departure of the East India fleet from Cork Harbour was now held up when an adverse wind blew up from the west causing them to put back into harbour and it was not until Saturday August 31st when, with the help of a favourable north-westerly, the fleet got under way. As the island of Ireland quickly faded out of sight the one hundred and thirty men and thirty six women would, no doubt, have said farewell in their own separate ways, but the thoughts of the Byrnes and Dwyers still must have been with their young children whom they had reluctantly left behind.

POSTSCRIPT

By the end of August, just as the Tellicherry was leaving Cork Harbour, the Government in Dublin was beginning the process of finally releasing other state prisoners and before the end of that year, the majority of them had been set free. These included John St John Mason, Edward Coyle, John Galland, Robert Carty, Nicholas Grey, James Byrne, Nicholas Lyons and John Kelly. Bryan Devlin was also released but not before he had to write a similar begging letter to Trevor. Ann Devlin was one of the last to be released at the beginning of 1806 and then only after the intervention of the new Chief Secretary Long.

On his release, St. John Mason demanded the sum of two thousand pounds in compensation from the Government to cover the losses he had incurred while in prison.and he had two fruitless meetings with Hardwicke, who would not accede to his demands. Following the death of William Pitt in 1806, Hardwicke was replaced by the Duke of Beford as Lord Lieutenant and he was supposed to be coming to Ireland with very liberal powers of redress. Mason drew up another memorial and had it presented to him by William Hume whom he described as 'his excellent friend'. Mason met with Bedford but was disappointed again when told by him that no funds were available to compensate him. Mason then published anonymously a savage pamphlet against Trevor whom he christened Pedro Zendono, the Inquisitor of Kilmainham, naming him after a character from the novel Gil Blas. The pamphlet was eagerly read by the Dublin public and quickly went into a second edition.

James Tandy, at the same time, had taken an unsuccessful legal action against Brabazon Morris and he also wrote a pamphlet about his ill treatment in Kilmainham which he dedicated to the Duke of York. St. John Mason then wrote another pamphlet against Trevor using his own name and then it was Trevor's turn as tried to answer his critics in a further pamphlet, having written to various members of past administrations asking them for letters of support. He received letters of varied enthusiasm from Hardwicke, Nepean, Wickham, Col. Flint and, of course, Marsden who proclaimed that if he thought Trevor had been responsible for any ill treatment he would not have allowed him to remain in his post for longer than one hour. Trevor's pamphlet also contained unconvincing versions of the death of Jimmy Devlin written by George Dunn and Thomas Brown and, in a final section, Trevor published as proof of his innocence a large number of letters of appreciation received by him including the letters from Michael Dwyer, Arthur Devlin, Bryan Devlin and the final letter signed by all five from the Tellicherry.

In July 1808, on the final day of the Parliamentary session in London, the playwright and politician Richard Brinsley Sheridan moved in the House of Commons for a Royal Commission to enquire into the abuses of state prisoners in Ireland although he expressed regret that William Hume who was to support him was not present on that day. Following Sheridan's motion, a commission was appointed, one of its members being Judge George Daly who had first come to Kilmainham Jail to hear the prisoners' complaints. The enquiry began that November in the Sessions House, Green St., but the state prisoners, who had gathered there to give evidence, were disappointed to learn that it was not, in fact, a public enquiry and, having been told that the Commission "could not listen to any matters injurious to Lord Hardwicke's Government", they withdrew. The shutters had gone up again and they now despaired of ever receiving an impartial hearing.

One final effort was made in 1810 by Mason when he published a final pamphlet which he dedicated to Sheridan and which was published by John Stockdale and Co. of Abbey St., the printer of Emmet's proclamation and a former state prisoner. But, with the death of Sheridan and with the Napoleonic

War reaching a climax, the issue, still unresolved, began to fade from the public mind. Mason received no compensation and Tandy was also unsuccessful in a further suit and Marsden, who was called to give evidence, predictably hid behind the cloak of Government secrecy; as for Tandy, his wine business slumped as loyalists in Dublin continued to snub him.

The Waterford-born General William Carr Beresford was soon to win fame and fortune in the Peninsular Wars and won the Battle of Albuera under Wellington who declared him to be "the ablest man I have yet seen with the army". He later was made a peer and died a wealthy man in Kent in 1854.

The Earl of Hardwicke, on his return to England, took his seat in the House of Lords and continuing to support Catholic Emancipation, voted for O'Connell's Bill in 1829. Ann Devlin, having partly recovered her health, married in Dublin and reared two children; but she had to earn a living as a washerwoman in order to survive and died in abject poverty. Alexander Marsden spent his last days in London and is buried in the same vault as his more famous brother William in Kendal Green. As for Dr Edward Trevor, still unabashed and untouched by both pamphlets' accusations and commissions, he continued to stalk the corridors of Kilmainham Jail as Superintendent, dispensing his own particular brand of justice there for many years to come.

In 1835, William Wickham, then in his seventies and living in Geneva, met up with two members of a delegation who had been sent by the Synod of Ulster to attend a religious meeting in the city. He had a long conversation with them and, a few weeks later, wrote a confidential letter to one of them, Dr Armstrong, outlining his plans for peace and prosperity in Ireland based on the sincere co-operation of all Christian denominations living there. With this letter he also enclosed another copy of Emmet's letter written to him thirty three years before which he had copied out yet one more time.

PART TWO

1

The Tellicherry was the fourteenth convict ship to have transported prisoners from Ireland to the penal colony of New South Wales; five of these ships had been sent out before the 1798 Rebellion, the first being the Queen in 1791 followed by Sugar Cane, Marquis Cornwall and the Britannia. Between the years 1799 and 1802, because of the policy of sentencing large numbers of rebels to terms of transportation, a further eight ships had been sent out, the Minerva, Friendship, Luz St Ann, Minorca, Hercules, Atlas I, Atlas II and finally the Rolla in 1802; and now a three year gap was being filled with the sailing of the Tellicherry.

The penal colony in New South Wales had been set up in 1788 after the loss of the North American colonies and following the rejection of other locations such as Tristan Da Cunha and the Guinea coast in Africa. It was Sir Joseph Banks, the President of the Royal Society, who first suggested New South Wales in 1779. As a young man, instead of taking the grand tour, he had sailed, at his own expense, as a naturalist with Captain Cook on his first voyage of discovery in the Endeavour during which expedition they landed in New South Wales and, having met with curious rather than belligerent natives, they named their landing place Botany Bay because of the abundance of previously unknown species of plants which they had discovered there.

In 1786, the Government in London finally agreed to locate a new penal colony in New South Wales and, with the prisons in Britain overflowing, the quite insane business of solving this problem by transporting convicts half way round the world, at a huge expense to the Exchequer, began. The First Fleet, as it became known, arrived at Botany Bay in January 1788 but its commander Phillip moved immediately up coast to a far more suitable harbour which was called Port Jackson. No convicts were subsequently landed at Botany Bay but its romantic sounding name caught the public imagination and it has since become synonymous with transportation: "thieves, robbers and villains they'll send them away, to become a new people in Botany Bay."

Sir Joseph Banks had recommended New South Wales because he felt that, because of its remote location, it would be a difficult place to escape from but he also wrongly believed, from his own observations on the brief visit he had made there with Cook, that the land surrounding Botany Bay was quite fertile and that the colony would become self-supporting within a very short time. But there were no lush meadows near the shore either at Botany Bay or Port Jackson and it would be many decades before the colony could provide enough food on a regular basis, to fend for itself and, in the first years, the inhabitants were, on occasions, close to starvation and had to rely on food supplies which had been shipped all the way from Britain and Ireland.

The habit of transporting convicts overseas had originally begun because of the need for cheap labour in the new colonies. There was no shortage of raw material in this regard because of the severity of the eighteenth century penal code which listed over a hundred and fifty crimes which were deemed to be punishable by execution and a far greater number of lesser misdemeanours which were subject to a variety of punishments including terms of imprisonment, whipping, burning of the hand, a sojourn at the stocks or transportation. With the rapid growth in the population of major cities in the latter part of the 18th century, urban crime was on the increase but, quite paradoxically, it was the gradual trend towards a modicum of leniency in the latter part of the eighteenth century which resulted also in the consequent overcrowding of prisons and the acceleration in the numbers of those who were sentenced to terms of transportation. The courts were no longer dealing out death sentences to those convicted of outrageous crimes such as the shoplifting of goods valued in excess of five shillings, the larceny of goods from a house in excess of fifty shillings or rural crimes such as the stealing of sheep and cattle or, that bane of the landed classes, the cutting down of trees in avenues. By the year 1795, in Britain certainly, there were already complaints that this new trend towards leniency was progressing far too quickly and it was pointed out that the mercy shown by judges to horse thieves had resulted in a wave of gangs being formed for that very purpose, the perpetrators being now safe in the knowledge that, if caught, they would not end up on the gallows.

In Ireland, prior to 1798, those sentenced to terms of transportation were, in the main, petty criminals with the exception of a small number who had committed more serious crimes but whose sentences had been mitigated. Jeremiah Fitzpatrick, the progressive Inspector-General of Prisons in Ireland, writing in 1790, a year before the first Irish convict ship had been sent to New South Wales, was of the opinion that only about thirty of the 'most atrocious offenders' in the country would be sent out every year but as these convicts tended to receive death sentences the main bulk of those transported tended to be those who had been sentenced for larceny, forgery or other petty crimes. But there were also in Ireland a number of agrarian offenders who were sentenced to terms of transportation; these were members of rural secret societies such as the Defenders, ruthless dispossessed peasant farmers who had finally resorted to violence, rebelling against the iniquities of the landed systems which took away even their dignity as human beings and who struck at night burning crops, houses and maiming farm animals. Governor John Hunter in New South Wales described them as 'horrid creatures' without even wishing or caring to know the reasons why they had been driven to such acts of desperation, but for Hunter and the small military garrison which was based in in New South Wales they represented, for the first time, a cohesive and potentially dangerous force among the convict population there. A rival Protestant secret society in Ulster at the time, proudly carried a banner on which was written the pointedly altered Cromwellian motto 'To Hell, Connaught or Butney Bay' although, with a curious but enduring double-think, they did not seem to consider themselves as possible candidates for the long voyage. In this belief they were also disappointed as sufficient of their numbers had arrived in the colony by 1795 to enable them to form a branch of the Orange Order proclaiming, with an unusual honesty, their loyalty to the Crown and Government for as long as they supported the Union.

But for a few years following the 1798 Rebellion in Ireland a new type of political prisoner was now being transported, drawn from the ranks of the Society of United Irishmen, a movement which had received support from all classes and creeds in the country, Catholics, Protestants and Dissenters and so for the first time, some of those transported were not criminals but tended to be committed and idealistic political activists and contained among their ranks teachers, doctors, priests, clergyment, merchants and master craftsmen. For the anxious authorities the arrival of another potentially powerful group of politically-minded prisoners was viewed with alarm, but the authorities quickly and wisely made use of their expertise, and it was left to the unskilled and the more disaffected among them to carry on their sense of grievance and they now threatened to complete unfinished business in the penal colony if the right opportunity arose.

But, by the year 1805, the number of political prisoners com-

ing to New South Wales was again negligible and they represented only a small number of the one hundred and thirty men
and thirty six women who sailed on the Tellicherry. Twenty different Irish counties were represented with the majority coming
from Dublin City and County where petty crime tended to be
higher and which provided no less than sixty-seven of those
who were on board. While the names of the prisoners and their
countries of origin is known there are, unfortunately, few surviving records as to nature of their crimes. There was, however,
a second Hugh Byrne on board; he was a native of County
Carlow and had been a member of a gang led by a Wexford
man, James Corcoran, who, like Dwyer, also had a reward of
five hundred pounds placed on his head at the end of 1803.
They operated in the counties of Kilkenny and Carlow but, in
March of 1804, following a gun battle with the military forces,
James Corcoran was badly wounded and died a short time
later. Hugh Byrne was captured and he would surely have been
executed but for the fact that he turned informer, or to be more
accurate because he managed to convince the local authorities,
in a written confession, that there were French spies in the area
and that a French ship bringing arms was due to land soon on
the Wicklow coast. For this imaginative piece of lying, his life
was spared and, although he, subsequently, offered to enlist in
a regiment overseas, he was sentenced to transportation for life
instead with two other members of the gang, Lawrence Fenlon
and John Fitzpatrick, both of whom joined him on the
Tellicherry.

  This trio could be loosely termed as political prisoners as
they had originally fought in the 1798 Rebellion and another
prisoner in this category was Walter Clare from Dublin, who
was also lucky to avoid execution. Walter Clare lived in
Thomas Court, off Thomas St. in Dublin, where Emmet's rebellion had taken place. He was living there in a rented house with
his wife and, in a typical example of the crowded conditions of
the time, they shared a single room with another couple and
their sick child. Walter Clare worked in a local brewery called

Roe's and, having spent three hours queuing up to collect his wages on the evening of the Rebellion, he was reported by a neighbour for having a pike in his hand outside his lodgings on that night and that, when the skirmishing began in the near-by Thomas St, he had rushed to his own door calling on his wife to let him in. Despite the rather flimsy nature of the evidence, this obviously unwilling and not too heroic rebel was brought to trial and sentenced to death with five others, but while they were hanged soon afterwards Walter Clare's life was spared because it was claimed that he had given information to the authorities and he was confined to Newgate Prison.

Margaret or Mary Kelly, an upholsterer from Dublin City was also on board the Tellicherry, as was Mary McNellis, or McNulty, a native of Co. Laois who had been sentenced in Dublin; Nicholas Prendergast from Wexford had been given a seven year sentence for "seducing soldiers to desert", but the vast majority of those on board seemed to have been transported for their involvement in petty crime. Pierce Condon from County Tipperary received a life sentence for stealing a cow, and among the large Dublin contingent were Thomas Holden and Edward Doyle on separate charges of stealing calico, Timothy Murphy for stealing eight bank tokens, fifteen dollars and a three and a half guinea note, and John O'Neill for stealing a promissory note of the Bank of Ireland from a house.

Newspaper records of the period show that less than a tenth of all those sentenced during the previous years were actually transported and there is on record at least one man who was given two separate transportation sentences but was finally left behind at Cork. Even allowing for the fact that was a three year gap between the Rolla and the Tellicherry, sentences of transportation seemed to be handed out at court hearings almost as a routine variation from relatively short terms of imprisonment and even the reputedly humane Chief Justice Kilwarden had sentenced a sixty year old man to seven years transportation in a cout room in County Offaly in 1802 for stealing apples from an orchard, and he also gave similar sentences to two boys aged ten and twelve. The various judges throughout the counties seemed quite oblivious as to the ramifications for prisoners of transportation sentences and indeed the ages of the prisoners on board the Tellicherry ranged from Edmund Burke from Limerick who was seventeen to Thomas Cuffe of Dublin who was fifty five.

What exactly lay in store for the prisoners when they reached their journey's end in the penal colony was something which they understood less than fully; they certainly would have been informed that if they remained on good behaviour they would not be confined to prison but, that instead the men would be required to work either for the Government or be assigned to individual landholders and become farm labourers; the women would be required to work as domestic servants in houses or at the one female factory in the colony. But, for the majority of prisoners on board, their perception of life in the penal colony was far bleaker; it was like being exiled forever into oblivion. At a trial in 1803 Mary and Andrew Harris were charged with forging and uttering notes supposed to be from the Bank of Ireland; Andrew Harris was given a death sentence and his wife transportation for life: "At this intelligence, which was apparently no more than moderate before, she burst into agonies of shrieking and crying". For all those on board the Tellicherry there was a sense of finality about their departure from Ireland; a sentence of seven years was virtually the same as a life sentence; in fact none of the Tellicherry prisoners would ever return and, for some of the married men, like Martin Burke, Walter Clare and James Sheedy from Clare, it meant leaving behind their wives as well as their families, whom they would never see again.

But, for the small educated minority in Ireland, who had access to newspapers, a more enlightened view was taking place concerning the rapid development of New South Wales as an emerging nation, particularly following the publication of the colony's first newspaper in 1803. When copies of the first edition of the Sydney Gazette reached London later that year the newspapers there republished some of its content and these articles were, in turn, reprinted by some of the city and provincial newspapers in Ireland as was the common practise at the time. The fact that the penal colony had already progressed so quickly took newspaper editors by surprise and the reaction of the Irish newpapers was enthusiastic if somewhat patronising: "There is, no doubt, a disagreeable idea attending the mention of Botany Bay and there are some whose levity will lend them to look contemptuously on the country but when we consider that such an establishment is raised from that part of society that was lost to the country and had justly forfeited their rights, how highly ought we to admire the humanity and the policy of those who converted the rigours of justice into so mild a channel and from the crimes and misfortunes of mankind raised a society that promises to become so respectable and worthy of protection". The Belfast Newsletter also welcomed the publication of the Sydney Gazette and regarded it as "an act which gives a sort of unity and character to the colony". The newspaper then went on, in a leading article, to make some quite prophetic claims for the future of New South Wales itself: "We see in it the beginning of a country which will, in a short time, exceed in power and energy Italy, Greece, Turkey and those parts of the world that, at one time, held all the rest in subjection and contempt".

It is extremely doubtful if such heartening sentiments had reached the ears of prisoners on board the Tellicherry as, in the company of the East India Fleet, they began the first leg of their voyage and sailed towards the Island of Madeira. And they were fortunate to have in charge of the ship the humane Captain Thomas Cuzens: the history of transportation is filled with stories of brutality, neglect, starvation, disease and death and for the female (and sometimes male prisoners) the added risk of sexual abuse. During the voyage of the Hercules from Ireland fourteen prisoners were executed, and a further thirty died on board, while another eighteen died on arrival, and during the voyage of Atlas I sixty-five prisoners died or were killed. The Captains in both these cases were charged with neglect as was the Captain of the Britannia in 1797, but they received only nominal fines.

But now, with an efficient and conscientious Captain in charge, and with a surgeon and assistant surgeon on board, there was no trouble during the first leg of the voyage to Madeira which took place in warm September weather; indeed, for the prisoners who were allowed to remain above deck, for at least part of the day, it was more than a welcome change from the wretched prison conditions where they had been kept in some cases for over two years. The Tellicherry duly arrived safely at Madeira within eleven days from where John Connellan, still carrying out his favourite role of Government informer, reported back to Marsden in Dublin.

"The Captain has been remarkable attentive and humane to the convicts, having taken whole charge upon himself to see the prison is washed, scrubbed, and swabbed and perfectly dry every day and fumigated occasionally. From the good conduct of the convicts he has taken the irons off twelve of them and all the rest have but one leg in irons. Their state of health, in general, is very good but we have not been free of fever since we came on board. The greatest discontent among them is the want of tobacco which I understood, was ordered by you but was neglected to be sent on board from Cork. But the Captain, always attentive to their complaints went on shore this day and for the purpose of buying as much tobacco as will be sufficient for them until we arrive at Rio Janeiro. Dwyer's party have behaved very well. Their women occupy one of the hospitals. The Captain has been remarkably civil to them, particularly to Byrne's wife, who is far advanced in pregnancy; he frequently sends her fresh soup, mutton etc., from his own table. In short, all the convicts, men and women, seem highly sensible of the Captain's humane attention to them, and I hope they will continue to deserve it".

At Madeira the Tellicherry now parted company with the East India Fleet although the female convict ship, the William

Pitt from London, for reasons of safety, remained with the Fleet as it made its way to the Cape of Good Hope to take on the Dutch. The Tellicherry now sailed on towards Rio De Janeiro, the usual route taken by ships on their way to New South Wales and a well-known port where they could renew their provisions and which provided an opportunity for the Captain, if he so wished, to purchase some goods which could be resold for a good profit on arrival in the colony. It is not clear if Michael Dwyer and his group were allowed to go on shore at Rio De Janeiro but it is likely that they bought a supply of fruits such as oranges, bananas, plantains, water melons and coconuts which they were probably tasting for the first time and would have been especially appreciated by the pregnant Sarah Byrne. There was no shortage either of tobacco, rum or wine at Rio and they, no doubt, purchased a quantity of butter also which was, usually, the first commodity to become scarce on board ship.

The journey from Maderia to Rio generally took about six weeks so the Tellicherry would have arrived there by November. By the beginning of the new year of 1807 they were well on their way again, travelling across the Indian Ocean, and it was during this period that Sarah Byrne safely gave birth to a daughter who was called Anne. She was assisted in her labour by Mary Dwyer and the happy event was no doubt suitably celebrated by, at least, the Wicklow group on board. But it may not have been the only birth during the voyage, as records show that, in addition to the three Byrne children, three other children arrived at the colony. One of these may have been a son of Eleanor Tyrrell from Co. Meath and the other two children may have been born to women who were pregnant coming on board. On the run across the Indian Ocean they encountered some bad weather and, even in the best run convict ships, there was a certain amount of hardship for the prisoners who were chained together in the hold. James Sheedy, a native of County Clare who lived on the banks of the Shannon River near the city of Limerick, was a prisoner on board who, later in his life, wrote a colourful if not always accurate account of life in the colony but this description of life below decks during the course of storm, is both graphic and authentic:

"The worst aspect of our trip out was being chained up at night as this made the night very long. The system of chains being that you had a small chain attached to your wrist and the other end on a ring attached to a round iron bar. There were two of these rings which ran the full length of the hold in which there were one hundred and thirty men. This system allowed you to be able to use the sanitary convenience which was situated at the end of the hold. For instance if you were number twelve at the bar to use the convenience ahead of you when any person was violently ill it meant the unfortunate victim had to have several of his shipmates up all night with him to allow him to use the convenience as it was impossible for these men to pass one another, the ring merely sliding along the rail which often led to complications.

However the worst position by far was when the ship struck a storm as the refuse was usually bailed out by pail through the hatch, but with a big sea running, the hatches were kept closed. This, of course, was essential but try to imagine, if you can, that these men were in chains and violently seasick with the ship tossing like a cork. Most of them had never been to sea in their life so became so sick that they could not walk or crawl under their own power. The position then was that the men behind them who were able to walk had to carry them forward so that they themselves could use the convenience. On one occasion we were battened down for two days. This was something no human would wish on his worst enemy".

There was now also some sickness and fever on board and a few men had already died but, for the bulk of the prisoners who remained healthy, a lesser problem was how to deal with the boredom which, inevitably, developed during the course of a long voyage. In the Irish convict ships, over the years, there was a certain amount of singing below decks and few ships would have been as lucky as the Providence which included among its prisoners an Irish piper called Denis Begley. On one voyage out of London the English prisoners on board, to relieve the tedium, regularly held mock trial sessions apeing the Old Bailey trials, with the prisoners acting out the various roles of judges, lawyers, clerks, jury etc., to the great amusement of everyone. The English generally divided themselves into two classes, namely townies and yokels, while, on the Irish convict ships, the prisoners tended to divide themselves into three classes, the Cork boys, the Dublin boys and the North boys, who were also called the Scots boys. Another account about the habits of the Irish states that "these are so zealous in upholding their respective tribes that when two individuals of different classes quarrel there is no possibility of driving at the truth since a dozen of each class will rush forward and bawl out at once in favour of their respective comrades of the most conflicting and contradictory nature". It was also noticed, over the years, that the Irish convicts were, for some reasons, more happy with their situation than the English and that "they possess an anxiety to please and have a light-hearted civility about them of which the English are totally destitute". The Irish were also known to frequently pray together in the holds "counting their beads and fervently crossing themselves and repeating their prayers from a book".

But while the Tellicherry was sailing steadily onwards towards New South Wales unfounded rumours were reaching London that there had been trouble on board. A British ship, having landed at San Salvador, was told that a convict ship had run aground there to the south of the island and that the Captain and crew had been murdered. When local fishermen were asked if the name of the ship was the Tellicherry they naturally replied in the affirmative and the story was given further credence, and was further complicated, when it was alleged that some of the female prisoners had been transferred to the William Pitt. The name of Michael Dwyer, inevitably, was linked with all of this and he was reported as having escaped an disappeared somewhere in the island. A naval officer logged this story and it was reported back to London and then to Dublin where the story was taken so seriously that an official search began in Wicklow to ascertain if in fact Dwyer had returned home again.

But, oblivious to all of these rumours, the Tellicherry was by then nearing the end of its voyage and, as the coastline of New South Wales loomed ever closer, new apprehensions began to grow in the minds of the prisoners as the uncertainty of what lay ahead of them began to prey on their minds. And for Michael Dwyer and his Wicklow group there were worries too, as they wondered if the promises made to them in Dublin and which were contained in Marsden's letter to the Governor of the colony, would be honoured and that they would be allowed to settle down to enjoy peaceful and prosperous lives in New South Wales.

2

By Friday February 14th 1807 the Tellicherry had arrived outside the Heads at the entrance to Port Jackson where the town of Sydney, the main settlement of the colony, was situated and the official despatches of the Colony recorded their arrival: "On Friday morning came in a six-oared cutter belonging to the ship Tellicherry with information that Captain Cuzens, apprehending detention from contrary winds had despatched from the Straits with advice to his Excellency of his approach: and yesterday morning the ship entered the Heads with 126 male and 35 female convicts from Ireland, having lost only four men on the passage. In the evening thirty convalescents were brought on shore and received into the General Hospital, all the others being in good health. At six in the morning boats were now in readiness to take the prisoners from on board, and at seven they left the ship for Parramatta". The female convict ship, the William Pitt, was however considerably delayed; when the East India Fleet arrived at the Cape of Good Hope it suffered a large amount of losses in an engagement against the Dutch and the Captain of the flagship of the Fleet, Sir Homer Riggs Popham, took over the William Pitt and used it for a short period as part of the military operation, before it was allowed to resume its voyage and reached New South Wales at the end of April 1807.

The Tellicherry now tied up at the King's Moorings in Port Jackson, having completed its voyage from Cork in one hundred and sixty eight days; several officials immediately came on board including three army officers, two doctors and a clerk from the Colonial Secretary's office who took charge of the ship's indents. The doctors, having examined all of the prisoners, were relieved to discover that those who were sick on board were suffering only from a mild form of scurvy and, of the thirty odd who were sent to hospital, all but one man quickly recovered. He may have been Richard Doyle from Carlow who died from tuberculosis in August 1806. In all a total of five men and one woman died during the voyage and this was one of the lowest mortality rates on record at the time for a convict ship.

As they had been housed in the relative comfort of the ship's hospital none of Dwyer's group had suffered from any ill effects during the voyage and Hugh and Sarah Byrne now must have been delighted and relieved that the gamble of bringing their two young children with them from Ireland had paid off. Their infant daughter Anne had also remained healthy but the Dwyers, now, must have been already regretting their decision to leave their young children behind.

The one hundred and thirty healthy prisoners were now transferred from the Tellicherry to small boats and were ferried up the Parramatta River to the second settlement of the colony, the town of Parramatta. It was here that they set foot on the soil of New South Wales for the first time and, having been provided with a meal they were then subjected to the expected indignity of a public inspection or muster before being assigned. It was Sunday and the Sydney Gazette having reported their arrival, a large crowd had turned up to judge the potential of the prisoners, both male and female. The Government had first choice and took all the building tradesmen who would be sent to join work gangs, mainly in Sydney, which were involved in various Government projects; next it was the turn of the military officers and ex-officer landholders and finally the small landholders in the colony who were, in the main, emancipated convicts. Within the space of two hours the muster was over and two thirds of the prisoners had been assigned. It seems likely that the majority of the thirty odd women would have been taken on as domestic servants by families in the colony but those who remained unassigned, including those unfortunate enough to have children, were sent to the Female Factory in Parramatta. The factory itself was involved in the making of woollen garments but was, in fact, only a loft situated above a jail where the accomodation was so poor that the inmates had not even beds and had to sleep on the raw wool at night. The majority of the women who worked there had to find lodgings in the town of Parramatta where, as one report stated, "they cohabit with the male convicts or any other person who will receive them". There is no actual breakdown available as to how the women in the Tellicherry were originally assigned but in time, as the records show, they fared reasonably well in the colony.

The men who had been assigned to work for the Government now became part of the various work gangs with an overseer in charge and with a superintendent, chosen from their own ranks, responsible for two or three gangs. Their conditions of work were strictly regulated and, in the context of the period, could be considered as being reasonably generous. They worked from six in the morning until three in the afternoon and were then free for the rest of the day but they were, however, prevented from moving freely about the colony unless they received a signed pass from a magistrate. They were housed, clothed and fed by the Government; their superintendents had no power to punish them but were obliged to bring them before one of the colony's magistrates when the usual punishment, inherited from the naval discipline for those found guilty, was twenty five lashes or "a Botany Bay dozen" as it was euphemistically called. For more serious breaches of discipline the sentence could be stepped up to three hundred lashes.

Those who were assigned to work with landholders were considered to be much better off as living with a family had a much more civilising effect in comparison to the regimentation of life in a Government gang and it also gave them a greater advantage with regard to their future prospects. In fact, in later years, many of the convicts on arrival were advised not to admit to having a trade, so as to avoid being chosen for Government work. On the farms the assigned servants could learn the business of agriculture and they generally were given plots of land where they could grow produce for themselves. They had a similar set of working conditions to those who worked for the Government and landholders also had to apply to a magistrate if they wished to discipline them. The servants, in turn, could report their masters to the same magistrate if they felt that they were being ill-treated. When their sentence expired single men received a grant of forty acres and were still fed from Government stores while they were establishing themselves. All in all their conditions of work were relatively benign and, at this early period in the history of the colony, with the relatively small population and with the prospect of other land tracts opening up there was plenty of incentive for the assigned convicts, both farmers and tradesmen, to obtain their freedom and have an opportunity of making worthwhile livings for themselves.

But, while the Tellicherry prisoners were being ferried up to Parramatta, Captain Thomas Cuzens along with Surgeon John Connellan and Michael Dwyer and his Wicklow group were landing at Sydney Cove and making their way up to the nearby Governor's House. The Governor, Philip Gidley King, a native of Cornwall in England, was then a forty eight year old crusty, hardbitten naval officer who was suffering badly from gout and who was nearing the end of his long sojourn in New South Wales. He had landed with the First Fleet in 1778 and was, soon afterwards, appointed as first commandant of Norfolk Island, a settlement which was situated a thousand miles from the coast in the Pacific Ocean and which was originally developed for its supposed flax-growing potential and as a supplier of timber for ship-building. Having returned briefly to England King was appointed as Governor of New South Wales in 1800 and returned to the colony with a dual brief from the Government in London to try and achieve self-sufficieny and also to curb the undue economic influence of the New South Wales Corps officer clique. King immediately applied himself to both of these problems with energy and determination, attempting at first to boost agriculture despite his own assertion that "he could not make farmers out of pickpockets". But, despite his reservations, under his guidance a renewal of public farming began; he arranged to have grain bought directly from growers and he established a Government store for this purpose which then resold the grain at a reasonable price.

But, despite his best efforts, King was less than successful in breaking the monopolistic hold on the economy of the New South Wales Corps squirearchy. The original convict guard which came to the colony consisted of marines but, in 1789, Major Francis Grose, a veteran of the American War of Independence, was given the task of raising a special New South Wales Corps to replace them and was also given the right to sell the rank of lieutenancies in the new Corps to the highest bidders, pocketing much of the revenue raised in this way for himself. Many of those who became lieutenants came to New South Wales determined not only to get their money back quickly but also to create a new ruling class in the colony and to make full use of the free convict labour to achieve this goal. Grose soon became the Lieutenant Governor of the colony succeeding Phillip, but a more influential figure was the Scottish born John Macarthur, who was the regimental pay-master and Inspector of Public Works. Grose ensured that the members of his New South Wales Corps were given preference to the detriment of the civilian population and soon they were monopolising the whole of the infant economy. When an

American cargo ship arrived in 1793 the hardnosed Captain refused to sell the goods on board unless his cargo of rum was also purchased. So the rum was bought and an irreversible trend began as the rum was sold for an exorbitant profit and soon became not only the common drink but was used also as the unofficial currency and as a means of barter; soon indeed it was claimed that there were two classes of people in the colony, those who sold rum and those who drank it!

King, on becoming Governor, soon arrested the leaders of the monopoly including Macarthur who was sent to London but the wily Scotsman, with his rapier sharp mind working overtime, soon gained the backing of the Royal Court with his ambitious schemes for the breeding of sheep in the colony and arrived back in triumph, to the dismay of King, bringing with him not only rams from the royal flock but the right to obtain further large grants of land. The hapless King could only bitterly remark that the rest of the colony should now be handed over to Macarthur as he owned one half of it already.

But if King had become paranoid about the New South Wales Corps clique he was equally intolerant of Irish convicts in the colony. His term as Governor had coincided with the arrival of the bulk of the 1798 rebel prisoners and, during his six years of office, rumour and counter rumour swept through the colony, on a regular basis, about supposed rebellions by the Irish. Even before the year 1800 there had been instances of Irish prisoners absconding in futile attempts to find the mythical overland passage which they thought would lead them to China and finally back to Ireland. It may have been a wild dream but it was their only dream and one that raised the faint hope of escape, liberation and freedom. At the end of 1797 fourteen Irish prisoners, helped by aborigines, commandeered a boat belonging to a settler in the area of the Hawkesbury River and, having killed the crew, made off towards the south before being captured. In 1800 there were rumours of an Irish rising also and, in March 1803, fifteen Irish prisoners escaped from Castle Hill but were soon captured with the help, on this occasion, of aborigine trackers. But the most serious outbreak had occurred at Castle Hill in the following year when three hundred Irish and English rebellious prisoners gathered at Castle Hill and marched towards Sydney, but without the benefit of an overall strategy, or a competent leader, the badly planned revolt was quickly ended by a New South Wales Corps detachment led by Lieut-Colonel George Johnston and the ringleaders were swiftly executed. The place where the rising was put down had been renamed Vinegar Hill but, despite this Irish historical connotation, it was more of a rebellion born out of frustration against living and working conditions, which accounts for the numbers of English prisoners who were also involved. It is interesting to note also that none of the Irish in the colony who had been pardoned had joined in the outbreak which was confined to those who were still working as convicts.

So it was a rather apprehensive Governor King who sourly watched as the group of tall and intimidating-looking Wicklow men made their way up from Sydney Cove to Government House on February 16th 1806. On the credit side King was very relieved to find that there had been little sickness or mortalities on board and he congratulated Captain Cuzens on this; the Tellicherry had also delivered its cargo of badly needed meat for the Government stores but King was annoyed to discover that, owing to a mistake in the Victualling Office in Cork, salted beef had been sent out in addition to salted pork. King's order had been for pork only as four pounds of pork, in terms of weekly rations, equalled seven pounds of beef and the pork would, consequently, last longer. But this was minor irritation compared to the shock that the Governor received when he read Marsden's letter addressed to him from Dublin Castle explaining the exact terms under which Dwyer and the others had been sent to the colony. King was due to leave for England within a few months; all he wished for now was a quiet life before retiring peacefully to his native Cornwall and the last thing he needed, or expected, was the arrival of these five rebel leaders from Ireland who had been promised the freedom of the colony. He, no doubt, read Marsden's letter for a second time but became even more despondent. Marsden, with his lawyer's skill, had tried to phrase the letter as adroitly as possible but despite this there was still no denying the central message of his letter:

"Among the number are five men - who were engaged in treasonable practises and who have requested to be allowed to banish themselves for life to New South Wales to avoid being brought to trial; and as it has been deemed expedient to make such a compromise with them, they are sent there. Not having been convicted, they claim the advantage of this destination the effect of which is not, however, to prevent their being subjected to all the laws and discipline of the settlement. And any further indulgence is to be earned by their behaviour of which there has been no reason to complain during the time of their confinement here. Three other men are also charged with treasonable practices and who have acknowledged their guilt, are embarked from Gaol of the County of Carlow. Their names are John Fitzpatrick, Hugh Byrne and Lawrence Fenlon - with these there have not any terms been made and they are considered to be of a very bad description".

The last sentence of the letter did little to improve King's disposition either and even though Captain Cuzens vouched for the good behaviour of the Wicklow men during the course of the voyage and they themselves assured King of their peacable intentions, all of this failed to convince him, as the texts of two official letters which he wrote a short time later reveal. The first letter, addressed to Lord Camden, the Secretary of State for the Colonies in London, stated that "the arrival of the five United Irishmen will call forth the utmost attention of the Officers in the colony". King now also replied to Marsden at great length regretting the fact that the five Wicklowmen were sent out without convictions and expressing his view that "more than half of the inhabitants were only too ready to renew the troubles of two years before if they were to receive leadership". But, despite his gloomy predictions, King realised that he had to comply with the law in their respect:

"As Dwyer and his companions are not liable to the restraints placed on prisoners sent here under the sentence of the law, they very rightly consider themselves entitled to all the rights and immunities of free subjects; but how far they may prove legal ones remains to be discovered by their further conduct. That no plea may be made by them of wanting the means to obtain their living by industry, and well knowing the capriciousness of the Irish character, I have clearly explained to them the footing they are on, and on their promise of being circumspect in their conduct and not giving any cause for complaint, I have allowed them to become settlers, with the encouragements given to free settlers sent from England. But how far these indulgences will operate on their apparent turbulent dispositions time will show".

James Connellan, having presented his letter of introduction from Marsden, was given the position of Assistant Surgeon in Norfolk Island but Captain Thomas Cuzens scarcely deserved what fate had in store for him for, having discharged his human and food cargoes he was now hired by the Government in the colony to deliver a cargo of rice from China and set sail again about six weeks later from Port Jackson. But, during the voyage, he had the misfortune to be shipwrecked in the Straits of Apo in the Philippine Islands and the Tellicherry was lost. The crew, however, managed to escape and succeeded in first reaching Manila and finally the Chinese city of Canton in August; later in the year the luckless Captain Cuzens arrived back in Port Jackson aboard the Admiral Wellesley which had come from Penang and it was an occasion for celebration among some of the Irish convicts who, despite his best efforts, did not appreciate life in the holds of the Tellicherry during the voyage.

But, for the Wicklowmen, the importance of being given the status of free settlers in the colony was now made more tangible when Governor King granted each of them a farm of one hundred acres of land in the direction of Botany Bay about nineteen miles to the south west of Sydney near the Georges River with each of their holdings bounding Cabramatta Creek. They were no doubt greatly relieved in their minds as they made their way back from the Governor's House and into the town of Sydney before travelling out to Georges River to take possession of their land grants. The town of Sydney, at the time, was a ramshackle affair, with badly planned streets and with very few public buildings. Some of the most successful business merchants had built some imposing houses but the majority of the houses were little more than cabins and the General Hospital which was constructed from prefabricated panels which were brought out on the First Fleet was now in a very bad state of repair. There were a fair number of shops and a collection of disreputable taverns in the area of the Rocks on the harbour front but there were very little visible signs of prosperity that might give credence yet to the recent Belfast Newsletter prophecy. In all, the European population at the time was less than eight thousand, made up of 3,500 men, 1,750 women and 2,000 children. Apart from the town of Sydney there were a few smaller centres of population such as Parramatta, the Hawkesbury settlement, the Government farm at Toongabbie, a military settlement at Castle Hill and, sixty miles to the north of Sydney, the newly established outpost of Newcastle where the bulk of those sentenced, following the Castle Hill outbreak, had been sent. There the convicts lived in extremely primitive conditions and worked long hours either quarrying from the recently discovered coal seam, making lime from the vast mounds of oyster shells on the shore, or felling the huge cedar and rosewood trees whose timbers were in great demand.

The European colony in New South Wales, at this time, apart from the Newcastle settlement, extended for only a distance of about thirty miles around Sydney and the population consisted of military forces, Government officials, landholders, convicts, and a small number of merchants, innkeepers, shopkeepers and tradesmen. There were signs of a settled community taking shape but the convicts still amounted to one third of the population and were a visible and integral part of the society, the raison d'etre for its very existence and the development of the colony would for many decades to come be underpinned by that stark reality. As for the native population, the members of the Iora tribe were too scattered and technologically inferior to mount a serious challenge to the new invaders and had either docilely accepted their alloted place at the lowest rung in the new society or were driven back to the fringes of the colony, where they were both attracted by the crop-growing capabilities of the new settlers and repelled by their strange habits of wishing to keep land for themselves by putting fences around it.

In view of his stated misgivings about the newly-arrived rebel leaders from Ireland it was surprising that Governor King now allocated land grants to all of the Wicklowmen in the same area rather than sending them to different parts of the colony. In fact all of the land grants were situated beside one another at Cabramatta, the farm of Martin Burke on the left and then John Mernagh, Hugh Byrne, Arthur Devlin and finally Michael Dwyer. As new settlers in the colony they were entitled now to draw free provisions from the Government stores for a period of eighteen months until they had established themselves and, quite ironically, in view of their past records, they were now also entitled to the services of two assigned convicts each, who would also be victualled by the Government. It is not clear if they all availed of this privilege, but Hugh Byrne soon had two men working for him and Walter Clare, the distillery worker from Thomas Court in Dublin, was taken on by Michael Dwyer and was soon learning, for the first time, the rudiments of agriculture and getting used to blisters on his hands. At Cabramatta they now met up with a fellow Wicklow man, James Meehan, who had been a friend of Martin Burke's; a surveyor by trade, Meehan had been transported following the 1798 rebellion on the Friendship and had arrived in Sydney in

1800. Owing to the scarcity of badly needed surveyors in the colony, his potential was quickly realised by the Government and, having received a quick pardon, he was appointed as assistant to Charles Grimes, the resident surveyor. Over a period of the next twenty years James Meehan (or Jimmy Mane as he was called by the Irish), laid out and measured the majority of farms in both New South Wales and Van Diemen's Land and in the process he became quite wealthy as a grateful Government awarded him large grants of land and he grandiosely called his own home Meehan's Castle.

But there was another surprise in store for the new settlers when, a short time after their arrival, the land beside Martin Burke's farm was granted to Joshua Holt, the son of Joseph Holt, the Protestant 1798 rebel leader who, following his surrender, was transported in the Minerva in 1800. Joseph Holt, the reluctant rebel, had been virtually forced into joining with the rebels in Wicklow in 1798 when his house was burnt to the ground by a local who held a personal grudge against him. But Holt soon discovered untapped military skills within himself and was soon vigorously leading the remaining rebel forces who had retreated to the Wicklow mountains following the defeats in Wexford. The circumstances surrounding Holt's surrender to the Government gave rise to friction between himself and the Dwyer faction and it is claimed that Dwyer had to intervene to save Holt from being executed by his own rebel forces. Relations between them had remained strained although it must have given Holt some measure of satisfaction to discover that, even though Dwyer, Byrne, Mernagh and Burke had held out for five years, they too had finally been forced to surrender and were likewise sent to New South Wales.

Joseph Holt, whose wife and family had been allowed to travel with him to New South Wales, had also received an early pardon by King and was given a grant of land which he successfully developed but had become under suspicion at the time of the Castle Hill rising in 1804 when false information

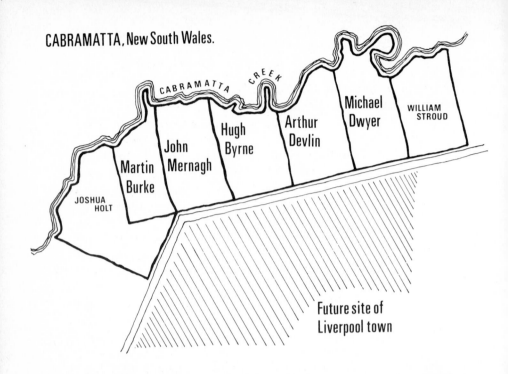

CABRAMATTA, New South Wales.

CABRAMATTA CREEK

JOSHUA HOLT

Martin Burke

John Mernagh

Hugh Byrne

Arthur Devlin

Michael Dwyer

WILLIAM STROUD

Future site of Liverpool town

Map of land grants of 100 acres given to Michael Dwyer and his comrades at Cabramatta, New South Wales 1806.

Michael Dwyer's house, 19 miles from Liverpool, New South Wales, probably drawn by Joseph Lycett in 1819 before the house was extended to become the 'Harrow Inn'.

was given to the authorities, mainly by Irish convicts, about his supposed involvement with the leaders. Holt was examined in court following which a nervous King exiled him initially to the outpost of Norfolk Island. He was later transferred to Van Diemen's Land and, having struck up a friendship there with the Lieutenant-Governor David Collins who valued Holt's agricultural expertise, he was allowed to return to New South Wales, arriving back just ten days before the Tellicherry had berthed. King had allowed him to return to his own farm, warning him to "beware of rocks and quicksands". But, soon after his return, Holt unwisely tried his hand at making illicit spirits and was again reported to the authorities and was lucky to escape with a fine. Soon afterwards he decided to live with his son at the new farm at Cabramatta and so, found himself living beside but, apparently, having very little contact with his fellow Wicklow rebels. Later in his life he was to accuse Hugh Byrne as being one of the two people who had informed the authorities of his illicit spirits operation but he may have been confusing him with the other Hugh Byrne from Carlow.

But now, the five Wicklow men were experiencing their first real sense of freedom in over eight years, and they now enthusiastically set about the task of building homes for themselves and of commencing the task of clearing some of their land and making it ready for the sowing of crops. But they were not initially helped by the weather as a very wet season had left the land rainsoaked which culminated in a deluge at the end of March which caused some flooding of the nearby George's River but which created havoc in the area of the Hawkesbury to the north where the river burst its banks, completely destroying the wheat and barley crops; some of the settlers drowned and the majority were left destitute as a result of the floods. But, at Cabramatta, despite the bad weather, their houses were quickly erected; they were made from wattle or plaster and split timber, the roofs being fashioned from sheets of bark or thatch which proved to be the coolest roof in hot weather and the warmest in cool weather. The timbers were put in rough and chipped all over with an axe to ensure adhesion to a subsequent coat of plaster which was made from a mixture of alluvial soil, dung and grass. When the plaster was dry it was finally whitewashed with a mixture of lime, plaster of Paris or apple tree ashes and sour milk. The houses had a single chimney and were divided into four compartments; there was also a loft for storage, the floor being covered with a mixture of soil and sand; a basic type of verandah was added to the front of the house.

In those early weeks and months living close to what was virtually still a wilderness, the New South Wales landscape must have been the source of endless fascination and diversion to them; there was a wide variety of birds with rich plumage, parrots, warblers and cockatoos, flocks of redbills and at night there were the sounds of the laughing jackdaws or settlers clocks as they were called to amuse them. Cabramatta was at the edge of the forest and they soon began to learn the names of the native trees such as eucalypts, acacias and various gum trees. They soon got to know about the trees at first hand as the back breaking task of clearing their land began. It was called hoe husbandry because of the fact that the common hoe had to be used extensively because of the presence of so many roots in the ground. Agriculture was still in its infancy and the records for the year 1800 show that there were only a thousand cattle, six thousand sheep and about a hundred and sixty horses in the colony at the time. But King, during the past six years, had been responsible for boosting these figures greatly; he had strengthened the Government herd and had recommended the adoption of plough husbandry. For this purpose he had offered for sale to landholders oxen which could be bought for twenty eight pounds a pair and which could be paid for over a three-year period with either cash or produce. It is doubtful however, if the new Wicklow settlers, who were now getting full value from the farm implements which Mary Dwyer had purchased for them in Cork, had the financial resources to avail of this offer as they laboriously tried to clear a few acres of land to sow the initial crops of wheat and maize. Wheat was mainly used for the making of bread and maize to feed animals and poultry and these were the two most successful cereal crops grown in the colony. Wheat was generally sown from April to June and harvested from the middle of November to the Christmas period while maize was sown in October and harvested from the end of March to mid-May.

All of the principal European vegetable crops had already been introduced but the potato did not fare too well, because of the climate, and was generally grown as a first crop. Pigs were to be seen everywhere, and especially in the town of Sydney and the numbers of sheep was steadily increasing owing to the keen interest of large landholders such as John Macarthur and the Reverend William Marsden who were experimenting with different strains to find a breed suitable to the colony's needs. These experiments, in the early years, had included two Irish ewes and an Irish ram which Macarthur had purchased from the Captain of an Irish convict ship, although the emphasis in latter years had been on the development of the Merino breed. There was an abundance of fish both in rivers and in the sea and a wide variety of fruits including apricots, oranges, lemons, cherries, almonds and peaches were so plentiful that cider was made from them or they were given as food to pigs.

But the quality of the soil in the colony differed greatly from area to area; for a distance of five and six miles from the coast the land was extremely barren with rocks which were covered with low flowering shrubs with scarcely a tree but with a great and beautiful variety of wild heath. Beyond this area the soil began to improve with a thin layer of vegetable mould resting on yellow clay. This type of terrain extended for a further ten miles but it required both skill and hard work to make it even tolerably productive, particularly after the first crop had been grown; it was in this general area that the farms of Cabramatta were situated but as they bordered Cabramatta Creek and were situated close to Georges River the soil seemed to be better than average. When Joseph Holt examined his son's farm there he reckoned it was a better area for feeding stock than his own land and this was the main reason why he moved there with the rest of his family. Holt, who was financially secure, soon built a house and stockyards for his son and he managed, in the first year, to clear forty four acres which may have acted as either a spur or became a source of understandable envy to his Wicklow neighbours who certainly had not the same financial resources as Holt at their disposal; in fact, reports suggest that John Mernagh, at the time, worked also for other landholders to supplement his meagre income.

But now there was a buzz of excitement in the colony as it became known that Philip Gidley King's six year term was coming to an end and that a new Governor had been appointed who was already on his way out from England. But this news scarcely mattered to the new settlers in Cabramatta. They were now busily developing their holdings and they were concentrating on becoming economically viable; with a few years the Dwyers would be able to send for their four children in Ireland. They would soon, hopefully, establish themselves as peaceable, responsible and prosperous citizens of the colony.

3

The new Governor of New South Wales was William Bligh, who is best remembered in history as Bligh of the Bounty. In 1789, Bligh was cast adrift in an open boat with eighteen of his crew by Fletcher Christian and his mutineers, and had to navigate without a chart and with little food and water for three months, covering a distance of over three thousand miles before reaching safety. He soon resumed his naval career only to become caught up with the Mutiny of the Nore when British seamen attempted to persuade the Admiralty to treat them a little better than convicts by trying to improve their conditions. Bligh had the misfortune to be ejected from his ship again and some of these seamen involved in the mutiny were, subsequently, transported to New South Wales including a Scotsman, Thomas McCann, who was certainly no friend of the incoming Governor.

Bligh was then given the less demanding task of surveying Dublin Harbour which he completed in 1800 and when it was suggested that he might publish his findings he was quick to insist that they should be published in London rather than Dublin so as to reach a wider market. In the following year, he also completed a survey of Holyhead Harbour in Wales but he was in trouble again in 1804 when a Lieutenant Frazier, who was serving on his ship off the Dutch coast, accused him of "tyranny and unofficerlike conduct". Bligh, in fact, was court-martialled on this occasion and restored to his command but he was reprimanded and warned to be more careful about his language in future, surely a unique rebuke for a sea captain. As in the case of the Bounty, Bligh seemed to be more sinned against than sinning on this occasion but he was correctly described as "a stickler for discipline and a martyr to naval efficiency; fiery and passionate, subject to outbursts of wrath accompanied by violent gesture". Bligh, who on occasions showed signs of schizoid behaviour, would savagely abuse an officer and moments later, having calmed down, would then invite him to dinner or having terrorised the sailors on board his ship would then take the trouble of spending an hour talking to a sick seaman in his bunk.

It was Sir Joseph Banks, the confidential adviser to the British Government on all matters connected with the colony and who was very friendly with Bligh, who recommended him as a possible successor to King. Bligh, who had a family of six daughters, hesitated before accepting, as his wife Betsy had a dread of the sea and could not face the prospect of the long voyage to New South Wales. Bligh who did not wish to become separated from his wife and family for a long number of years again was on the point of turning down the offer but the persistent Joseph Banks kept urging him to accept the post, offering him an income of two thousand pounds a year, the promise of further promotion on his return and even went as far as trying to make the less than convincing argument that Bligh's unmarried daughters would have the opportunity of making more suitable marriages in the colony. Bligh finally accepted the position of Governor and, in the absence of his wife, who still refused to travel, brought with him his daughter Mary, who was married to a Lieutenant Putland who was also appointed to his staff. But there was trouble also on the voyage out when Bligh quarrelled with Captain Short who was in charge of the two-ship convoy. Bligh began to take decisions without reference to Short and when finally Bligh changed course without reference to him an enraged Short, in the second ship, ordered Bligh's own son-in-law Putland to fire a shot across the bows of his ship. When they landed in Sydney Bligh, who was now in command, had Captain Short arrested and sent back to England, thereby ruining his plans of making a new life for his family in New South Wales and, indeed, Short's wife died during the return voyage.

The new Governor arrived with basically the same set of instructions which King had received six years before, namely to stimulate agriculture, to halt the drain on the British Exchequer by making the colony self-sufficient, and to curb the power of the New South Wales monopolists, with particular reference to the control of the rum trade. Bligh, on his arrival, was thoroughly briefed by King who remained on in the colony for a few months and the new Governor, who lacked even a modicum of common sense and who had, seemingly, neither the desire nor the capability of making valid judgements based on his own observations, now accepted without question all of King's warnings and so inherited his two great hates, namely an aversion to the New South Wales Corps clique and a conviction as to the supposed ever-present threat to the peace of the colony by the dreaded Irish convicts.

All factions in the colony now hurried to present flattering addresses of welcome and support for Bligh, the first coming from the unabashed and opportunistic John Macarthur, who took it upon himself to represent the views of the colony. But his address was quickly repudiated by the worthy citizens of the town of Sydney who directly attributed to Macarthur the recent rise in the price of mutton, accusing him of witholding a large flock of wethers until he got the price he wanted. The landholders from the Hawkesbury now also drew up a separate address objecting also to Macarthur's and pointing out that the monopolists had recently caused ships to leave Sydney laden with badly-needed merchandise in order to keep them at inflated prices. They also complained generally about the low

Governor William Bligh, from a miniature.

price for grain and, above all, about the depreciated currency which was in circulation. It was an impressive document from the Hawkesbury settlers, which set the parameters for the emergence of democracy and an independent voice in the colony as they looked forward also to the prospect of free trade, the prevention of monopolies, and demanded that the law should take its course without control in matters of property and that justice in general should always be administered according to the known law of the land.

Bligh attempted to meet at least some of their immediate demands by giving help to those who had suffered because of the recent floods and he also gave notice of his intentions to the monopolists by making an order banning the use of rum as barter. He then supported Andrew Thompson, his own farm bailiff and one of the biggest emancipist settlers in the colony, when Macarthur demanded repayment from him for a promissory note expressed in wheat at the currency inflated price. But Bligh's heartening support for landholders in the Hawkesbury did not extend to the Wicklow settlers at Cabramatta. Even though they had taken possession of their farms and had begun to develop them they had not received the relevant legal documents registering their ownership. Hugh Byrne, becoming impatient at what he considered to be an undue delay in this regard, took his courage in his hands and travelled into Sydney where he confronted both King and Bligh, who happened to be together at the time in Government House about the matter. James Meehan had, in fact, long since drawn up the necessary papers but King had refused to grant permission to have them registered, believing that the Wicklow rebels were still on probation as to their behaviour in the colony and Hugh Byrne received only an evasive answer at the time. King, no doubt, used the occasion again to warn Bligh about what he still believed to be the potential danger to security in the colony from these rebel Irish settlers.

It scarcely helped matters when rumours now began to circulate during the Autumn that another rebellion was being planned by Irish convicts with the aim of avenging the defeat at 'Vinegar Hill' two years before and while the Wicklow settlers at Cabramatta had no intention of becoming involved ever again in any such activity, news of their arrival would have spread quickly among the Irish in the colony and it is likely that the name of Dwyer would have been hinted at by disgruntled convicts as a possible leader.

Although there is plenty of evidence to show that Dwyer himself worked extremely hard on his farm during that first year he may have, inadvertently, contributed to the spreading of such rumours because of his increasing dependence on alcohol. During his five year period spent as a fugitive in the Wicklow mountains the combination of the cold winters and of spending long periods of time in local sheebens had led to a situation where the drinking of whiskey had become the norm; in the early months of his confinement in Kilmainham jail also, Dr Edward Trevor ensured that he was supplied with as much alcohol as he needed in an effort to loosen his tongue and, on his arrival in New South Wales with its prodigious rum drinking he found it difficult to shake off either his own rambling habits or his drinking of spirits; towards the end of 1806, certainly, he seems to have spent a fair amount of time travelling up to the Hawkesbury and into Sydney where he frequented some of the taverns in the area of the Rocks owned by Irishmen. At these gatherings he was, more than likely, introduced as a great Irish rebel leader rather than a Cabramatta settler and, as the drink flowed, and as he regaled his audience with anecdotes from the Wexford and Wicklow campaigns, a certain amount of loose talk, naturally, began to circulate as the night progressed with dark threats emanating as to what would happen in the colony if the Wicklow boys got their hands on some guns and pikes. Given the extremely volatile state of the colony such talk, however fanciful, was highly dangerous because there was no shortage of informers, especially amongst the Irish convicts themselves, who would gladly pass on and embellish such information to local magistrates in the fervent hope that it would help to obtain for themselves a remission of their sentences or the ultimate goal of a free pardon. Such was the nature of life in the colony but Dwyer seemed to be oblivious to the danger signs.

It was during this period also that Michael Dwyer and Arthur Devlin quarrelled; there could have been any number of reasons for this falling out, going back to the period of Emmet's rebellion, but certainly the temperate Devlin would scarcely have approved of Dwyer's loose talk in the colony, fully realising that he himself might, involuntarily, become caught up in the consequences of such unwise behaviour which had the potential of destroying them all.

Another likely reason for their quarrel may have stemmed from the fact that, shortly after their arrival, Arthur Devlin had met and fallen in love with the sixteen year old Priscilla Mason, a currency lass - one of the first native born girls of the new settlement. She was the step-daughter of a former English convict, James Squires, who was a brewer and reputedly the first man to have grown hops in the colony. The romance quickly blossomed and they were married at the beginning of April just seven weeks after Devlin's arrival. Priscilla Mason, however, was a Protestant and, as no Catholic priest was allowed by the Government to minister to the substantial Catholic population in the colony, the marriage may have been performed by a clergyman, which would have upset staunch Catholics such as the Dwyers and the Byrnes, who would have regarded such a wedding as a betrayal of their faith and which was something they would not have accepted without comment.

Three Catholic priests, Frs Dixon, O'Neill and Harold had, in fact, already arrived in the colony having been transported following the 1798 Rebellion, but Fr O'Neill was soon allowed to return to Ireland. In 1803, in an effort at conciliation, Governor King, despite opposition mainly from the Rev William Marsden, had allowed Fr Dixon a conditional emancipation, and he was permitted to say Mass every third Sunday at the three main settlements at the Hawkesbury, Parramatta and

Sydney. He celebrated his first Mass probably in James Meehan's house but he was not allowed to officiate at weddings or to give baptism and, in the wake of the Castle Hill rebellion of 1804, King withdrew this permission although Fr Dixon still remained in the colony.

This created many personal problems over the years for the Catholics in the colony, particularly in the area of marriage as they were faced with the prospects of either conforming, which many did, or being officially categorised as cohabiting together; there are many instances also of Catholic women living with Protestant men but refusing to marry them and, after their deaths, being buried in a Catholic cemetery apart from their families. Even though they were not allowed to practise their religion the early Catholics in the colony were determined at least to be buried in their own graveyard and they often buried their co-religionists in secret to achieve this.

But despite the fact that the friction between Arthur Devlin and Michael Dwyer deepened, the fruit of their labours on their farms began to be realised and, by the end of the year, Michael Dwyer had nine acres of maize ripening and he was now planning to sow a further six acres of maize and some wheat also. In January 1807 Bligh sent James Meehan to the area of Georges River to check the progress of the settlers there and while he was in the locality Dwyer, already thinking in terms of expansion, asked him to calculate how many bricks he would need to build a barn forty feet long and ten feet high. The rest of the Wicklow men were also making good progress on their land although it seems that John Mernagh may have still been working with other landholders and had bought a house in the town of Parramatta.

But rumours of the supposed Irish rebellion continued to spread and Bligh now became convinced that not only his own arrival but the recent arrival of HMS Porpoise had already prevented it but that the conspirators were still waiting to strike at another suitable time. The Hawkesbury settlers, who were very heartened by Bligh's support for them since his arrival, now signed a declaration of support for him and the signatories included both Michael Dwyer and Hugh Byrne. On February 22 1807 an order was issued from Government House "that a return be made immediately to the magistrates at Hawkesbury, Parramatta and Sydney of all persons who have arms of any description - distinguishing the different kinds of which they are in possession, and the quantity of powder, ball or shot which is to be registered in a book to be kept by the magistrate. And the magistrates are hereby directed to enroll the names of all of His Majesties subjects as are ready and willing to defend the country against war and tumult administering them the oath of allegiance, as is customary on such occasions".

On the same day the Sydney Gazette gave an account of the supposed plan of action of the rebels which, no doubt, was supplied to them by Bligh: "They were to have destroyed the Governor, who they supposed would be going into the country as soon as the Buffalo sailed, on his way to the Hawkesbury, and which was to have been the commencement of the general insurrection; the New South Wales Corps were to have been surprised; the leading gentlemen of the colony were to have been killed at the same time; the Porpoise and shipping were to have been seized; and a general massacre was to have taken place".

This article naturally helped to bring the rebel scare to a level of near hysteria and, just three days later the Hawkesbury settlers felt impelled to present a second address to Bligh their saviour which was signed by over five hundred people in which they thanked Bligh for his wise and unwearied solicitude over the public welfare at all times. They also agreed wholeheartedly with the proposal to make themselves available for the defence of the country and added significantly "but (we) sincerely hope that your Excellency, in your wisdom, and judging from the real and presumptive proofs exhibited in this country now and for many years past by those disaffected people of their relentless and incorrigible spirit of rebellion, murder and atrocity, that you will be graciously pleased to dispose of the ringleaders and principals so as to prevent future conspiracy amongst them and to restore public tranquility which blessing of peace and happiness may your Excellency long continue to give and enjoy in your gracious government over us is the earnest prayer of your Excellency's devoted etc etc".

In addition to voicing their genuine fears about the supposed Irish rebellion the Hawkesbury settlers did not wish to see any harm coming to a Governor who seemed at last be taking on the New South Wales monopolists of whose economic policies they had been the principal victims. Their request to Bligh "to dispose of the ringleaders" of the disaffected was something which Bligh could not ignore and just two weeks later he ordered a military guard to go to Cabramatta and to arrest Michael Dwyer and the other Wicklow settlers whom informers had claimed were the leaders behind the revolt. Dwyer, as the principal leader, was imprisoned aboard the HMS Porpoise in Sydney Harbour and Devlin, Burke, Mernagh and Byrne were all lodged in Sydney Jail. Dwyer's servant Walter Clare was also arrested as was an English convict William Morris and the Scottish former seaman Thomas McCann who had acted as a standard bearer during the period of the Nore Mutiny when the seamen marched each day in procession through the town of Sheerness and who had been one of those who had ejected Bligh from his ship.

Bligh now called a meeting at the house of Andrew Thompson, his farm bailiff, to prepare the book of evidence against the prisoners and Thompson was assisted in his work by the ex-English lawyer, George Crossley.

These sudden arrests came as another savage blow to the Wicklow men and their families who had just completed their first year in the colony. It was particularly heartbreaking for Mary Dwyer and Sarah Byrne to witness the arrests of their husbands and the breaking up of their families just as they were beginning to settle down to some kind of normalcy in their lives again. They had begun to believe that the years of hardship which they had endured in Ireland were over and now, in a nightmarish fashion, they were plunged into a deeper crisis which they did not even understand. They could see no valid reason for the arrests; their husbands were hardworking settlers rather than being disaffected convicts and, once more, they began to feel a deep despair when confronted with what they believed was the brutal and uncomprehending power of the law. Both of them were now pregnant again, expecting their first children to be born in the colony and there was now also the added responsibility of suddenly being left to cope with looking after the farms as well. There was anguish too for the young Priscilla Devlin who was expecting her first child and she returned to her stepfather's house.

But in Sydney the evidence in the case against the eight prisoners was now being assembled and they were to be tried before the Court of Criminal Judicature on the charge of being the leaders of a conspiracy which was attempting to raise a rebellion in the colony. If they were found guilty of these charges they would, in all probability, be sentenced to be hanged.

4

The trial of the eight prisoners was due to begin in Sydney on May 11th 1807 and, as friends and witnesses gathered at the Courthouse on that morning, the main question now centred around the quality of the evidence which the prosection had gathered in the intervening weeks and whether the prisoners would be able to counter it successfully. Bligh when writing to William Windham, the Home Secretary for the Colonies in London shortly after the arrests had taken place, was less than convincing when describing the background to the charges: "In general we are improving and have every hope that we shall do well, notwithstanding a late attempt to insurrection, which has been preparing for eighteen months past, and was to have been put into execution the date before I arrived, but was prevented by my appearance off the coast, and of which Governor King had an alarm. No arms have been found, or any positive overt act been committed, our information leading only to declared plans which were to be put into execution by the Irish convicts, headed by O'Dwyer and some of the Irish State prisoners, as they are here called.

It appears that in order to avoid detection, they determined to rest their success on seizing the arms of the loyal inhabitants; and in order to affect this, the Irish servants of the inhabitants were on a certain time fixed to massacre their respective masters, and the principal persons of the colony, and to possess themselves of their arms.

Of this determination I continued to have proof, more or less, when I determined on seizing the persons represented as the ring leadres and effected my purpose. O'Dwyer I have put on board the Porpoise. Byrne, Burke and some others are in jail for trial and will be brought forward as soon as the evidence are all arranged and prepared".

It is obvious from Bligh's letter that the evidence to be presented by the prosecution would be mostly in the realm of hearsay and in stating that the conspiracy was being planned for eighteen months he conveniently overlooked the fact that the Wicklow men arrived in the colony only a year before. His description of them as being state prisoners rather than free settlers was also rather ominous and would also become an issue during the trial.

The Court of Civil Judicature was presided over by Richard Adkins, the Judge Advocate of the colony, and he had the assistance of six officers drawn from the military forces to assist him in coming to a verdict. This was the usual composition of the Court of Civil Judicature which dealt with treasons, felonies and all other criminal offences. The best known, and most senior, of the officers was Lieut-Colonel George Johnston who had put down the Castle Hill rebellion in 1804 and the other members were Lieut William Minchin, Lieut James Simmons, Lieut William Ellison, Ensign William Lawson and Ensign Cadet Draffin. Richard Adkins could hardly have been described as the jewel of the legal profession. In fact he had very little legal background, having arrived in the colony with Major Grose and the New South Wales Corps and having been appointed as a Justice of the Peace soon afterwards. But he had now fallen out with the New South Wales Corps and became a sworn enemy of John Macarthur. This, naturally, endeared him to Governor King who described Adkins as "a man of abilities and exceedingly clever" but added the necessary codicil that "he is, unfortunately, some time addicted to liquor". Another settler described Adkins as "an infamous drunken character" and Bligh himself, no man to mince his words when he disapproved of someone, is quoted as saying about Adkins that "sentences of death have been pronounced in moments of intoxication, his determination is weak, his opinion floating and infirm, his knowledge of the law insignificant and subservient to private inclination". Despite these reservations Bligh allowed him to preside over the trial during which he had to carry out the role of prosecuting attorney and was in possession of the book of evidence which had been largely assembled at the meeting in Andrew Thompson's farm. The format of the trial was that prosection witnesses were first called, examined by the court on the basis of their written evidence and the prisoners were then given the opportunity, if they wished, of cross examining them. When the case for the prosecution had ended the prisoners would then be allowed to call and examine their witnesses following which a verdict would be arrived at and delivered by the Judge Advocate.

The trial, which would last for almost a week, with over thirty witnesses being called, opened with the prosectuion calling on a rather surprising witness, namely James Squires, who was Arthur Devlin's father-in-law. Squires, a former convict who had been arrested as recently as 1802 on a charge of possessing arms, was taking no chances on this occasion and had written a letter to a magistrate, Dr. John Harris, having received information as the court put it "that the croppies were going to rise", the word croppy being defined by the court as "dissatisfied persons opposed to the lawful government of the colony and using arts to raise a tumult and rebellion against the state".

Squires told the court that his son-in-law Arthur Devlin asked him if he could have a hogshead of beer to take with him to the Hawkesbury for the purpose of collecting wheat and he also promised to take some beer into Sydney to supply some of Squires' customers. But, just as Devlin was about to leave, James Kavanagh who worked for Captain Kent came in to see

Devlin: "Immediately afterwards my son-in-law came to me and said 'Father I want to speak to you... I cannot go to the Hawkesbury on Tuesday as I intended for Kavanagh has been up to Parramatta on Saturday for his provisions and was told there that Dwyer was going to the Hawkesbury with a cask of beef to see what he could do with the people up the country". Squires then added that Devlin had told him not to take any notice of what he had said but that he had felt it his duty to report the matter.

It seemed, at this stage of Squire's evidence, that he was trying to distance Devlin from Dwyer but then he went on to inform the court that Kavanagh had spoken further to Devlin but that he did not know the subject of their conversation. It was an unsatisfactory ending to his evidence and certainly he did not show any great support for his new son-in-law.

The second prosecution witness was Edward Abbott, the residing magistrate at Parramatta, who had arrested Joseph Holt on the charge of illicit distilling but who would soon fall foul of Bligh when it was discovered that Abbott had imported an illegal still from England himself. Abbott claimed that he had received information about the rising on a number of occasions as far back as the previous August but that, in January, he had received definite information that "it was the intention of the dispossessed to come into Parramatta on a Friday evening and to seize the barracks and its arms while the soldiers were receiving their provisions". Abbott felt that he had forestalled the rebellion on that date by placing extra sentries and constables on duty. He also received information that the detachment of soldiers stationed at Castle Hill were to be attacked and was even more suspicious when the convicts at Castle Hill did not apply for their usual week-end passes on a certain Friday at the end of February.

At this stage of the proceedings Adkins, in his role as prosecuting counsel, put his first leading question to Abbott by suggesting to him that if he had not taken these precautions and that if Dwyer and the other prisoners had not been arrested an insurrection would have taken place. It was the type of question which would have pleased Bligh and Abbott duly obliged by agreeing wholeheartedly with the sentiments expressed, adding that it would have been attended with "the most atrocious proceedings contrary to the peace".

Up to now the proceedings seemed to be taking an ominous turn as far as the prisoners were concerned and Dwyer must have felt this as he made his first intervention and asked Abbott if he had seen anything suspicious in his conduct since he came to the colony. Abbott truthfully replied that he had not but the court then asked him if Dwyer's conduct had been peaceable. The reply came "No. It was not. I was obliged to bind him over to the peace but it was for nothing seditious". It seems clear that Abbott had bound Dwyer to the peace for being drunk but the Judge Advocate, for obvious reasons, did not choose to ask Abbott to expand on this statement and the next witness was quickly called.

It was, in fact, John Macarthur, the Judge Advocate's own sworn enemy, and a surprising witness in view of his recent row with both Bligh and Andrew Thompson. Adkins, for the only time during the course of the trial, addressed a witness as "sir" and somewhat frostily put another leading question to Macarthur.

Court: Was you not informed that O'Dwyer made an observation, on seeing a flock of sheep passing by, and on being informed they belonged to Captain Macarthur what was his observation?

Macarthur: To the effect that they should not continue as they had done, that there was a plan among the Irish prisoners to break out into an insurrection and that Dwyer was to lead it.

Macarthur went on to explain that the same man had given him information a few years before and on being further asked by Adkins "that such an insurrection had it broke out would have been attended with the most sanguinary of atrocious proceedings even to the massacre of all those who were not actuated by their principles" to this colourful assertion Macarthur readily agreed and, without being questioned by Dwyer, stepped down.

The next prosecution witness was the superintendent at Castle Hill, a Mr Knight who once served as a private in the New South Wales Corps. Knight, for the first time, mentioned the names of Hugh Byrne and Arthur Devlin as being directly involved although the nature of his testimony was far from convincing:

"On the fourteenth of February last Devlin and Byrne came to Castle Hill about half an hour before the sun setting and brought an order for two sows. The sows not being in I kept them in conversation until they came in as I had received information from Captain Abbott that they were coming and he had desired me not suffer them any intercourse with the prisoners at that place. I delivered to each one a sow and they both went away with them. Some time after I saw Devlin in camp who said that he had lost his sow and came back to find her. Devlin asked permission to stay in the camp that night. I told him it was contrary to orders but, as it was a very bad night, I suffered him to stay in my house. The next morning the sow being found he got her and went away".

This was the extent of Knight's testimony which added absolutely nothing to the prosecution's case and he was immediately challenged by Arthur Devlin:

Devlin: Did you see anything in my conduct to lead you to suppose I came for any other purpose than of getting my sow?

Knight: No. I did not.

Court: Have you seen Dwyer after at Castle Hill?

Knight: Not more than twice and then it was to buy corn of me.

Hugh Byrne: You have known me ever since I came to the colony. What is your opinion of me?

Knight: I always considered you as an industrious man. You drew your provisions at Castle Hill and I never knew anything improper of you.

Knight seems to have been a reluctant Government witness

and indeed one of the most striking aspects of the trial was that the majority of the prosecution witnesses like Knight invariably gave good character references to the prisoners when they were cross-examined by them. But now, following some inconsequential hearsay evidence by the Chief Constable Thomas Oakes and his Irish servant James McCarthy, the first of the two chief prosecution witnesses was called. He was a forty-six year old Irish convict by the name of Dominic McCurry who had come out on the Hercules in 1801 and his evidence was directed against Dwyer only as he stated that he did not know any of the other prisoners on trial.

McCurry claimed that he met Dwyer when he was driving some sheep up Constitution Hill and that when he told him that he was not a free man Dwyer had assured him that soon every prisoner in the colony would be free and that he himself was going up to the Hawkesbury to contact some people in this regard. With the help of some leading questions from the court McCurry claimed that Dwyer had told him that the rising would take place a fortnight after the Buffalo had sailed from Sydney and when the Governor was on his way to Parramatta and the Hawkesbury and he also mentioned the names of Lieut-Colonel George Johnston (one of the sitting officers), Dr Harris, Mr Palmer and Mr Laycock as being others who were to be 'checked' as he put it. The court tried to give one of their main witnesses every assistance:

Court: Did any person inform you of any particular number of pikes Dwyer had or was to have?

McCurry: O'Dwyer informed me that he could get from one hundred to one hundred and fifty pikes.

Court: Did he tell you the place where they were secreted?

McCurry: He did not.

Court: Did not O'Dwyer in your presence, and to your knowledge, say if he had fifty or one hundred Wicklow boys with himself at their head, he would not be afraid of anything?

McCurry: He told me that if he had a hundred or a hundred and fifty of the Wicklow boys he could do a great deal.

Mc Curry, whose evidence seemed to be the basis of the Sydney Gazette article of Feb 25th, went on to claim that Dwyer had offered to "take on any one who would run with him" and but for his arrest a rising would definitely have taken place. He finally made a rather surprising admission that he had heard that Hugh Byrne would have nothing to do with the rising.

Dwyer now questioned McCurry closely, concentrating on the early part of his evidence about his supposed meeting with him on Constitution Hill and asked him to state when it took place and if there were any other persons present at the time. McCurry replied that the meeting took place a few days before Christmas and that no one else was present. But Dwyer kept pressing him.

Dwyer: Have you ever spoke to me in any person's company?

McCurry: I never did.

Dwyer: Was you ever in conversation with me before?

McCurry: Yes. Several times, at the Lumber Yard when you asked me to give you half a pint of whiskey which I did at Graham's which was served by Graham's man, Thomas Bartlett, and after we drank the half pint we separated.

This last statement by McCurry would be raised again by Dwyer later in the trial but now on the first day of the trial the time being three o'clock the court adjourned.

The trial recommenced on the following morning and the prosecution continued to call its witnesses beginning with J.W. Lewin who had come out on the Minerva and was one of the colony's first artists. Lewin certified as to the good character of McCurry and pointed out that he had been recommended by Rev William Marsden, sometimes known as the flogging parson, who owned huge land tracts in the colony and whose reference as to McCurry's good character was enough to raise doubts.

Two other witnesses now also gave evidence as to McCurry's unblemished character and the prosecution then called its second main witness who was another Irish convict by the name of Daniel Grady who came out on Atlas II. Grady was assigned to a settler called Thomas Ramsay who lived in the area of the Field of Mars and who had reported his information to the magistrate Dr. John Harris having received it from a Thomas Connell. For the first time the names of Walter Clare and John Mernagh were mentioned in court as Grady claimed that Clare had informed him that Dwyer was going to the Hawkesbury two days before the rising was due to take place and that he also told him that Dwyer intended to lead a rebellion there and that John Mernagh was to take charge at Parramatta. Grady claimed that both Dwyer and Clare had told him they expected to get some pikes at Captain Kent's farm, that it was their intention to take over both the HMS Porpoise and the Lucy with sixty of their men in addition to seizing the barracks at Parramatta, and that they would not be called cowards this time.

This last remark of Grady's probably encapsulates the whole of the affair, namely the overhearing of some loose talk by some disaffected convicts who were expressing a hope that the arrival of Michael Dwyer in the colony might provide the necessary spark for another Castle Hill rebellion. Dwyer, likewise, may have compounded this by talking drunkenly about his exploits in Wicklow, remarks which were seized upon and blown out of proportion by Grady and McCurry in an effort to obtain their own freedoms. But the net result of this was that Dwyer and seven other prisoners were now fighting for their lives in a Sydney court.

Grady now was closely questioned by Dwyer as to when he had spoken to him and Grady replied that it was at John Mernagh's house in Parramatta but added that Mernagh himself was not present and that Dwyer had sent Walter Clare down to the wharf for a cask of rum at the time. Grady then claimed that he had omitted to tell some of his evidence namely that Dwyer would not tell him the date of the rising until he had returned from the Hawkesbury and that if he got hold of the Governor, Lieut. Col. Johnston and Captain Abbott he did not care a damn for the country. This evidence almost echoed the previous day's statements made by McCurry and again Dwyer pursued Grady asking him in great detail when this last conversation between them had taken place. Grady claimed that he had spoken to Walter Clare in Dwyer's own home having been sent to Georges River to bring a gun home to his master John Ramsay from Andrew Cunningham and to collect further information about the rising at the request of Dr Harris and Captain Abbott. He also claimed that he had spent the night in the home of Dwyer's next door neighbour Sergeant Stroud. Grady was now also questioned by Walter Clare and when he was stood down he was followed to the stand by his master John Ramsay, who gave Grady a good character reference. Ramsay was later described by Harris as a notorious character but he now answered the following questions in a favourable manner for the prisoners:

Dwyer: What is your general opinion as to my conduct during the time I have been your neighbour?

Ramsay: Nothing but that was good and proper.

Martin Burke: What opinion have you formed of me from my general conduct?

Ramsay: Nothing but what was good and reasonable.

This was one of the few occasions when Martin Burke spoke during the trial and in fact, no evidence of any kind was offered against him by any of the Government witnesses. But now, for the first time, the next witness gave evidence against the two remaining prisoners Thomas McCann and William Morris. His name was Denis Stacey, an Irish convict who had also come out on the Atlas II and he told the court about a conversation he supposedly had with McCann at Parramatta, claiming that McCann had talked about the good times which were coming, for there were men now concerned, that would go through with it, but that it would not begin at Castle Hill. Stacey also claimed that William Morris had asked him to go with him to Castle Hill to try and steal arms from Mr Knight saying that Stacey's own life would be respected after the rebellion. When

Stacey asked for more information Morris told him that a rebellion would take place and that Dwyer was up at the Hawkesbury drinking at Clarkes.

Once again the link between Dwyer and the Hawkesbury is mentioned and it seems that this part of the evidence was well rehearsed in advance by Stacey, McCurry and Grady in an attempt to co-relate at least some of their evidence. Stacey then told the court that William Morris had taken out a small book and asked him to take hold of it and that he would then tell him more but that he refused. Two weeks later, when Dwyer and the others had been arrested, Morris again came to him saying that it was time to get the arms before those people who were in jail were sent out of the colony or disposed of. Stacey then claimed to have told Morris that he was going to inform the authorities against him. William Morris, strangely, did not cross-examine or challenge Stacey on these points but Thomas McCann now questioned Stacey about his supposed meeting with him and asked him significantly if it was true that the magistrate in Parramatta had said that if Stacey had come to him again with such a cock and bull story he would flog him. McCann finally accused Stacey of sending Grady to Georges River looking for information, an accusation which Stacey denied.

The next prosecution witness was a watchman from Castle Hill who stated that he heard Morris telling Stacey that the sooner they could get the arms from Castle Hill the better, "for fear those men who were now confined should be sent out of the colony". Again it seems to have been well rehearsed evidence and one wonders why Morris should speak so loudly so as to be overheard. The next witness, Mathew Lock, a constable at the Hawkesbury, denied, however, that he had heard of any improper behaviour by Dwyer there and the next witness George Bear was even more unforthcoming.

Court: Have you heard O'Dwyer speak about any cruelties committed on the Loyalists of Ireland by him and his party?

Bear: I never did. Thompson put it down wrong!

Despite these setbacks the prosecution case ploughed onwards and the evidence of the next three witnesses concentrated on an incident which had occurred at a farm on New Year's Day which had little bearing on the charges themselves but showed that the sectarian differences between the Irish back home were now surfacing in the colony. The first of these witnesses was William Chalker, a farmer whose New Years Day party did not turn out quite as he had intended.

Court: Had you not a good deal of company at your house on New Year's Day and was not O'Dwyer there?

Chalker: O'Dwyer was there.

Court: Did not O'Dwyer among others sing a song?

Chalker: Not to my recollection.

Court: Was not a man by the name of John Hewit in the house at the time?

Chalker: He was.

Court: Did he sing a song?

Chalker: He did - several.

Court: Was not a good deal of disapprobation expressed at one of the songs?

Chalker: Not to my recollection.

Court: Did you see John Hewit knocked down by any person with a pailey?

Chalker: I cannot say that I did.

The apparently absent-minded Chalker, who had stalled impressively, was now replaced on the stand by the aforementioned John Hewit, an Ulsterman who had come out on the Minerva and who was mentioned by Joseph Holt as being disruptive during the voyage. Hewit was now also questioned about the New Year's Day party at Chalker's farm.

Court: Did O'Dwyer sing?

Hewit: He sang one song.

Court: What was the tendency of the song? Was it disaffected?

Hewit: I think it was.

Court: You sang a song. Was it a loyal song?

Hewit: I sang an Orange song.

Court: Did you hear some person say 'Knock him down the bloody Orange scoundrel'?

Hewit: I did but I cannot say who it was. He was drunk.

Court: Did you not, in consequence of such an expression, receive a blow from a pailey?

Hewit was apparently reluctant to give a reply to this question and the equally forgetful Ulsterman, having been asked to stand down, was replaced on the stand by a James Metcalfe who willingly told the court that he was in a neighbour's house on New Year's Day when he heard a commotion. He went to Chalker's house to investigate and saw the owner and Dwyer fighting but he added that most present were intoxicated anyway. With that final revelation the court hastily adjourned for the day and the case for the prosecution ended or rather petered out. The court was due to meet again two days later and then it would be the turn of the prisoners to present their defence.

By any standards the prosecution case as stated in court was a weak one. As Bligh admitted in his letter to Windham, there had been no evidence of any meetings being held, no discovery of arms, no incriminating documents presented. With regard to the individual prisoners not a single word of evidence had been offered against Martin Burke; the evidence against Hugh Byrne and Arthur Devlin was tenuous to say the least; there was only one reference also during the proceedings to John Mernagh; the accusations made against Thomas McCann were equally vague and Walter Clare was only arrested because he was a servant of Dwyer and had, supposedly, spoken to Grady. The case against William Morris rested on the testimony of Stacey whose confidential conversation was apparently quite readily overheard by the watchman at Castle Hill.

But the prosecution's main case was directed against Dwyer and the majority of their witnesses had testified that he was to be the leader of the supposed rising. Here again most of the testimony against him was in the realm of hearsay and had been successfully challenged but, given the mood of the colony, the disposition of the Judge Advocate and, above all, the conviction of Governor Bligh that the prisoners were guilty, their defence would be crucial if they were to avoid a guilty verdict being handed down.

At the end of the second day's hearing Dwyer was again returned to solitary confinement on board the Porpoise while the others were locked up in Sydney Jail where they had some access to those who were helping to gather witnesses for their defence. In the meantime, those two courageous wives Mary Dwyer and Sarah Byrne, with the experience of Kilmainham Jail behind them, were already canvassing support for their husbands and loudly proclaiming their innocence. And they were not without hope; one of the military court members, Lieut James Minchin, owned some land near Cabramatta and he believed that Dwyer and the others were hardworking and peacable men. In addition many of the settlers who had appeared for the prosecution had likewise agreed, when asked, that they had found no cause for complaint against the Wicklow men.

So the manner in which the prisoners would carry out their own defence was now all-important and, if they could manage to contradict the testimony of McCurry and Grady in particular there was still hope that the Court just might bring in a not guilty verdict.

5

The friends of the defendants now had two days to complete the line-up of their witnesses but they had the advantage, at least, of knowing the full extent of the prosecution's case. These two days were spent, not only in contacting witnesses and ensuring that they would turn up, but in trying to isolate areas of the prosecution witnesses' evidence which they might be able to contradict. The third day of the trial began on the morning of May 17th but before the prisoners were allowed to begin their defence the Governor's secretary appeared in court and, in a move obviously initiated by Bligh, produced the letter which Marsden had sent to King outlining the terms on which the Wicklow men had been sent out from Ireland. Although Marsden had stated categorically in his letter that they had come out without conviction the Court now came to the surprising conclusion that they were, in fact, prisoners for life and that it, presumably, superseded their claim to be free settlers. This judgement, unfortunately, went unchallenged by the prisoners but when they produced their first witnesses it became obvious that both Mary Dwyer and Sarah Byrne had been active behind the scenes as the first three witnesses called were landholding neighbours of theirs in Cabramatta who incidentally were all Englishmen, Samuel Higginson, Stephen Share and John Emmerson. They all now testified separately as to the industry and peacable nature of the Wicklow men and, having achieved this initial advantage, the defence now decided to concentrate their efforts on refuting the evidence of McCurry and Grady. They now called Andrew Cunningham, a landholder who had been mentioned by Grady in his evidence.

Dwyer: Do you know a man by the name of O'Grady?

Cunningham: He came to me for a gun for his master, John Ramsay and I put him over the water in my coracle. He says that some time past he was speaking to Dwyer about the rebellion at home. O'Dwyer said, "Damn the rebellion, every time I think of it makes my mind shudder to think of the desolation it has occasioned so many families at home".

This was a far cry from what Grady had told the court about his conversation with Dwyer and the first cracks in his testimony began to appear. The next witness to be called was a respected name in the colony, namely their fellow Wicklowman James Meehan and who, given his Government position, was taking a risk by speaking in their favour. When asked by Dwyer, Meehan described to the court the progress that they had all made on their farms since their arrival and when Hugh Byrne asked him to confirm the fact that he had personally visited Government House asking that their land grants should be registered Meehan agreed, although he, cautiously, added that he could not recall if Bligh had been present on the day in addition to King. The next witness was Thomas Dargin, who had signed the Hawkesbury settlers' address and who later opened the Red Lion Inn at Windsor, and he testified that he was with Dwyer all of the time on the way from Parramatta to the Hawkesbury on the day during which Grady claimed that he had spoken to Dwyer. Dargin was followed by Malachy Ryan, a native of Co. Limerick, who had come out on the Tellicherry and who was now an assigned servant with Dwyer's next door neighbours the Strouds.

Dwyer: Did you ever see me going to Morrison's house in Parramatta and in whose company was I at that time?

Ryan: To the best of my recollection the Sunday after Christmas Day. Between ten and eleven o'clock I was at this time in company with Grady and Jeremiah Griffin.

Dwyer: Did you expect anything from Sydney by the passage boat?

Ryan: Yes. Our provisions from Sergeant Stroud then living at Sydney.

Dwyer: Did you go more than once to the wharf to if the passage boat had arrived?

Ryan: I went three or four times in company with Grady to Kirwan's house where the provisions were usually left to see if it was come.

Dwyer: Did you hear me speak to Grady in the course of the day?

Ryan: I did not.

Dwyer: What time had elapsed from the first time of your seeing me that day to the last?

Ryan: Six or seven hours. I never left Grady during that time and I did not hear or see him speak to O'Dwyer during that time. Grady went with me to George's River where he remained two nights. Grady did not stop at O'Dwyer's farm the evening that he arrived at George's River and Clare, at that time, had not arrived home but was left behind at Parramatta for a cask of beef.

Two other witnesses now also gave evidence in the prisoners' favour and, having partly demolished Grady's testimony, Thomas Bartlett was called to deny having served Dwyer and McCurry with drink as McCurry had claimed. Bartlett's testimony was immediately corroborated by the innkeeper John Graham.

Dwyer: Did you ever see me and McCurry together?

Graham: I never did.

Dwyer: Did you ever suffer Thomas Bartlett to draw any spirits?

Graham: I never did.

Dwyer: Did you ever draw spirits and give it to him to serve your customers?

Graham: I might have done but seldom and then I always pointed out the company he was to serve.

The final witness of the day, Bryan Donnelly, now further discredited McCurry by telling the court that McCurry had not honoured an IOU which he had written and the court then adjourned not having cross-examined any of the defence witnesses during the day but having plenty to think and talk about concerning the trustworthiness of the main prosecution witnesses.

On the following day the last of the defence witnesses were called and Thomas Lynch who had briefly appeared on the previous day was now recalled by the court.

Court: On what part of the Rocks do you live?

Lynch: On the furthest part of the Rocks.

Court: You say that you saw O'Dwyer at your house on the two days preceding Christmas Day. For what purpose did he come?

Lynch: He came to my house for some spirits.

Court: Did he come for any other purpose?

Lynch: He did not.

Court: How long have you known O'Dwyer?

Lynch: I have seen him often since he has been in the colony, but I never had any discourse with him before.

Court: At what time of the day was it when he came to your house the first day preceding Christmas?

Lynch: About twelve o'clock.

Court: And you positively swear that you was not at work at that time at Mr Campbells?

Lynch: I came home for my dinner between twelve and one on that day and I then saw O'Dwyer at my house.

Court: Who was at the house besides yourself at the time you mention?

Lynch: I believe my woman.

The next defence witness was Michael Howlin, who was questioned first by Dwyer and then by the Court.

Court: Do you remember seeing Grady at Georges River?

Howlin: I do.

Court: How many nights did he stay at Stroud's farm?

Howlin: Two nights.

Court: Did you go into Parramatta with him?

Howlin: I did and we had a pot of beer at Mernagh's. We then separated and he went to the road leading to his master's John Ramsay's house.

Court: What time of the evening was this?

Howlin: Between six and seven and he never spoke to any person whatever in the streets of Parramatta that night whilst I was with him.

The reason why Thomas Lynch had been recalled was now made clear when the magistrate John Harris was called who told the court that he had received information that "something improper was intended among the Irish" and that hearing that Dwyer had gone into Sydney he saw John Redfern the Chief Constable to get further information about it. Redfern had come back and told him that Dwyer had been seen drinking in some houses but had returned to his farm before a constable had arrived to make an enquiry.

Harris, now having been asked in turn by Hugh Byrne, John Mernagh and Martin Burke, agreed that he had never heard anything prejudicial to their character. Up to now the defence witnesses who were called had been testifying for the Wicklow men but the other two prisoners, McCann and Morris, now both called witnesses in their defence. Captain Laycock told the court that McCann had done his duty as well as any other person but was then asked by the court "Has the prisoner in your presence boasted to the gang or otherwise of his being active in the Mutiny of the Fleet or that he was the person who handed Captain Bligh over the side of the ship at the time?" Laycock replied that he had and McCann must have regretted having called him as a witness. William Morris now called his witnesses to testify to his good character and Arthur Devlin then recalled John Kavanagh to the stand and asked him to clarify the conversation which took place between them at Squires at the beginning of January.

Kavanagh: You informed me that you were going up to the Hawkesbury with a load of beer. I told you that O'Dwyer had gone up with a cask of beef on which you replied that as yourself and Dwyer had some differences you would not go.

Walter Clare finally denied the charges made against him and the case for the defence having concluded the court adjourned for four days.

On May 18th it met again. During that period Dwyer, Devlin and McCann had papers proclaiming their innocence drawn up and these were now delivered to the court and were read out by the Judge Advocate. The court then adjourned to consider the verdicts and reconvened for a final time on the following day when, to a hushed and apprehensive courtroom, Judge Advocate Adkins read out the verdicts.

Michael O'Dwyer	- Not guilty
Hugh Byrne	- Not guilty
John Mernagh	- Not guilty
Thomas McCann	- Guilty
William Morris	- Guilty
Arthur Devlin	- Not guilty
Walter Clare	- Not guilty.

The immediate expressions of relief in the courthouse, no doubt, as the verdicts were read out exceeded the expressions of disappointment but now there was silence again as the Judge Advocate continued:

"After the most mature deliberations in the respective testimonies that has appeared before the Court, the Court is fully of the opinion that the Charge as set forth in this indictment is fully proved against the prisoners Thomas McCann and William Morris and the Court, therefore, doth adjudge and sentence the said Thomas McCann and William Morris to receive one thousand lashes and the Court further recommends that the said prisoners Thomas McCann and William Morris being delinquent of the most dangerous principles of character be removed by the most speedy consequence to a remote place where the baneful influences of their example, cannot be expressioned nor disseminated among other ignorant and deluded convicts".

The relief of the Irishmen was now surely tempered on hearing of the savage sentence meted out to McCann and Morris as one thousand lashes was almost the equivalent of a slow and painful death sentence. The irony of the verdict was that the six Irishmen were cleared of the charges brought against them while the Scotsman and the Englishman were both found guilty. But the verdicts could equally be seen as the five settlers and one of their servants going free while the two convicts were punished.

What were the main considerations which caused the members of the court to come to this conclusion? From the outset there were two distinct trials going on simultaneously and, as can be judged from the verdicts, there seemed to be little or no evidence offered as to a link between the Irishmen and the other two prisoners. But in coming to their decisions the members of the court had to look at the evidence offered against each of the Irishmen. Martin Burke had no case to answer as his name had not come up at all during any part of the proceedings expect when he himself asked a few settlers to vouch for his good behaviour in the colony. Likewise, there was very little evidence offered against either Mernagh, Byrne or Devlin. The assertion by Grady that he had received information from Walter Clare had been contradicted so finally it was the case against Dwyer which occupied the minds of the Court members when they were trying to reach their verdicts.

Dwyer had been mentioned by a succession of prosecution witnesses as the leader of the supposed rebellion and, even though it was hearsay evidence, it had been given by some of the most prominent people in the colony. But the case for the defence had been marshalled extremely well and Dwyer himself had contributed in no small way to this by his intelligent line of questioning, as did his witnesses who, in very short time, demolished the evidence of both McCurry and Grady. Later reports indicate that the members of the Court discovered that McCurry was thought to be an unreliable character in the colony and this factor also helped them in arriving at their verdicts. There is little doubt also that Minchin in particular may have been put under strong pressure to bring in a not-guilty verdict by the settlers at Cabramatta and Lieut-Colonel George Johnston was known for his fair-mindedness and liberal views. The votes of only five of the sitting members of the Court were needed to bring in a guilty verdict and this also may have had a bearing on the final verdicts.

With regard to the guilty verdicts brought against Morris and McCann it could be argued that these were merely a sop to Bligh who was confidently expecting guilty verdicts in all cases which would rid the colony, in his opinion, of dangerous rebels and leave him free to take on the monopolists. The case against them certainly was also based on hearsay and in the case of Morris on the evidence of Stacey who was backed up by the watchman at Castle Hill. It was unfortunate that Morris did not choose to challenge Stacey's evidence and, as for McCann, Captain Laycock's revelations of him boasting about what he had done to Bligh during the Nore Mutiny did little to help his overall cause.

The Court, however, had shown at least a modicum of courage in finding the Irishmen not guilty but their relief was short-lived as a furious Bligh refused to set them free, roundly abused Minchin on hearing the verdicts and proceeded to send them all back to prison again. On the following day, in a flagrant abuse of the law of the colony, Bligh illegally summoned a Court of Magistrates and, in what surely constituted the first kangaroo court, disregarded the verdict of the Court of Civil Judicature and now found each of the Irishmen guilty. It was Bligh at his autocratic worst: "The law sir", he had barked on one occasion, "Damn the law. My will is the law and woe to any man that dares to destroy it". He now carried out that threat and sentenced the six Irishmen as well as McCann and Morris to be deported in pairs to separate outposts of the colony. Writing again to William Windham in London a few months later Bligh defended his actions:

Bligh to Windham, 31 October 1807.

"Referring to my Letter of the 19th of March, stating an Insurrection was on the Eve of breaking out, and that the leading persons were taken up, I have to inform you, Sir, they have since been tried, and the fact, in my opinion, proved, yet they were acquitted - except two, who were sentenced to corporal punishment; the whole being Prisoners for Life I immediately divided the Gang and sent two to each of the Settlements of Norfolk Island, the Derwent, and Port Dalrymple, and kept two here. The two Men who informed me of this Conspiracy gave their Evidence so steadily as to induce me to give them Free Pardons, and they remain here without any apprehension of being molested by the disaffected Irishmen".

Bligh claims in this letter that the Wicklow men were prisoners for life and puts forward this as an excuse for not freeing them when they were adjudged to be not guilty. It also leads one to believe that the intervention of his secretary on the third day of the trial may have been the result of a conversation he had with Adkins who may have alerted him to the feelings of the Court and indeed Adkins, having studied Marsden's letter to King on that morning, quickly decided that they were prisoners for life.

Bligh's assertion to Windham that Grady and McCurry gave their evidence steadily is a pathetic effort by Bligh to justify his own lack of judgement in the whole affair and indeed it is worthy of note that Grady and McCurry were the only two convicts to be given their freedom by Bligh during his period as Governor. Dr John Harris, the magistrate who gave evidence at the trial, later that year wrote a letter to King in England which implied that he had now fallen out with Bligh and made reference to the trial:

"Two of the men who swore against them being for life, one of them a servant of that scoundrel Ramsay and a notorious character, His Excellency thought proper to give them free pardons and which will be also of the kind he will ever do, as he does not seem to have much of the milk of human kindness about him".

Bligh now ordered Michael Dwyer and William Morris to be deported to Norfolk Island on board the Porpoise which was commanded by his son-in-law Lieut Putland and he was given a letter of instructions signed by Bligh which was addressed to the Commandant of Norfolk Island, Captain John Piper:

"Michael O'Dwyer and William Morris, two convicts for life, being found to be persons necessary to be removed from this settlement, you are directed to receive the two said men and victual them accordingly, taking care that they are not allowed to quit Norfolk Island unless by authority from under my hand. And the said William Morris, having received 525 lashes pursuant to his sentence of 1,000, you are required to direct the remaining part of the 475 lashes to be inflicted according to the warrant sent herewith by the Judge Advocate".

Before the Porpoise sailed Mary Dwyer went down to the wharf to say goodbye to her husband but she was refused permission to see him.

Martin Burke was one of two prisoners who were deported to Port Dalrymple in the northern part of Van Diemen's Land. The exact destinations of the others is not known but it is likely that Hugh Byrne and Arthur Devlin remained in New South Wales, perhaps in the Newcastle settlement and that John Mernagh, Walter Clare and Thomas McCann were sent to the Derwent or to Port Dalrymple in Van Diemen's Land.

So the short-lived joy of Sarah Byrne and Mary Dwyer had turned into despair once more and they returned from Sydney to their homes without their husbands. But now some of the neighbours at Cabramatta who had given evidence in favour of the Wicklow men rallied round and helped the women as best they could in the running of their farms, the irony being that they were largely members or ex-members of the New South Wales Corps. Sarah Byrne in the midst of this crisis gave birth to a daughter, Catherine Agnes, and now had four young children to rear on her own while Mary Dwyer had her infant son James to look after.

But Bligh remained firmly convinced of their guilt and referred to the trial also in a letter which he wrote to his wife Betsy in London. She mentioned it in passing to William Marsden, the Secretary of the Admiralty, the brother of Alexander Marsden. He was born in Co. Wicklow and seemingly knew Hugh Byrne and when Betsy Bligh replied to her husband's letter she passed on a piece of advice to him from Marsden:

"The idea of the mutiny and the massacre by the Irish convicts terrified us, but Mr Marsden made light of it, and said it was an impossible thing and that the informers were the people he mistrusted most. Byrne, he said he would not believe anything against".

But Marsden's words of wisdom to Bligh went unheeded and out at Cabramatta, as the farms of John Mernagh, Martin Burke and Arthur Devlin began to grow wild again, Mary Dwyer and Sarah Byrne struggled on, realising full well that no further recourse to the law was possible for them and that they would be unlikely to see their husbands until Governor William Bligh had departed from the colony, something which seemed a forlorn hope for the foreseeable future.

6

Norfolk Island, situated in the South Pacific about a thousand miles from the coast of New South Wales, had not fulfilled the initial high hopes of the Government that it might provide a steady supply of timber for ship building and that flax would be grown successfully there. But a number of free settlers had been sent to establish farms there and the settlement was also used to house some of the colony's recalcitrant convicts. When the great mass of United Irishmen were sent to New South Wales many of them were transferred to Norfolk Island and Governor Hunter sent out Major Joseph Foveaux, one of the most senior officers of the New South Wales Corps, to take charge.

But the seemingly virulent Irish rebel scare fever had also reached Norfolk Island and in December 1800 Foveaux received information that the Irish were planning to seize control of the island and two Irishmen, Peter Maclean and John Whollohan, were summarily executed on a beach by him as a warning to the others. This illegal action taken by Foveaux was the beginning of a sadistic reign of terror which he carried out over the next few years during which neither male nor female prisoners were spared the agony and humiliation of ritual floggings. But, despite all of Foveaux's savagery, a few of the Irish convicts are reported to have made their escape aboard American whaling ships which often called to the island.

In 1803 a decision was taken in London to colonise Van Diemen's Land, an island roughly the size of Ireland which lay close to the south-east coast, mainly to protect the developing whale fishing industry there, and with it came the decision to abandon Norfolk Island. But the Castle Hill rebellion of 1804 caused King to postpone this decision and many of those who were involved were shipped there, including Joseph Holt who, like Dwyer, had come into the colony without conviction. On arrival Holt, to his surprise, was ordered to work with the other convicts but when he refused he was quickly advised to change his mind "for if Major Foveaux, the Governor, was disposed to hang, he would do so".

But by August the evacuation of Norfolk Island began with the removal of most of the convicts and half of the military forces who were sent back to Sydney. Foveaux was also recalled to Sydney at this time, much to the relief of the remaining convicts, and his successor, Captain John Piper, was an easy-going genial officer and as his main problems came from the free settlers who naturally were reluctant to leave their farms, the few remaining prisoners such as Joseph Holt now spent their time fishing at night from the rocks. But Governor King had not sufficient resources at his disposal to enable him to transfer over seven hundred people with their livestock and possessions to Van Diemen's Land and so the evacuation dragged on for another two years.

In 1805 King also deported from Sydney four additional prisoners whom he regarded as "characters who are well known who would lose no means of stirring those deluded up to any act of atrocity". These were Maurice Margarot the combative Scottish political activist with republican tendencies, Michael Massey Robinson the colony's first poet and two Irishmen William Maum and Sir Henry Brown Hayes; William Maum was a native of Charleville Co. Cork and a Trinity College graduate who had been transported following the 1798

Rebellion and who, like Holt, had become a victim of King's paranoia following the Castle Hill rebellion. Finally there was the larger than life figure of Sir Henry Brown Hayes, the Cork city luminary, who had attempted to abduct Mary Pike, a Quaker heiress, and, although she had escaped unharmed, he was tried before Justice Day in Cork in 1801 when, to his great surprise, the jury, inspired by the eloquence of the prosecuting counsel John Philpot Curran, sentenced him to transportation for life. Hayes on arrival in the colony was immediately given six months imprisonment for insulting the ship's surgeon at Rio de Janeiro but was soon freed and, because of his wealth, purchased a large estate which he named Vaucluse. He then applied to King for permission to form a Masonic Lodge in the colony but was refused and ended up in Norfolk Island when King discovered that he had gone ahead and secretly formed the Lodge. Margarot and Hayes remained on Norfolk Island for a short period as King sent out fresh orders to separate the four prisoners and they were transferred to Van Diemen's Land. By the time that Michael Dwyer and William Morris had arrived there Michael Robinson had been allowed to return to Sydney and William Maum had also gone to Van Diemen's Land where, in time, he would become a very large landholder.

But Bligh now received fresh instructions from William Windham in London insisting that Norfolk Island should be abandoned as a settlement and giving him renewed orders to transfer the remaining settlers and convicts to Van Diemen's Land and these orders were passed on to be implemented by Captain John Piper. As there were only a handful of convicts left on the island it is probable that Dwyer and Morris were involved in the preparations for the final evacuation and it seems likely that given the relaxed atmosphere which prevailed on the island at the time that Morris may have avoided the remainder of his flogging sentence. There is no record as to whether Thomas McCann received his full sentence but it is likely that Bligh would have insisted on his old adversary receiving the full sentence and it is equally likely that McCann would have stood up to his horrific sentence without flinching.

A large contingent of settlers left for the Derwent on the Lady Nelson in November and Dwyer and Morris were among the last two hundred who completed the evacuation, arriving at the Derwent on the Porpoise on the 17th of January 1808. So Norfolk Island, after twenty six years of settlement, was left to the few remaining pigs, goats and sheep but within two decades it would become a penal colony again and would, with some justification, be compared to Devil's Island.

But now, at the beginning of 1808, six of the eight prisoners exiled by Bligh were in Van Diemen's Land although there was little or no contact between the two settlements of Port Dalrymple in the north and the River Derwent and the town of Hobart in the south. On arrival Dwyer and Morris were probably assigned to Government work and must have expected to remain so employed for a considerable period of time. But, quite unknown to them, a major confrontation was looming on the mainland between Bligh and the New South Wales Corps faction led by John Mcarthur which culminated in Bligh ordering the arrest of Macarthur on a series of charges which ranged from sedition to the illegal possession of a still and for resisting arrest. Macarthur secured bail and spent the weeks before his trial drumming up support for himself in the colony and loudly proclaiming that Judge Advocate Adkins had already made up his mind and had pronounced him guilty.

On January 22nd 1808, a few days before his trial was due to take place, the wily Macarthur asked Bligh's permission to inaugurate a mess dinner for the New South Wales Corps and the unsuspecting Bligh consented and even presented Macarthur with a gift of wine for the inaugural dinner. It took place on the night before the trial and all of the six military members of the Court were present in addition to Lieut-Colonel George Johnston. The main topic was, of course, the following day's trial and although Macarthur himself did not attend he spent the evening walking up and down outside on the Parade listening to the regimental band. Inside wine flowed freely; Macarthur was no doubt toasted and his absence bewailed and Lieut-Colonel George Johnston became so drunk that he fell from his carriage on his way home and became hors d'combat.

When the trial commenced on the following morning Macarthur tried to disrupt the proceedings by immediately questioning the impartiality of Adkins and he was given tacit support by the members of the military court. The trial broke up in confusion and, as a highly charged atmosphere began to develop, Bligh ordered his Provost Marshal on the following day to arrest Macarthur although legally he was still on bail. Bligh also summoned the six military officers of the Court to meet him at Government House where he intended charging them with treason but they refused to attend. Lieut-Colonel George Johnston, who had already refused Bligh's call for assistance, now sprung into action and released Macarthur from prison on a warrant which he signed as Lieutenant Governor and with the encouragement of Macarthur and with the regimental band striking up 'The British Grenadiers', a military party accompanied by a drunken rent-a-crowd marched to Government House. There they were met, initially, by Bligh's daughter Mary Putland whose husband had been buried a short time before and who now barred their way: "You traitors, you rebels, you have just walked over my husband's grave and now you come to murder my father!" Bligh, who had some advance notice of their intentions, now attempted to hide before attempting to make his way to the Hawkesbury where he felt he would receive support, but after a search of two hours the soldiers finally discovered him hiding under a bed and he was placed under arrest at Government House while Lieut-Colonel George Johnston took over as Lieutenant Governor.

Bligh's arrest was greeted with acclamation in Sydney and the occasion must have been viewed with genuine delight and astonishment by the convict population in general as they witnessed a Governor overthrown, at last, not by the actions of the disaffected Irish rebels but by his own military forces. As they relished this delicious irony there were frantic celebrations in the streets, bonfires were lit, the taverns did a roaring trade, Lieut-Colonel George Johnston was declared the saviour of the colony and one enterprising Irishman, John Reddington from Roscommon, was later reported as having adopted the sign of the harp without the crown outside his tavern.

As Lieut William Minchin was a leading member of the military party which had arrested Bligh, the news of his overthrow quickly reached Cabramatta where he lived and the delighted and surprised Sarah Byrne and Mary Dwyer immediately began to petition for the release of their husbands and the other prisoners. As both William Minchin and George Johnston had been members of the military court in the Dwyer trial whose verdicts had been set aside by Bligh they were now in favour of such a move and indeed it was in their own interests to highlight such cases and to cite them as glaring examples of Bligh's disregard for the law and the abuse of his powers.

Mary Dwyer left immediately for Van Diemen's Land taking her infant son James with her to find her husband and to inform the authorities there that the Bligh convictions had been quashed and that he had been given permission to return to Cabramatta. The other prisoners were likewise contacted and soon Hugh Byrne and Arthur Devlin were allowed to return home and Devlin saw for the first time his son James who had been born in the previous September.

Lieut-Colonel George Johnston, no doubt contemplating the inevitable wrath of the British Government, was not anxious to retain his position of interim Lieutenant Governor for any great length of time and sent a message to Lieut-Colonel William Patterson, the veteran ex-Administrator of the colony and the commanding officer of the New South Wales Corps in Van Diemen's Land, to return to New South Wales and take over as Governor until, as he hoped, a new appointee would be sent out from England. But Bligh had not yet accepted defeat and wrote also to Patterson ordering him to reinstate him as

Governor and, while Patterson hesitated and remained in Hobart, Col James Foveaux, who had returned from leave in England in July, now took over from Johnston.

Bligh now spent his time busily writing to London complaining bitterly about the conduct of the new regime and defending his own actions as Governor including his handling of the supposed Irish rebel scare:

"The chief of this conspiracy Dwyer, who had been banished to Norfolk Island, and was to have been left at the Derwent, has been sent for by the present rulers - an extraordinary circumstance, for which no reason can be assigned unless they purpose by their indulgence to him hereafter to unite with his old party in an opposition to Government should they feel his assistance necessary".

But despite Bligh's wild speculations Michael and Mary Dwyer did not return to New South Wales for a further six months. They were well aware that Bligh was still in Government House and decided to remain in Van Diemen's Land until they were guaranteed that he would not return to power.

When Col Foveaux first arrived back in the colony from England Bligh was hopeful also that he might restore him as Governor but Foveaux sided with his New South Wales Corps colleagues and, having taken charge, now tried to persuade Bligh to leave the colony. But Bligh, who could afford to lose a ship but certainly not a colony, refused to budge until he had received direct orders from London and remained under arrest in Government House. Foveaux now, surprisingly, dismissed John Macarthur who had been appointed as Colonial Secretary and both Johnston and Macarthur prepared to leave for London to explain their actions to the authorities there.

Lieut-Colonel William Patterson, having dithered for the best part of a year, finally made up his mind to take over from Foveaux and arrived in Sydney in January 1809 a full year after the Rum Rebellion had begun and Michael and Mary Dwyer travelled back on the same ship as him having presumably received guarantees from him concerning their safety. The Dwyers were probably the last of the Wicklow settlers to return to their farms at Cabramatta and records show that Mary Dwyer had given birth to a daughter in Van Diemen's Land at the end of 1808 which is possible as she had arrived there at the beginning of February.

Bligh again appealed to Patterson to restore him to power but Patterson refused and following long negotiations he came to an agreement with Bligh that he could take custody of the Porpoise on condition that he would leave the colony. Bligh agreed and sailed out of Port Jackson but immediately broke the agreement and sailed only as far as Hobart. He was initially welcomed there by Lieut-Colonel Collins but his attitude towards Bligh soon changed when he received a letter from Patterson ordering him to have no more dealings with him.

The ailing Patterson was now installed as Lieutenant Governor but the real power still remained with Foveaux, and Patterson, who was described as "a weak but honest man" soon resorted to the familiar colony habit of appearing to be drunk most of the time. Foveaux now embarked on a massive spree of giving large grants of land to his friends and supporters and an incensed William Gore, who was Bligh's Provost Marshal, wrote to Bligh's wife in London about what he considered to be the slide towards anarchy in the colony:

"Free pardons and emancipations have been indiscriminately granted to almost all the atrocious criminals that have been transported to this colony - all the principal Irish rebel chiefs have been pardoned, many of whom conscious of the invalidity of these instruments, are now hastily quitting the country for Ireland previous to the arrivals of the expected succours".

But Gore was to be disappointed in his expectation of help from England as, with the Napoleonic War still raging, news of the overthrow of Governor Bligh in the far-off penal colony created very little interest either in Government circles or among the public. With regards to Gore's assertion that Irish rebels were quitting the colony, there appears to be very little evidence to support this. One surprising departure however was that of Fr Dixon, who also returned to Ireland during the year, although Bligh in a letter written to Castlereagh was of the opinion that he was still in the colony:

"Colonel Patterson has become very lavish in his favours to a great number of persons in order that when reforms takes place it may produce as much discontent as possibly he can effect. Among their iniquities and designing acts, they have been lavish in their gifts and indulgences to some of the worst characters particularly to the Irish rebels, Dwyer, Holt and other principal ones and the Romish priest is now following his functions where before kept within proper bounds and must again be limited by wise and mild measures".

Bligh may have been referring to Fr Harold who had continued to keep a very low profile in the colony and was given permission to return to Ireland about the same time and afterwards became parish priest at Rathcoole, Co. Dublin.

It is interesting to note also the reference to Joseph Holt in Bligh's letter as Holt's name never appeared in any of the reports concerning the Dwyer trial even though he was living then beside them at Cabramatta. Fr Dixon's return to Ireland at this juncture is harder to fathom if, as Bligh claims, he had been allowed for the first time in four years to function as a priest and administer to the Catholic population, but perhaps he also feared a return to harsher times.

Meanwhile at Cabramatta, less than two years after they had been first arrested, the five Wicklow men were at work again at their farms. But while they were still victualled from the Government stores they had very little money and some had already contracted debts. In January 1809 shortly after the Dwyers had returned Martin Burke received another serious setback when his house was burnt to the ground and although the others rallied round as best they could it must have seemed to them as if their misfortunes were never going to end. But there was some good news in May when Patterson confirmed their ownership of the Cabramatta farms and Hugh Byrne received an extra grant of seventy acres for his wife and children. They now officially regained the status of free settlers and Myles Dolan, a veteran of the 1798 Rebellion and a native of Carlow, was assigned to work for John Mernagh and Michael Dwyer to help them burn and clear off some of their land and make it ready for the growing of badly needed crops.

About this time also a notice appeared in the Sydney Gazette informing the Dwyers that letters had arrived for them from 3, Browne St., the Earl of Meath's Liberty in Dublin where their four other children were being reared. The question of sending them out to New South Wales was obviously being raised again as their ages now ranged from six to ten years and decisions would have to be made about their futures. But the Dwyers, because of the recent disruption in their lives, were in no position to send on any money to pay for their fares and it was obvious now that Trevor had reneged on the agreement made before they left and that the Government were not going to pay for their passages out. So the Dwyer children remained in Ireland although further letters continued to be exchanged over the next couple of years.

Meanwhile as Patterson and Foveaux continued to lavish large land grants on all and sundry and as the economy began to stagnate news finally arrived from London concerning the appointment of a new Governor to replace Bligh. Within a few weeks of this announcement William Patterson, responding perhaps to a petition from Dwyer, granted him a full pardon but as the year 1809 drew to a close and as the colony awaited the arrival of the new Governor all the old anxieties must have returned to the Wicklow settlers about their future. There was some relief, initially, when it became known that Bligh was not being reinstated but it was also known that he was still at Hobart and it was possible that he might have the ear and sympathy of the new Governor rather than Patterson and Foveaux.

On December 30th 1809 the small convoy of ships bringing

the new Governor arrived in Port Jackson and anchored off the Governor's wharf at Sydney Cove. In the town itself that night bonfires again blazed as a welcoming gesture and they were answered by the firing of festive rockets from the ships in the harbour. But nineteen miles away that night in Cabramatta there was little jubilation as the Wicklowmen waited and hoped and prayed that some pattern of normal living might be in store for them in the colony at last.

On New Year's Day 1810 a large crowd watched, with more than passing interest, as the new Governor Lachlan Macquarie assumed his powers on the Grand Parade in Sydney when he broke the wax upon the Patent and handed the Great Seal of the Territory to the incoming Judge Advocate Ellis Bent, who officially displayed it to the somewhat bewildered onlookers. Members of both Macquarie's 73rd regiment and the New South Wales Corps stood guard as ceremonial volleys rang out and bands played 'God Save The King'. Macquarie now addressed the crowd in his rich Scottish accent stressing that it was his intention to exercise the authority vested in him with strict impartiality and expressing his optimism that "all the dissensions and jealousies which had unfortunately existed in the colony for some time past would now terminate for ever, and give way to a more becoming spirit of conciliation, harmony and unanimity among all classes and descriptions of inhabitants".

It had been the intention of the Government in London that Bligh should officially remain as Governor until that day and that he should receive Macquarie as his successor at Government House where Macquarie was to have opened his Patent, but Bligh had remained at Hobart and having consulted with the new Judge Advocate, Macquarie had proceeded without him.

Lachlan Macquarie, a forty-nine year old army officer, was a native of the island of Ulva in the Inner Hebrides and was a member of the poorer of two septs of the Macquarie Clan who owned a castle in Mull. His father died when he was young and he was, subsequently, reared by his mother in relative poverty on a rented farm. His uncle Murdoch Mclaine of Lochbuy became responsible for his education and, following the outbreak of the American War of Independence, he joined the British Army and, later, spent many years on active service in India where his first wife died. Some years later he married Elizabeth Campbell from Airds in Scotland and she readily agreed to come with him to New South Wales where their only son would be born. Macquarie, originally, had been offered the post of Lieutenant Governor but, when the designated Governor became ill, Castlereagh quickly offered him the post of Governor with the promise of a full pension if he remained in New South Wales for eight years. Macquarie brought with him the 73rd Regiment which had fought with him in India and which were to replace the New South Wales Corps.

Among his staff were two quite interesting Irishmen; his Lieutenant General was Colonel Maurice O'Connell, a debonair member of the famous Kerry family who had the typical background of an 'Irish Geese' officer of the period. He was the younger son of John O'Connell of Ballinabloun, a tall strapping lad who was first intended for the priesthood until his famous uncle, Count Daniel O'Connell, arranged to have him sent to military college in Paris. When the Irish Brigade was taken into British pay in 1794 Maurice O'Connell was appointed Captain and, having adroitly conformed to the Church of England, he served in the British Army in a variety of exotic locations such as Surinam, St Lucia and Dominica before his appointment to New South Wales. The second Irishman on Macquarie's staff was John Thomas Campbell, the efficient and sober Unionist who had previously worked in the Bank of Ireland and was a founder member of the Bank of the Cape of Good Hope.

For Macquarie his unexpected appointment as Governor was to become the great challenge of his life and he looked forward to it with almost a child-like enthusiasm. He was indeed the right man for the right job and, above all, he came at the right time. He was down to earth, bluff, full of reforming zeal and he possessed a great deal of common sense in addition to a keen organisational ability while his no-nonsense upbringing in Ulva meant that he lacked the artificiality of manners, pomposity and the hideous class consciousness which was the hallmark of so many of his contemporaries.

Colonel Joseph Foveaux, deputising for Patterson who was ill, greeted Macquarie on his arrival and soon became indispensable to the new Governor, being now the essence of civility and reasonableness, a far cry from his Norfolk Island days. As the British Government had ruled that Bligh officially had remained as Governor until the arrival of Macquarie it meant that all of the grants and pardons which Patterson and Foveaux had lavished on their supporters were invalid and there was consternation in the colony, initially, when Macquarie issued a proclamation ordering all those who had received grants or pardons to return them to his secretary J.T. Campbell.

Even though it was immediately explained that Macquarie would reconfirm the great majority of these grants and pardons, the Wicklowmen at Cabramatta, once again, found themselves the victims of an ongoing type of musical chairs and they now also had to surrender their grants and pardons. Hugh Byrne was the first to reapply and on January 22nd he had a memorial written and sent to Macquarie in which he described himself as a free settler. In this petition he also described how he had been brought to trial and imprisoned falsely by Governor Bligh:

"During this period he (Hugh Byrne) had to lament the misfortune of his wife and five children (three) who were left unprotected and their pitiable state during that period will no doubt be felt by your Excellency, altho' almost surpassing description - deprived of every indulgence, his men taken from him, and his property exposed to the merciless world, by which means he was under necessity of incurring debts that he has not yet surmounted".

Hugh Byrne finally asked Macquarie to allow two servants to be assigned to him again to help him with his farm and also that they should be victualled from the Government store "and in the meantime that you will be pleased to confirm the Title of his Land and allow him to return to the enjoyment thereof". Macquarie, in fact, officially regranted their farms to those who had surrendered them, the titles being backdated to New Year's Day although it is not clear if he allowed Hugh Byrne to have the service of two assigned convicts on his farm. But their status as free settlers was still not clarified and, in fact, the legal definition given by Judge Advocate Adkins during their trial that they were prisoners for life now also was accepted by Macquarie and Dwyer, having surrendered the pardon he had recently received from Patterson, would now have to go through the process of receiving first a conditional pardon and then a full pardon before being legally adjudged to be a free settler again.

The colony was soon feeling the full brunt of Macquarie's spirit of reform and there was great unease as he began to insist on a strict adherence by everyone to the observance of the Sabbath and even went as far as sending constables out to arrest anyone whom they found working on the Lord's Day. He now ordered all couples who were living together in the colony to get married as he felt that the children of such marriages were often neglected in terms of education and Mathew Hughes, the Protestant teacher from Co Down who had been a corporal in a militia regiment before being transported, was asked to open a Charity School at the settlement in Windsor which was subsidised to the amount of eight pence per week per pupil for spelling and reading and one shilling for accounts. There was still no respite however for Catholics who were still without the services of a priest to function to their religious needs.

Macquarie now turned his attention to some of the colony's innkeepers whom he termed "in defiance of all law and decency scandalously kept open during the night, the most licentiously and disorderly houses, for the reception of the abandoned of both sexes and to the great encouragement of dissolute and disorderly habits". He now curtailed the granting of spirit licenses which had multiplied during the period of the Rum Rebellion and he encouraged the growing of barley so that beer might, at least, begin to replace the demon rum as the common drink. This was obviously good news for brewers like James Squires and Arthur Devlin also took advantage of the new policy when he was granted a beer license in March 1810. It meant that he was now allowed to sell beer without having to go to the expense of running an inn. With regard to the rum trade, the Colonial Office had instructed Macquarie not to allow rum to be used in future as barter and that no rum should be imported into the colony without his permission. Macquarie now, in a rather novel attempt to regularise the trade and benefit the colony financially, entered into a contract with some of the leading traders who agreed to build a new hospital, soon to be called the Rum Hospital, in exchange for an exclusive rum franchise and, although the project became a controversial issue for the new Governor, it was apposite, at least, that the new magnificent hospital built on the sale of rum should cater for many of its victims.

Macquarie now also revelled in his self-appointed role of town planner and he quickly set to work on improving Sydney's appearance; streets were regulated, sidewalks were built, cattle drovers were warned about their straying herds and the Governor's populatity rose dramatically when he allowed horse racing to take place in Hyde Park while Elizabeth Macquarie became equally popular with the Irish when she gave a dinner on St. Patrick's Day for almost sixty Irish convicts and overseers who were employed with the Government, probably the first official recognition of the Irish national day in New South Wales.

But it was Macquarie's enlightened attitude towards the convict population in general which marked him out as the Governor who would first determine the future shape of the colony when he stated "that long-tried good conduct should lead a man back to the rank in society that he had forfeited and do away, in as far as the case will admit, all retrospect of former bad conduct". It was to be the cornerstone of his reforming policy during his eleven-year tour of duty and one which, almost inevitably, brought him into conflict with those in the colony whose philosophy was that the convicts should always remain subservient to their masters and that, even when they became emancipated, the major offices in the colony should always remain the preserve of the so-called exclusives. The fact that this latter policy was echoed by Government officials sent out from London added to Macquarie's ongoing problems in this regard.

But while the Wicklowmen at Cabramatta worked their farms and waited for news of even conditional pardons being granted to them, John Mernagh formed a liaison with Mary Johnson, a native of Co. Meath, who had also come out on the Tellicherry and a daughter Elizabeth was born to them in July 1810 although the place of birth was given as the Hawkesbury rather than Cabramatta. But, at least, the Wicklowmen had the satisfaction of knowing that Bligh had finally left the colony but not before he arrived back in Sydney on the leaking Porpoise and proceeded to make all sorts of demands which soon alienated Macquarie. When Bligh finally departed for London to indict Johnston and Macarthur, Macquarie wrote to Castlereagh stating that he found Bligh "certainly a most disagreeable person to have any dealings or public business to transact with; having no regard whatever to his promises or engagements however sacred". He also described him as being tyrannical in the extreme and "a very improper person to be employed in any situation of trust or command". But there was a final disappointment for Bligh as he had to leave behind his widowed daughter Mary Putland who had fallen for the dashing Col Charles O'Connell and, despite Bligh's initial opposition, he attended their wedding before he left the colony.

Macquarie now also set about reorganising the administration arm of the colony; among those whom he promoted was the emancipated D'Arcy Wentworth who was then acting as

Government medical officer at Parramatta. D'Arcy Wentworth a native of Portadown, was the son of an innkeeper, and he began his colourful career when he joined a local regiment of the Irish Volunteers as a medical ensign. He then moved to London to continue his medical studies but, to supplement his income, took the unusual step of becoming a highwayman. He soon found himself in the Old Bailey defending three charges of robbery, but although he was initially acquitted, further charges were brought against him. Through the influence of the Fitzwilliam family, to whom he claimed a relationship, he was allowed, prior to being sentenced, to take up a position of assistant surgeon on a convict ship going to Botany Bay. Ironically he was, subsequently, acquitted but was now committed to a life-long career, initially in Norfolk Island and finally in New South Wales. By 1810 he had also become a prominent businessman and landholder in the colony and Macquarie, who was also acquainted with the Fitzwilliam family in London, soon appointed him in quick succession to the posts of Principal Surgeon of New South Wales, Chief Police Magistrate of Sydney and Superintendent of Police. D'Arcy Wentworth also became one of the main contractors involved in the building of the Rum Hospital although this latter venture did not prove to be as profitable as he had anticipated.

Macquarie's reorganisation of the police force included the appointment of new constables in outlying areas of the colony including the area of George's River. There was soon great surprise expressed among the Irish population when in August 1810 it was announced that Michael Dwyer had been appointed as one of the new constables at Georges River. Some reports claim that it was D'Arcy Wentworth who had approached Dwyer - certainly they would have had a lot in common - but it is more likely that the request to Dwyer came from Macquarie himself. There was in the local area of Bankstown a settlement known as Irishtown which had sprung up on a hill and, as the name suggests, was composed of various Irish people including those who were on ticket-of-leave or had been granted some remission of sentence.

The area was known to be a trouble spot for British born constables and so, with the need being recognised for the appointment of an Irish constable, Michael Dwyer, with his acknowledged position as former rebel leader, was an ideal choice to deal with his potentially turbulent countrymen and it would also neutralise Dwyer's own position as a potential rallying force for the disaffected in any future plans for rebellion.

From Dwyer's point of view it was an offer, particularly if it came from Macquarie, that he could scarcely afford to refuse. He was now being asked to give positive proof of his declared intention to live peaceably in the community and he now had to show cause as to why the new Governor should grant him a conditional or a full pardon. If he had refused the offer it surely would have been seen as proof that he still retained his rebel sympathies; it might have the effect of delaying the chances of his and his Wicklow comrades of receiving their pardons. Dwyer, no doubt, discussed the proposal with Martin Burke and Hugh Byrne and they would have supported his decision to accept. His wife Mary would also have encouraged him to accept the offer; for her it would remove at last the threat of sudden arrest and of their home being broken up again; they now could become part of the settled community and there would be some continuity in their lives. She and her young family would feel protected at last from the crudities of a legal system which had caused her so much anguish since her husband surrendered in 1803; she would no longer have to flinch every time a military person approached.

But even though the vast majority of constables, many of them Irish, were ex-convicts, for this very reason alone Dwyer would not have been comfortable within himself at the prospect of becoming a constable. He regarded himself as a free settler and, in this context, it was something of a loss of face in the eyes of the community. He would also in some way, have to justify his decision to the many Irish convicts he would now meet in the course of his duty and who still regarded him as a leading Irish rebel chief; there could no longer be any more singing of Irish rebel songs at night at Clarke's in the Hawkesbury or at Lynch's in the Rocks. The man who refused point blank to wear the splendid military uniform which Emmett had sent down to him in Wicklow now found himself stoically donning the constable's blue coat with its red collar and heading out to Irishtown with a lot of explaining to do.

Just ten weeks after the announcement of Dwyer's appointment as a constable Governor Macquarie made an official visit to the area around George's River, one of his many energetic visits to the outlying areas, and the inveterate diarist left the following account of his visit, date Friday 9th 1810:

Friday 9th. At 6 am I set out to see the remaining farms in the Banks Town District towards Botany Bay along George's River and Harris' Creek. After we had looked at the southernmost farm on the latter creek, we crossed the country with the intention of returning home by the upper part of George's River in a south west direction; but missing our way we lost ourselves in the woods and wandered about in a boundless forest for upwards of three hours without knowing where we were. At length we stumbled on the river, and got home a good deal tired about 1/2 past 10 o'clock; finding Mrs M and Mrs Moore waiting impatiently for our return. Breakfast was ready for us and we soon got over all our fatigues.

I had sent Mr Meehan early in the morning to lay out the ground for the town of Liverpool, which deprived us of his services as a guide, and good honest Mr Moore had never before explored that part of the country in which we had lost ourselves this morning. We must have rode at least 20 miles before breakfast.

After resting ourselves and our horses for a couple of hours, I set out to explore the remaining farms in the Minto district and to look once more at the site of the intended town of Liverpool, leaving Mrs M to follow and meet me in the afternoon at Dwyer's farm along with Captain Antill; it being our intention to return in the evening again to Parramatta, and therefore, now took leave of our kind hostess Mrs Moore from where I set out with Mr Moore etc. etc., at 1 o'clock, crossing the river in the boat to meet our horses on the opposite bank.

We proceeded first to Liverpool, where having marked out the square for the church etc. etc. I continued my tour to the adjoining farms belonging to Holt, Burn, Devlin, etc. etc. and ended up at Dwyer's where I found Mrs M. and Captain Antill waiting for us. Here we took leave of our worthy guide and Mr Moore, who returned home, and we pursued our way to Parramatta, where we arrived at 1/2 past 5 o'clock in the evening; and Mr Broughton who had come with me on business to George's River, dined with us.   ✗

Thomas Moore was in fact one of the largest landholders in the district, a man of strong religious belief who would bequeath all of his estates in trust to Bishop Broughon. It was significant of Dwyer's new official status in the area that Elizabeth Macquarie and the Governor's aide de comme Captain Antill should choose to stay at his farm that afternoon and while one can only imagine the conversation which took place between the two women it can be assumed that Mary Dwyer left Elizabeth Macquarie in no doubt as to the extent of her sufferings at the hands of Bligh. She, no doubt, received a sympathetic hearing as Macquarie's final comment about Bligh when he was leaving was that "he was heartily glad to be quit of him". Macquarie was, on the other hand, still completely taken in by Major Foveaux whom he described as "a man of very superior talents, of strict honour and integrity, the fittest person he had ever met with in any country in thirty years for improving and conducting an infant colony to maturity". He recommended Foveaux for a post in Van Diemen's Land without success and Foveaux returned to London and spent the year 1814 in charge of a military group in Co. Waterford.

In March 1811 the Wicklowmen at Cabramatta finally received the titles to their farms as part of a general amnesty and the titles were backdated to New Year's Day 1810 with the provisos that the land should not be sold for the space of five years, that the Government had the right of making a public road through it if necessary and that it had first claim also on such timber as "may be deemed fit for naval purposes".

In July they all received conditional pardons and at the same time were granted free stock from the Government herds to boost their incomes. With the founding of the town of Liverpool all of the constables in the area were now based there and Dwyer was given a cottage in the tiny settlement although he continued to live on his own farm which was less than a mile away. His first real embarrassment as a constable came when a warrant was issued for the arrest of Arthur Devlin on a charge of grand larceny; although there had been a disagreement between them Dwyer must have been very unwilling to arrest his fellow Wicklowman although reports suggest that he did so. Devlin was tried in court but was found not guilty and discharged. This might have seemed to be the final break between them but, according to James Sheedy who with John Mernagh was now helping to look after Lieut-Colonel George Johnston's farm while he was in London defending himself against Bligh's accusations, Mernagh, Sheedy, Dwyer and Devlin joined forces over the next few years in an arrangement to rear and sell cattle together as Dwyer was spending most of his time attending to his duties as a constable.

Meanwhile in London, during the month of May 1810, a Court Martial was held at Chelsea Hospital at which Lieut-Colonel George Johnston was charged with mutiny against the Crown for deposing Bligh. William Minchin was asked during the proceedings about the Dwyer trial, and having described Dwyer as a peaceable man he was duly savaged by the prosecution when, owing to a lapse of memory, he told the court that Lieut-Colonel Patterson had been present when Bligh reprimanded him after the court verdicts had been announced. Patterson, in fact, had returned to Van Diemen's Land before the trial had begun and the whole of Minchin's testimony was consequently called into question. In addition Minchin revealed that during the Dwyer trial the military court had discovered that Dominic McCurry was of bad character in both the colony and in Ireland and that his evidence was therefore discounted. Minchin was also asked if he was aware of Dwyer's reputation in Ireland and whether that had been taken into consideration. Captain Edward Abbott, who had given evidence against Dwyer in the same trial, also had an uncomfortable time trying to explain away how he had later changed his mind about Dwyer's guilt, but when the court asked Minchin if it was true that a Sergeant Trotter had given evidence as to McCurry's good character Minchin, at least, had the satisfaction of replying that it was well known that McCurry was making illicit spirits at George's River for Sergeant Trotter's wife! At the conclusion of the trial George Johnston was found guilty of mutiny but was sentenced only to be cashiered and the Prince Regent, confirming the lenient sentence of the court martial, described it as "so inadequate to the enormity of the crime of which the prisoner has been found guilty have apparently been actuated by a consideration of the novel and extraordinary circumstances, which by the evidence on the face of the proceedings, may have appeared to them to have existed during the administration of Gov. Bligh both as effecting the tranquillity of the colony and calling for some immediate decision".

So George Johnston escaped with a relatively light sentence and both he and Macarthur were allowed to return to the colony within a few years. As for William Bligh, still retaining the protection of Sir Joseph Banks, he was promoted to the rank of Rear Admiral of the Blue in 1811 and to Vice Admiral in 1814 but he never held office again and died in London in 1817.

In 1812 Joseph Holt also received a free pardon from Macquarie and he decided to return to Ireland having spent twelve years in the colony. He proceeded to sell his own farm at Glen Bride for the sum of a thousand pounds and all his livestock and grain for the same figure. James Meehan purchased his horses and harness for an undisclosed sum, and Holt also received two hundred pounds for five English bred cows and finally sold a smaller farm for a hundred and fifty pounds. In

December Holt, with his wife and one of his sons, left on the Isabella bound for London and he also brought with him his servant John Byrne who had left behind a wife and seven children in Ireland. Also on board was the formidable figure of Sir Henry Browne Hayes who had been also given permission to return to Ireland. But in February, owing to the bad seamanship of the Captain, who was drunk, they were shipwrecked in the Falkland Island and, having been marooned there for some time, were finally picked up by an American ship and Holt and his family finally made their way back to Ireland. Soon after his arrival he bought a public house in Dublin but, as both Catholics and Protestants regarded him as a traitor, business was very slack and he finally built some houses in the town of Dun Laoghaire and made a modest living from the rent he collected, bitterly regretting his decision to leave New South Wales.

In 1812 also Michael Dwyer was given the additional post of pound keeper and was soon advertising the fact in the Sydney Gazette that he had impounded a bay colt and a grey mare. It was a source of some extra money for him and his main qualification for the post was that he was able to read and write. He was, in fact, the only one of the five Wicklow men to have this facility even though Hugh Byrne may have learned to write his name after his arrival in the colony. The ability to read and write, at a time when literacy among the peasant population was low, gave Dwyer an added status and a big advantage especially when dealing with the authorities, although many of the constables who were taken on at the time often signed their names with the customary X. Dwyer with the bonus of his two official position in addition to the farm now seemed to be in a position to make a good living but the others were still struggling and a combination of circumstances would see them go their separate ways over the next few years as one by one they were forced to sell their farms at Cabramatta.

7

There now followed a very harsh period for the farming community in the colony as the usual March rain did not fall in 1813 and by August the situation was becoming desperate. But the dry spell continued and, by October, more than five thousand sheep and three thousand cattle had perished. With the consequent shortage of grain the government was finding it difficult to buy sufficient wheat locally to feed those who were victualled from their stores and the situation was further exacerbated when speculators began to hoard their remaining stocks of grain and waited for prices to rise.

The drought persisted into the following year and many of the smaller farmers were now forced out of business. They now could no longer afford to keep their assigned servants, some whom turned to bushranging in preference to returning to the drudgery and discipline of the Government work gangs. It now became increasingly dangerous to travel the roads of the colony particularly at night and the Sydney Gazette warned its readers to travel always in groups so that they could defend themselves more easily. The whole landscape had now become parched, springs and rivers had run dry and there was no relief until the year 1815 when, after a disastrous three-year dry spell the rains finally came. During this period Michael Dwyer's combined income as constable and pound keeper cushioned him from the worst effects of the drought but Martin Burke had already sold his farm and became a publican for a short period. Hugh Byrne with a family of six children to feed had no other source of income apart from his farm and he now was forced to lease fifty acres of his land to a Lawrence Brady. Arthur Devlin was still operating his beer license and John Mernagh was still helping to look after George Johnston's farm. But the three year drought had again made it increasingly difficult for them to become financially secure.

The first major census of population or muster in New South Wales took place in 1814 and it gives a fair indication as to how the Tellicherry transportees had fared since their arrival eight years before. The census- taking was spread over a period of four weeks in the middle of October and the various categories of people had to report to the four main settlements at Windsor, Parramatta, Liverpool and Sydney. On November 4th all free men and ticket of leave prisoners were asked to attend the school house in Liverpool and the following day was confined to free women, female prisoners and "such of the stock keepers as were unable to attend on Friday". Settlers and landholders were required also to give an account of their cultivated stock and mothers were asked to give details of their children. Failure to attend was to be punished with the utmost severity but despite this warning the census naturally is somewhat defective and a number of men and women from the Tellicherry, who are not listed, turn up fourteen years later in the 1828 census. For example, the name of Hugh Byrne is missing although his wife Sarah and his children are all listed. Michael Dwyer is decribed as a constable rather than a landholder, Martin Burke as a publican, Arthur Devlin and John Mernagh as landholders and Mary Johnston is listed as living with Munar (no-one in the colony could ever master Mernagh's name) and she is credited with having three children.

With regard to some of the other Tellicherry prisoners, James Sheedy, having been sentenced to death but reprieved shortly after his arrival, is credited as working for George Johnston but Pierce Condon from Tipperary had repeated his crime of cow stealing and had been hanged. Hugh Byrne from Carlow is also missing for similar reasons. He had been given a conditional pardon by Macquarie in 1811 as part of a general amnesty but the shock must have proved too much for him, and now bearing the nickname for obvious reasons of Hughie the Brander, he was tried in Sydney in 1813 on a charge of stealing Government cattle and was sentenced to be hanged. He was however reprieved by the magnanimous Macquarie "on account of some favourable circumstances in mitigation of his offence" and he was given a life sentence with hard labour in the Newcastle settlement. But the life style in that particular establishment would scarcely have suited Hughie's tastes and, having no doubt absconded, he turned up next in Van Diemen's Land, the haven of many bushrangers, where reports were issued in May 1815 that an attempt was being made to apprehend him. Hughie 'The Brander' Byrne was finally arrested in August and, having failed to cheat the hangman's rope for a third time, he was finally executed on September 3rd 1815.

Of the one hundred and twenty five men and thirty five women who landed safely on the Tellicherry in 1806 about seventy five men and twenty women are listed in the 1814 Census which was confined to New South Wales and did not include a small number who may have gone to Van Diemen's Land. The majority of the men are described as labourers but eleven at least, excluding Dwyer and his fellow Wicklow men, had gained their freedom and were now classified as landholders. They include John Cogan from County Kildare who had received his pardon from Macquarie "for considerations of his successful exertions in making the recent discovery of good land to the Westward of the Blue Mountains". Cogan, who was described as being five feet two inches tall and aged forty, was one of the servants who had taken part in a recent expedition headed by Gregory Blaxland, William Lawson (probably the

Ensign Lawson who had been a member of the military court at the 1807 trial) and the youthful William Charles Wentworth, the son of D'Arcy Wentworth, which had made the first successful attempt to extend the boundaries of the colony by crossing the, seemingly, impassable Blue Mountains. According to the 1814 Census several others of the Tellicherry transportees, who had received their pardons, were making good livings as tradesmen including blacksmith Edward Jones from Derry, carpenters Thomas Shaughnessy from Co. Dublin and Jeremiah Griffin from Co. Clare, baker John Connolly from Co. Dublin and butcher Hugh Woods and tailor Henry Austen from Dublin City; Patrick Mulhall from Carlow is described as a grass cutter while Nicholas Prendergast from Wexford had become a stock keeper, but Charles McMahon from Waterford was in jail and Denis O'Sullivan from Tipperary was in the Sydney Benevolent Asylum.

Twelve of the women listed in the Census were now married; Mary Bradshaw from Dublin to Sergeant Kaye with two children; Eleanor Burke from Dublin to Darby Murray who was also on the Tellicherry and was now a landowner; Catherine Fynnes of Dublin to a Constable Gavigan (Britannia I); Anastasia Shanley from Dublin to an English labourer called William Cooke; Mary Smith from Dublin to Thomas Brown; Bridget Shea from Limerick City to another Tellicherry man Michael Fitzgerald and who had a family of three children, one of whom she may have brought with her from Ireland; Eleanor Tyrrell from Co. Meath to an Englishman John Grant with two sons whom she also may have brought with her from Ireland; Mary Kennedy from Co. Clare to Thomas Kelly with a family of two children; Ann Mathews of Dublin to Constable Tutty; Margaret Hayes of Co. Clare to an Englishman, R. Parsons and Mary Lamb of Dublin to Constable Francis Wilde (Queen). There is a listing also for Mary Golledge (maiden name not given) who was married to an ex-soldier and already had four children.

A further three of the women are described as living in the Female Factory at Parramatta. These were Catherine

McLaughlin from Dublin with four children, Bridget Johnston also from Dublin with three children and Abigail Kelly from Dublin (who is not listed in the ship's indent) with one child. Mary Rice from Limerick City is listed as living with Hugh Mulhall and Mary Gough from Dublin, who had two children, as living with a Henry Williams who worked as a waterman. Two of the remaining women, Catherine Hinchy and Honora Molony from Limerick City are listed as being single and Mary Nagle from Westmeath as being confined to jail.

Other entries in the census include Malachy Ryan, the Tellicherry prisoner who worked for Sgt Stroud, the owner of the farm next to Michael Dwyer. Ryan, who had given evidence in support of Dwyer at the 1807 trial, was still working as a labourer but within a few years would, like Dwyer, become a constable. The two chief witnesses against Dwyer are also listed: Dominic McCurry, despite receiving a pardon, was still working as a labourer while Daniel Grady had become a small landholder. Edward Morgan, an English convict, was working for Michael Dwyer while Irishman Michael Tolan, who had recently arrived on board the convict ship Three Bees (which caught fire and sank in Port Jackson soon after its arrival), had been assigned to work for Arthur Devlin. Missing from the Census are the names of both Walter Clare and Thomas McCann who may have remained in Van Diemen's Land, but there are no less than four men listed with the name of William Morris.

While the tradesmen in the colony were now earning as much as three pounds per week the smaller farmers were still struggling and John Mernagh, despite working for George Johnston and rearing cattle with Devlin, Sheedy and Dwyer was in severe financial trouble by the year 1817. His farm was already partly mortgaged to the newly founded Bank of New South Wales for a sum of twenty five pounds and he was soon forced to put it up for sale on the suit of Darby Murray, one of the Tellicherry landholders to whom Mernagh owed thirty pounds. The farm was duly bought by Joseph James who was described as "a gentleman from Sydney" for ninety three pounds, a very low price which may have indicated that Mernagh had done very little with his land in recent years. This left Mernagh with a residue of only twenty pounds but Joseph James, obviously a land speculator, quickly turned his purchase into a profit when he sold it soon afterwards to John Hosking for one hundred and fifty pounds. Hosking was in charge of a Methodist day school and had originally come to the colony, on the invitation of the Rev Samuel Marsden, to take charge of the Orphan School, but was also involved in commercial activities. In 1818 Hosking also purchased the farms of both Hugh Byrne and Arthur Devlin which gave him a three hundred acre holding as the three farms adjoined one another. Ironically, in the following year, Hosking quarrelled with Marsden and returned with his family to England but two of his sons returned to New South Wales a few years later to take over their father's property.

The plight of the smaller farmers in the colony during this period was well summed up by J.T. Bigge, a Government official who was sent over from England to write a report on the state of the colony, when he analysed what he termed "the failure of some emancipated convicts as farmers":

"They constitute the middle and lower order of settlers in the colony and having in general began with very limited means, they have been obliged to depend solely upon the produce of the land. It is through their means, therefore, that the greatest quantity of grain has been produced for the consumption of the colony; and it is also through their want of means and their want of capital and skill, that the productive powers of the soil, that is not generally a fertile one have been exhausted by repeated cropping. Many of the original grantees are now either reduced to a state of dependence upon their creditors, or are seeking for opportunities for redeeming themselves by removal to some now and more productive tracts near the rivers Nepean and Hawkesbury".

Hugh Byrne, having sold his farm, received a grant of land in the more fertile area of Airds not far from Cabramatta. It was a wise decision and having invested the money he had received into developing it from now on managed to make a comfortable living. His family was now growing up and the eldest members, who were in their late teens, were able to help with the farm work. Arthur Devlin received a new grant of land in the area of Ryde at Botany Bay and moved there with his family. Martin Burke had by now relinquished his spirits license and, following Dwyer's example, became a constable in the nearby area of Bringelly.

By the beginning of 1819 Michael Dwyer was the only one of the Wicklowmen still living at Cabramatta and it seemed, on paper at least, that he was by far the most successful of them as reports show that he had increased his acreage and that he was tendering for the supply of fresh meat to the government stores. But the extremes of weather still continued and during the winters of 1816 and 1817 rain now fell incessantly and with the assigned convicts being let go by impecunious landholders again they were more inclined to opt for a life of crime. In addition to the inevitable spate of robberies the Government herd at Cowpastures, despite the presence of a military guard, became much depleted and those convicted of cattle stealing were shown no mercy.

But the attention of the Catholics in the colony was diverted in 1817 with the arrival in Sydney of the maverick Trappist priest Fr Jeremiah O'Flynn who was appointed in Rome in the previous year as Prefect of the Mission of 'Bottanibe'. Jeremiah O'Flynn was a native of Tralee, Co. Kerry, whose chequered career began when, having been ordained in England by the largely French order of Trappists, he had a row on his way out to the West Indies with his Lord Abbot whom he had threatened to strike. He was, subsequently, suspended but proceeded to minister to the poor before being recalled. His appointment to New South Wales was opposed by the Vicar Apostolic in London, Dr William Poyntor, mainly because he had not been

Governor Lachlan Macquarie, from the portrait by Opie.

View of George's River near Liverpool, New South Wales,
1819, the property of George Johnston.
(probably by Joseph Lycett).

The town of Liverpool, New South Wales, from an etching
drawn about 1830.

informed by Rome about it and also because he believed that O'Flynn was not a suitable priest to go to New South Wales. O'Flynn was known for his anti-British views and had refused in the West Indies to pray for the King during religious services. Having been brought up as a native Irish speaker in his native Kerry, Jeremiah O'Flynn had never mastered the English language and when he originally had written for permission to Lord Bathhurst to minister in New South Wales he was refused, partly because 'the orthography of his letter induced a suspicion of his fitness'. The Colonial Office in London had also enquired of Poyntor as to his suitability and were told 'that the person in question was a most improper one to be entrusted with the care of souls'.

Undismayed by Lord Bathhurst's refusal to grant him official permission, Jeremiah O'Flynn departed on the Duke of Wellington from London and duly arrived in Van Diemen's Land in October 1817 where he was welcomed by the new and moderate administrator Lieut Gov William Sorrell, who gave him permission to say Mass there. At the beginning of November he left for Sydney but received a frosty reception from Macquarie and when O'Flynn tried to bluff his way by claiming that he had received official permission from Lord Bathhurst, written proof of this was demanded, which of course was not forthcoming. O'Flynn then resorted to making a personal plea to Macquarie asking him to recognise the fact that there were a very large number of Catholics in the colony without the benefit of a priest, but Macquarie bluntly replied that he wanted to make them all Protestants and his secretary, the Ulster Unionist J.T. Campbell, added that one religion was enough for any state and that he realised only too well the consequences of the differences of religions for twenty years in Ireland - Protestants knocking the brains out of Catholics and Catholics knocking the brains out of Protestants and all, supposedly, for the pure love of God. Macquarie decided to deport O'Flynn immediately and, showing some of the prejudice of his predecessors, even expressed the fear that the Irish convicts in the colony ' "might be worked upon by a designing priest, so as to excite a spirit of resistance". But while O'Flynn was waiting to be put on a ship to take him back to London he managed to celebrate Mass in a private room daily with only nine or ten people present so as not to arouse any undue hostility, and he left behind a consecrated host which was kept in a cupboard in the home of William Davis in Sydney. Davis, formerly a blacksmith from Co. Laois, had received a full pardon in 1814, became a publican for a time in Parramatta and now was a successful farmer in addition to owning property in Sydney. He now, together with Michael Dwyer, Hugh Byrne, John Lacey and James Dempsey, secretly founded the Council for the Protection of the Blessed Sacrament and, reputedly, held constant vigil at the cottage of William Davis in Sydney where St. Patrick's Cathedral is now situated.

But Fr O'Flynn's efforts were not in vain, as petitions were now sent to the Government in London to officially sanction the provision of a Catholic priest for the colony. Dr Edward Slater had been appointed by the clerical authorities in Rome as a Vicar Apostolic for the vast region which stretched from the Pacific to the Cape of Good Hope and he travelled to Ireland looking for priests to volunteer for service in New South Wales. Fr O'Flynn, on his return, also kept up the pressure and, having met with Fr Joseph Therry, a young Cork priest, mentioned his name to Edward Slater who in turn wrote Fr Therry in Cork. Joseph Therry was then in his late twenties having been ordained by Dr Troy the Archbishop of Dublin in Carlow in 1815. Having been sent briefly to work in a parish, he was then appointed as secretary to Dr Murphy, the Bishop of Cork, and became interested in the welfare of transported convicts following an incident which had taken place a short time before. He was walking along the streets of Cork when he noticed a wagon passing by which contained a group of convicts handcuffed together and guarded by a military escort who were on their way to board a convict ship in the harbour. Thinking about their spiritual, rather than their physical needs, Fr Therry rushed into a nearby bookshop where he bought two dozen prayer books and racing after the waggon threw them in among the prisoners. While the reaction of the convicts to this unusual gesture has not been recorded, the incident made a deep impression on Fr Therry and when Edward Slater wrote to him from Liverpool in England in 1818, he readily accepted his proposal, his only reservation being that he had no knowledge of Irish which was the only language of many of the convicts. Dr Slater felt that this was not a major obstacle and, at the same time, Fr Richard Connolly, a native of the North of Ireland who was working in the Kildare diocese, also volunteered to go to New South Wales. Their applications were vetted and agreed in London by the Earl of Bathhurst and by the Prince Regent and an annual stipend of one hundred pounds each per annum was granted to them.

A convict ship, the Janus, with a complement of one hundred and five female prisoners was diverted to Cork to pick them up in December but Fr Therry was soon shocked to discover the extent of the cohabitation between the crew and the female prisoners on board. He immediately complained to the Captain who listened gravely and agreed to put an immediate stop to it. But when Fr Therry discovered that one of the female prisoners was in the habit of spending the night in the Captain's own cabin he decided to wait until he reached Sydney in May 1819 where he then made his views known to a genuinely disapproving Macquarie. Frs Therry and Connolly, on arrival, were put up by William Davis in his house in Charlotte Square, Sydney and they celebrated Mass on the following two days at the home of John Reddington in Pitt Row. Even though they had received official permission they were, initially, tolerated rather than encouraged by the authorities in the colony; Government premises were refused to them to say Mass and as the prosyletising spirit still remained reports in 1820 still show that many Catholics, when seeking grants of land, were refused because they were not known to a Protestant clergymen. On the other hand Frs Therry and

Connolly received a great deal of assistance from individual Protestants, especially when funds were being raised to build the first Catholic church.

That first fund raising meeting which took place in 1820 was chaired by Fr Connolly but a committee was then formed and the elected chairman was James Meehan. Fr Connolly soon went to Van Diemen's Land leaving the energetic Fr Therry with the onerous task of administering to the scattered Catholic population and he, consequently, spent a great deal of his time travelling on horseback between the various settlements. The treasurer of the Church Fund, surprisingly, was J.T. Campbell, Macquarie's secretary and founder of the recently established Bank of New South Wales. Both William Davis and James Dempsey were also involved in the fundraising but neither Hugh Byrne nor Michael Dwyer was among the committee members, and for Dwyer in particular, it was the period when the myth of his apparent prosperity soon vanished.

8

The year 1820 began in a very positive manner for Michael Dwyer, as J.T. Bigge's report on the state of the colony showed that he was credited as being one of the biggest emancipist landholders in New South Wales with an acreage of six hundred and twenty acres, two hundred acres of which were cleared. It is difficult to confirm if Dwyer in fact owned that much land and further statistics in Bigge's report reveal that whereas comparable landholders were heavily stocked with cattle and sheep Dwyer is credited with having none and his livestock consisted of one hundred and twenty pigs, an indication of his lack of capital. But there was further good news for him in May when he was appointed Chief Constable of Liverpool and now had three constables working for him. Although there was a sizeable population in the district around Liverpool the town itself still had only a population of about two hundred and Dwyer continued to live at his own farm about a mile outside the town.

The first hint of trouble began when on July 26th the following order was issued from the Court of Magistrates in Liverpool:

"Whereas Arthur Devlin of the district of Botany Bay stands charged with felony these are to charge all constables and others to apprehend and lodge the same Arthur Devlin in one of His Majesties gaols, and all persons are directed not to harbour the same Arthur Devlin upon pain of prosecution, to the utmost rigour of the law".

The nature of Arthur Devlin's felony was not revealed but Dwyer, as Chief Constable, would again be responsible for his arrest. Martin Burke who had been a constable in the neighbouring area of Bringelly had resigned on the first of July but soon became a constable in the area of Pittswater near Broken Bay, north of Sydney. But Arthur Devlin went into hiding, did not appear in court to face the charges which were to be brought against him, and was declared a missing person.

About the same time Denis Molloy, a Limerick man who had come out on Atlas 2 and who was listed as a labourer in the 1814 census, was arrested on a charge of bushranging and, with a number of others, was brought to Sydney Jail to await trial. Denis Molloy had previously been charged with bushranging in 1807 and was sentenced to a term of imprisonment but he was released in 1813. He had become friendly not only with John Mernagh and James Sheedy but also with Michael Dwyer and was living with Jane Black, a native of Northumberland who had been transported on the William Pitt for "political offences". One report suggests that Molloy was previously married and that following the death of his wife two of his children were reared by Mary Johnston and the Dwyers. Molloy, having been brought to trial, was found guilty of bushranging, sentenced to death and was hanged at the end of August. Two others who died with him confessed their crimes on the scaffold but Molloy remained silent.

Michael Dwyer had by now resumed his old drinking habits but Molloy's execution seemed to have triggered off a sustained bout of drinking which came to a head less than two months later when in October 1820 Dwyer was summoned before a Magistrates Court in Liverpool charged with being an unfit person to remain in the post of Chief Constable because of his continuing drunkiness. The charge was brought by the worthy citizens of Liverpool led by Thomas Moore and the two magistrates on the bench were William Redfern and Richard Brooks. Redfern was one of the ablest men in the colony, a Canadian-born doctor who at the age of eighteen while serving in the British navy as an assistant surgeon had given some advice to the Nore mutineers and was duly transported. He was a most conscientious doctor who had given selfless service both on Norfolk Island and in New South Wales, but Macquarie, who recognised his worth, was prevented from appointing him as Chief Medical Officer owing to the concerted opposition of the exclusivists who blocked his promotion on a legal technicality and Redfern consequently retired to his estate although Macquarie did succeed, again with difficulty, in making him a Justice of the Peace.

The case against Chief Constable Michael Dwyer was held in public in Liverpool Courthouse and a number of witnesses were called to give evidence against him. The first of these was William Klensendorlffe who, with his wife, had arrived in the colony as free settlers on the Ocean two years before and had opened the Elephant and Castle Inn at Liverpool and who had an interest also in horse breeding and racing. He told the court that when he refused to lend money to Dwyer he was accused by him of lending money to a man called Burcher even though he knew that Burcher had stolen pumpkins and melons! It could hardly be called a startling revelation but it showed that Dwyer must have been short of money and that he may have been drunk on that occasion. Klensendorlffe went on to tell the court that he had seen Dwyer "so beastly intoxicated on the day of Tuesday August 29th - about the time that Denis Molloy was hanged - that he had to be led away in a cart being totally incapable of walking home unprotected".

Klensendorlffe then recalled to the court an incident which had taken place in April when Dwyer had been seen drinking with Molloy and other supposedly disreputable characters who had come into his inn and who had remained there drinking until nine o'clock. Molloy had ordered the drink but Dwyer finally had to pay for it. Klensendorlffe finally declared that, on another occasion, Dwyer was so drunk that he had lost some official letters which were due to be posted and the Court then asked him to confirm that Dwyer had complained to him that he had been robbed by Mr Moore of the sum of five pounds seven shillings and six pence.

The second witness was a local schoolmaster, John Cutler, who also gave evidence of having seen Dwyer in a drunken state, and mentioned an occasion when Dwyer had to be taken home in a cart by a neighbouring farmer, Andrew White, and that, as recently as a month before, he had seen Dwyer drunkenly sitting on the ground near the jail.

Richard Guise whose farm was close to Dwyer's now told the court that he also had seen Dwyer drunk on a number of occasion and that he had to be led home by Constables Morgan and Bradley. Guise also recalled the day when Dwyer had been seen drinking with Molloy at Klensendorlffe's Inn and that he and his companions had gone into the parlour by themselves but Guise added that Molloy had not been charged at that time. Another of the local constables, John Brady, now gave evidence that Dwyer was so drunk that he could not answer a question when asked and that he sometimes had to be led home by his wife and by a man called McNally, who was the Watchman of the Jail. Brady also accused Dwyer of neglecting his duty and of failing to attend the military camp. He was then asked by the Court to confirm that Dwyer had not given his constables their share of money received from the sale of cedar even though he was requested by Thomas Moore to do so and that a sum of two pounds had not been paid to them.

Andrew White and a Mrs Mary Neal again recounted the events of the night when Dwyer was brought home in a cart and White told the court that when he arrived at Dwyer's house his young son James, then aged thirteen, helped his father in and that Mary Dwyer became very angry with White and, blaming him for her husband's condition, had slammed the door in his face. White denied this assertion completely and said that Dwyer himself had asked for drink and had told him that he had taken five glasses of spirits in the nearby barracks before coming to the Elephant and Castle Inn that night. Mary Neal reiterated most of Andrew White's evidence but drew attention to the fact that Michael Dwyer was suffering from 'a bad leg' but the circumstances which caused it are not recorded. Thomas Moore, the biggest and most influential landholder in the district, now took the stand and was asked by Dwyer if he had ever seen him incapable of performing his duty and Moore limited himself to stating that he had seen Dwyer in a state that he should not be. The Bench then pointedly asked Moore if, in his opinion, the Chief Constable should be resident in the town and Moore readily agreed, saying that the inhabitants had frequently complained that there was no one to direct the constables in their duties. Michael Dwyer was now asked to defend himself against the charges and he denied having said to Klensendorlffe that Burcher had stolen melons and pumpkins and he also denied all of the other charges brought against him except the principal charge of being drunk. He explained to the court, however, in a somewhat unconvincing manner, that the night he was brought home drunk in the cart he had come into Liverpool for the purpose of getting something to cure a cold. He finally agreed to give the constables their share of the cedar money although he still claimed that the money belonged to him.

With that the hearing of the Court of Magistrates came to an end and the two magistrates soon issued the following verdict:

"After minutely examining the evidence in support of the charges brought forward by Thomas Moore and the inhabitants of Liverpool, we are of the opinion that Mr Dwyer, from his unfortunate propensity to drunkeness and his not residing in the town, is an unfit person to fill the situation of chief constable in the town of Liverpool".

In issuing their findings Brooks and Redfern had tried to lessen Dwyer's embarrassment by referring to the fact that he lived outside the town but a week later, a much more direct official notice emanated from the Civil Department in Sydney: "Michael Dwyer, Chief Constable at Liverpool is dismissed under the present date from that situation in consequence of irregular and improper conduct". The main questions which emerge from the court hearing and which remain unanswered, concern Dwyer's exact relationship with Molloy. What business were they discussing that was so secret that they had to go into the parlour in the month of April, and why had Dwyer become so affected by his execution? But there is little doubt that Dwyer was very relieved to be rid of the position of Constable which he had held for ten years, and was far from being demoralised by the outcome of the court hearing. He was now given some Government work to compensate perhaps for his loss of earnings as Chief Constable and with a partner called Murphy was paid thirty seven pounds in November 1820 for repairing watch towers.

In the same month Arthur Devlin died at the early age of forty eight and was buried in Botany Bay cemetery. Very little is known of his movements after he went missing following the issuing of a warrant for his arrest in Liverpool four months before, although one report suggests that he was killed accidentally by a falling tree, perhaps on his own property at Ryde. After his death his widow Priscilla and her five children returned to her stepfather's house and she had Arthur Devlin's beer licence transferred to her name.

But Michael Dwyer now decided to solve his financial problems by following the example of many of his fellow Irishmen and applied for a license to sell spirits. A fellow Wicklowman called Andrew Doyle, one of two brothers who came out on the Rolla in 1802, had recently purchased the Lord Nelson Inn at Windsor and would make a fortune from it. Other successful Irish publicans at the time included the schoolteacher Farrell Cuffe who opened the Macquarie Inn in Sydney, Patrick Cullen who owned the Ships Fame, Hugh Kelly the proprietor of the Halfway House which was situated between Parramatta and Windsor while it is interesting to note that two of the taverns in the Rocks area not recommended for a license by Macquarie, as they were reckoned to be of "bad fame, injurious to the morals and sobriety of the troops" were called 'The Harp' and 'St Patricks'.

Dwyer was now granted a temporary spirits license for six months, probably through the good offices of D'Arcy Wentworth, who was responsible for the issuing of licenses, and he now decided to convert his own house at Cabramatta so that it could provide accomodation for guests as the law required. The name he chose was 'The Harrow Inn', an attempt to exorcise the memory of the past ten years and in memory of one of the most decisive victories won by the Wexford rebels in 1798.

He now proceeded to borrow heavily from two local businessmen, Daniel Cooper and Robert Campbell, to finance his new enterprise, and no effort was spared to make the Harrow Inn superior to Liverpool's other inn, which was of Klensendorlffe's Elephant and Castle. Daniel Cooper who lent Dwyer most of the money he required was a native of Lancashire who had arrived in the colony just five years before with a life sentence for larceny but possessing a great business flair he had become so successful that he was on the point of setting up his own banking firm, even though he only received a full pardon in 1821. Robert Campbell who lent Dwyer a lesser amount of money was a Scotsman who had come to the colony as a free settler with his uncle in 1806 and is described as being "convivial, charming and with the flair of a bon viveur", and soon all these admirable qualities of his would be tested in full. In addition to being a successful businessman he was a close friend of D'Arcy Wentworth with whom he shared a passionate interest in horse breeding and his Persian stallion Hector is regarded as being the foundation line of Australian bloodstock. Michael Dwyer spent the year 1821 in converting and extending his home and he also received an additional land grant and spent some of the money he had borrowed buying additional livestock.

Following the return of George Johnston to the colony James Sheedy and John Mernagh were no longer required to look after his farm. Sheedy was given forty acres of land by Johnston and soon both he and Mernagh became joint tenants of Kemp Farm, Cabramatta and they also leased land from Isaac Nichols at Liverpool, where they reared cattle and supplied wheat to the Government stores. For Hugh and Sarah Byrne the year 1821 was a happy one as their eighteen year old daughter Rose whom they brought with them on the Tellicherry, married William Craft, the son of a local constable, and Hugh Byrne was also selling wheat from his farm at Airds to the Government stores. Fundraising for the Catholic church had got under way and Michael Dwyer made a generous contribution of ten pounds together with five pounds from his wife Mary and one pound from each of his three children. Other major contributions received by treasurer J.T. Campbell included fifty pounds from William Davis, thirty pounds from James Meehan, ten guineas from Farrell Cuffe and five guineas from his wife, ten pounds from D'Arcy Wentworth and twenty pounds from Lachlan Macquarie who agreed to lay the foundation stone for St Mary's Church while jocosly remarking that it was an unusual ceremony for an old mason to undertake. But the proposed size of the church, as envisaged by Fr Therry, was too elaborate to be funded from public subscriptions alone and, without the provision of a Government grant, the church remained without a roof for many years despite Fr Therry's best efforts and a totally unsuccessful fundraising journey by James Dempsey to India!

In 1822 Michael Dwyer still felt confident about the financial success of the Harrow Inn and presented an official memorial for the renewal of his license for a further twelve months:

"That your memorialist is the proprietor of the Harrow Inn near Liverpool on which he has been lately expending considerable sums of money to render it commodious for the reception of travellers. That your memorialist is induced to hope that his conduct during the term of his former license has been such that his Worshipful Bench will grant him a license to sell spirituous liquors for the ensuing year". The fact that he had been dismissed from his post as Chief Constable for drunkness was not considered to be a prohibiting factor and he was granted a further extension of his license. Given his Irish connections and the fact that he was well known in the area it should have been a highly profitable venture, particularly as the Harrow Inn was still one of only two such establishments in the Liverpool area, but there were ominous signs from the very beginning. On the very first night that the Harrow Inn opened for business Dwyer, having unlocked the front door, in an extravagant gesture proceeded to take the key of the door in his hand, walked to a nearby well and threw the key in, declaring that the door of the Inn would never be closed again. The resulting cheers, no doubt, could be heard one mile away in the town of Liverpool. The Harrow Inn was soon described, with very good reason, as the liveliest in the history of the colony and while this should have augured well for its financial success it also became known that if anyone had not enough money to pay for drink or lodgings he was not pressed very hard and with the fifteen year old James Dwyer in charge, helped by his fourteen year old sister Bridget, and with the proprietor being one of its best customers, the ghost of Constable Dwyer may have been well and truly laid but the financial consequence of such bad management was soon to follow.

9

On the ninth of December 1822 Richard Campbell the Younger made an application to the Court of Civil Judicature in Sydney, to obtain a judgement against Michael Dwyer for the sum of three hundred pounds to be repaid to him. The judgement having been granted Dwyer made a repayment of eighty pounds but Campbell was back in court three days later before Justice Barron Fields who directed the Provost Marshal J.T. Campbell "that the goods and chattels, lands, tenements and hereditaments of the said Michael Dwyer he should cause to be made the sum of two hundred and nineteen pounds eight shillings and sixpence to render to the said Robert Campbell".

But Dwyer's troubles were only beginning and on the very next day Ann Stroud, the widow of Sgt. John Hawley Stroud, who owned the Warwick Park farm next to Dwyer's, brought a separate court action against him alleging that Dwyer had taken over her land without her permission and had put it out for rent for his own gain. This case also came before Justice Barron Fields at the New Hospital Sydney on December 16th and the charges against Dwyer which were read out were quite specific and claimed that he had "with force of arms broke and entered her property in the district of Bankstown amounting in all to one hundred and sixty acres of arable land, meadow, pasture, woods and furze and heath making a total of eight hundred acres and that he had received for his own use the rents issues and profits for the said tenements". Ann Stroud claimed that Dwyer had taken over these lands during a three year period from 1819 until the issuing of the writ and she further claimed damages of a hundred pounds which Dwyer had allegedly received from the renting of her land. Dwyer was represented in court by his attorney James Norton who entered a plea of not guilty to the charges. There are no reports of Dwyer himself giving evidence in his own defence but judgement was found in favour of Ann Stroud and she was awarded damages of the one hundred pounds which she had sought.

The exact background to this case is unknown but it is important to note that Dwyer was a local constable in the area at the time and that Ann Stroud claimed that he had ejected with force of arms. One presumes that Ann Stroud during this time lived at her original farm at Warwick Park and was not actually living on the lands at Bankstown which obviously were lying idle. As Dwyer was found guilty in court of the charges brought against him, one can only speculate that his actions may have been prompted by his deteriorating financial situation. But the question remains as to why Ann Stroud delayed for three years before reporting his actions to the authorities. Surely she should have complained at the time when he was dismissed as Chief Constable two years before?

But Dwyer now was unable to pay the one hundred pounds damages and on the same day that judgement was given against him, he proceeded with the help of attorneys James Norton and Frederick Garling to effectively declare himself bankrupt against the money that he owed to his principal creditor Daniel Cooper which amounted to one thousand, nine hundred and seventeen pounds, four shillings. Cooper, Campbell and Stroud now all informed the Government of Dwyer's declaration and three weeks later, on January 9th 1823, an official notice from the Provost Marshal's office appeared in the Sydney Gazette:

Father Joseph Therry in 1819, from a miniature.

"Campbell V Dwyer.
Cooper V Dwyer.
Stroud V Same.

By virtue of several writs of Fieri Facia to me directed in the following cases I will put up for sale by Public Auction at the place and times hereafter mentioned the property of several defenders in said case. In these causes I will sell at the Market Place, Liverpool on Saturday Jan 25th, 64 Head of Horned Cattle, 5 Horses, 7 rams, 20 pigs, 1 cart, 1 chaise, 20 gallons of rum, 2 casks of wine, without household furniture and other property. Also a farm of land containing about three hundred acres all fenced in, in nine paddocks in possession of the defendant and situated about one mile from the town of Liverpool, with the erection therein, a good house and several outhouses - with a good garden attached unless the several executions thereon be previously discharged".

So the extravagance of the Harrow Inn was now threatening to destroy him and Dwyer faced the prospect of total ruin with even his house being sold to meet his debts. But this official notice also showed the extent of the monies he must have spent also on the purchase of livestock when compared to his situation two years before, when he was credited with having neither cattle nor sheep. He had reduced the number of pigs he owned to twenty but he had over sixty cattle and his purchase of seven rams seems to indicate that he was about to concentrate on the breeding of sheep. He also had bought five horses which might have been an attempt to become involved in horse breeding and racing, like his rival William Klensendorlffe of the Elephant and Castle Inn.

Dwyer now approached Daniel Cooper and through Cooper's solicitor tried to make a deal which would enable Cooper to recover his money and leave Dwyer with at least some of his possessions. A separate notice now appeared in the next two issues of the Sydney Gazette and which paradoxically ran alongside the original notice from the Provost Marshal's Office which was also repeated:

"Liverpool - to be sold by private contract 100 acres of ground more or less situated within one mile of Liverpool on which there is a neat dwelling place, barn stalls etc. There has been lately 1000 pounds expended in improvements. The land is subdivided into nine paddocks and fenced in and well watered in the driest season it being bounded on the North by Cabramatta Creek the same being too well known to need any particular description it having for some time being a licensed house and would also answer for a private residence for a genteel family. The house contains twelve rooms. One two or three hundred acres can be given if agreed upon. Also in the town of Liverpool eight allotments of ground with tenements thereof known by Holt, Smith, Marquis Love, and Dwyer's allotments the whole included with paling. Application to be made to Mr. Michael Dwyer, Liverpool the present proprietor or to Mr. Daniel Cooper and Mr. P. Garrigan George's St., Sydney".

The main differences between the two notices were that Dwyer now proposed to sell his original farm and home which was now incorporated in the Harrow Inn but not his livestock and, for the first time, it is revealed that he also owned eight allotments in the town of Liverpool. One of these originally belonged to Joseph Holt which Dwyer may have bought from him before Holt's return to Ireland and which would indicate some contact between them. While on paper these allotments in Liverpool seemed to indicate hidden wealth the fact was that property in Liverpool at the time was of a low value and leases were given solely on condition of erecting a dwelling on them.

But the office of the Provost Marshal was not impressed by this notice and went ahead with the scheduled sale of Dwyer's farm at Cabramatta on January 25th when it was sold to Alexander McLeod from the Newcastle settlement for the sum of five hundred and seventy pounds. This amount, however, fell far short of the amount that Dwyer owed and the January 30th issue of the Sydney Gazette contained another notice of sale from the Provost Marshal's office:

"On Friday February 14th, at my office in Hunter St Sydney at 11am, all the right title and interest of the defendant Dwyer of, in and to the several allotments hereafter mentioned, all situated in the central part of the town of Liverpool and known by the names and descriptions following viz. Dwyer's allotment - 6 1/2 acres, Morgan's allotment 1 1/2 acres subdivided in four parts, Smith's allotment - 1 1/2 acres. Each of the above (except Dwyer's) being well enclosed and having a dwelling house thereon, Love's allotment with a brick house of two rooms and one house with four rooms unfinished. 50 acres of land at Cabramatta known by the name of Newman's Grant, 30 acres known in the name of Dove's Grant. And in the same case I will sell on February 8th next on defendant Dwyer's premises near Liverpool, his household furniture of all descriptions and the remainder of his stock in cattle unless the several executions thereon be previously discharged.

J.T. Campbell Provost".

This notice indicates that most of his livestock had already been sold and that it was intended also to sell even his household furniture which must have been the final indignity for Mary Dwyer. But there was now a further delay in the sale of his farm when Alexander McLeod was unable to raise the money and the sale finally fell through. Dwyer was allowed to remain in possession of his house and, although the remainder of his assets were sold off, the farm at Cabramatta was not put up for sale until August when a final notice appeared in the Sydney Gazette listed as Dwyer V Cooper only. On August 8th Dwyer's farm and house was now purchased by John McQueen of Sydney for the much lower figure of three hundred and twenty pounds by McQueen who promptly resold it to John Ovens for four hundred and twelve pounds ten shillings, making a quick profit of over thirty per cent. But John Ovens had little spare cash either and he sold the property on December 27th, for the same price, to Thomas Moore, the biggest landholder in the area, and the man who had instigated the proceedings which led to Dwyer's dismissal as Chief Constable three years before. As Moore was more interested in the land rather than the house he, no doubt, came to an arrangement which enabled Dwyer and his unfortunate family to remain in possession of their home and he even may have employed Dwyer to look after it for him. The low price which Dwyer finally received for his farm did not materially make any difference to him but rather to Richard Cooper who, in the end, had to settle for about fifty pence in the pound, receiving a final payment amounting to a little over nine hundred pounds. Shattered by the traumatic events of that year Mary Dwyer turned to religious practises as her only consolation as she saw everything which she had worked so hard for since her arrival in the colony sold to meet their debts. Fr Joseph Therry gave the Dwyers what little help he could, and a public notice which appeared in February 1824 stated that "Catholic Books, Religious Moral and Polemical were to be obtained at first cost from Mrs Dwyer, Liverpool". James Dwyer, now aged seventeen, opened his own inn which was probably unlicensed, although there is no report as to whether it became financially viable or not.

By now Lachlan Macquarie had returned to England, having transformed the colony in the intervening eleven years, but, owing to the opposition of the exclusivist faction supported by London, he failed in his attempts to integrate the emancipated convicts fully into the mainstream of life in the colony. His successor Sir Thomas Brisbane was a moderate also by nature and when he introduced an assisted passage scheme which enabled relatives of the colony's inhabitants to be brought out from Britain and Ireland, Fr Therry informed the Dwyers who now, even though they were destitute, decided to send a memorial to the new Governor seeking permission to bring out their four children from Dublin. But before the memorial could be forwarded to Sir Thomas Brisbane, Ann Stroud, who still had not been paid her one hundred pounds damages, had Michael Dwyer committed to a debtor's jail in Sydney in May 1825. The bankrupt Dwyer had no means now of repaying this amount and would have remained in prison but for the passing of a recent regulation in the colony which put the onus on those who committed debtors to jail to pay for their upkeep. On arrival in prison Dwyer immediately invoked this new regulation:

"To Justice Francis Forbes. That Your Honour's petitioner is at present under confinement for debt in His Majesty's Jail at Sydney under the suit of Mrs Mary Anne Stroud. That your petitioner is unable to support himself and entreats that Your Honour will order him a maintenance according to the usage in this case".

But Ann Stroud, who must have found the new regulation difficult to fathom, did not keep up the weekly payments and three weeks later Dwyer again wrote to Justice Francis Forbes:

"That petitioner lately received from Your Honour an order of maintenance which was duly served on the plaintiff directing a weekly allowance of one Spanish dollar to be paid to your petitioner on, or before, two o'clock on Monday of each and every week. That, in pursuance of the said order your petitioner was furnished on Monday the 16th with the maintenance but on Monday the 23rd plaintiff wholly unattended to and neglected Your Honour's order and therefore your petitioner entreats Your Honour will direct petitioner's liberation from gaol according to the usual custom in such cases and petitioner as in duty bound will ever pray etc. etc.
Michael Dwyer,
Sydney May 24th 1825".

Dwyer, for a last time, signed his name with a rather shaky hand to an official document and he was released a short time later. For the very first time in his life justice had rallied to his side but, ironically, only when he appeared to be in the wrong. Michael Dwyer returned to his home at Cabramatta which he continued to hold on sufferance and he died there, barely three months later, on Tuesday August 23rd 1825 at the age of fifty three, surrounded by his grieving wife, his eighteen year old son James and his two daughters Bridget, aged seventeen and Eliza, aged thirteen. Five days later he was buried without ceremony in the Irish burial grounds. His death certificate indicated that he had died from dysentery which was reckoned to be one of the two most prevalent causes of death in New South Wales at the time and which for the most part was "greatly exaggerated by the excessive use of spirituous liquors to which the mass of the colonists are unfortunately addicted". The Sydney Gazette reported his death in a single line: "Deaths: At Liverpool, Mr Dwyer formerly Chief Constable". It was not the description he would have preferred.

There was still the question of the hundred pounds damages which was owed to Ann Stroud and there may have been other debts outstanding as in September Mary Dwyer publicly thanked Stephen Blake, an Irishman who had come out on the Boyd, for his help in settling her affairs. The Dwyers now left the family home at Cabramatta where Mary Dwyer had lived since she had arrived in the colony seventeen years before but which had been held only on sufferance since 1822. She was destitute but Fr Joseph Therry came to her assistance and she moved to Sydney with her family and became Fr Therry's housekeeper, a position which she held for many years.

Fr Therry now began the process of applying for assisted passages to bring out Mary Ann, Esther, John and Peter Dwyer from Ireland and in January 1828 John Dwyer, then aged twenty seven, and Peter Dwyer, aged twenty six, arrived in Sydney on board the Marquis of Huntley. They were now reunited with their mother whom they could scarcely remember and met for the first time their brother James and their two sisters Eliza and Bridget. The happy reunion was dampened somewhat by the fact that their father was already dead for over two years and must have been particularly poignant for Mary Dwyer who, no doubt, saw in her sons the image of her husband as he had looked at the time of their marriage thirty years before. And there was further comfort for her in October of the same year when Esther and Mary Ann Dwyer also arrived from Dublin on board the Sir Joseph Banks. Esther, who had been born while her father was in Kilmainham Jail, was then twenty four years old and Mary Ann, the eldest of the family at twenty nine, already had her share of grief as her husband William Hughes had died before she left Ireland, leaving her with an infant son, William, whom she brought with her. Shortly after their arrival Eliza Dwyer, the youngest of the family, who had married Peter Bodicene in 1827, gave birth to a daughter and she was named Mary Anne after her newly arrived eldest sister. Eliza Dwyer was not yet sixteen when she married and her husband Peter, who was then aged thirty three, had arrived in the colony in 1820 aboard the Saint Michael. He had a wool business in Georges St., Sydney and he gave Peter his first job in the colony as a wool sorter, while John Dwyer worked as a warehouseman with J.B. Bettington. Bridget Dwyer, also with the help of Fr Therry, became a teacher in his Catholic school, working at various periods of the year in both Parramatta and Sydney teaching about eighty children in each area for which she was paid two pence per week per pupil by the Government. Esther Dwyer also became a governess at the Catholic school in Hyde Park.

But while the Dwyer children, slowly but surely, began to achieve self sufficiency these were years of mixed fortunes for Hugh and Sarah Byrne. In 1824 their son Michael who, as a five year old boy had come out on the Tellicherry, married Jane Warby, the daughter of a local constable in Airds, and in 1825 their eighteen year old daughter, Catherine Agnes, married John Feighran who became a mill owner in Campbellstown. But in March of that same year their daughter, Rose Craft, who had already given birth to a son and a daughter, sadly died at the early age of twenty two. In 1826 Ann Byrne, who was born during the Tellicherry voyage, married a namesake, William Byrne, who was the son of Michael Byrne and in that same year the amazing Sarah Byrne, at the age of fifty two, gave birth to the last of her fifteen children, a daughter who was named Rose in memory of her recently deceased sister. Hugh Byrne continued to make a good living from his new farm at Airds, managing to feed his ever- increasing family and still having enough wheat left over in 1825 to supply the Government stores with two hundred bushels at a price of nine shillings a bushel.

Martin Burke remained in the position of constable in the district of Pittswater and one report suggests increased his agricultural holdings to two hundred acres and that he. had become a Protestant. John Mernagh was described as a landholder living in Liverpool in 1820 and may also have been given land by George Johnson on his return from England but, by 1828, he had obviously sold the land and was living with James Sheedy on his holding at Liverpool which now amounted only to 14 acres. John Mernagh, surprisingly, is described as a shoemaker and James Sheedy had now married Jane Black who previously had been living with Denis Molloy before his execution in 1821. Sheedy had, by his own admission, left behind a wife and children in Co. Clare but it was not unusual for men in similar circumstances in the colony to remarry although it seems doubtful if Fr Joseph Therry was asked to officiate at the ceremony.

In 1826 John Mernagh's daughter Elizabeth was married at the age of sixteen to Daniel Canvin, a native of Bristol who had been transported on the aptly named Elizabeth in 1820. Canvin was a blacksmith by trade and soon went with his young wife to work for a Mrs Badgery in South Creek, Bringelly. Arthur Devlin's widow Priscilla had remarried in 1821, one year after his death. Her second husband was Thomas Small, eight years her junior, who owned an inn on her property at Ryde and she would rear a second family of eight children.

10

The New South Wales Muster of 1825 and the major census which took place in 1828 both provide further opportunities for checking on the fluctuating fortunes of the surviving Tellicherry transportees twenty years after their arrival in the colony. Of the men who were described as landholders in 1814 only John Cogan and Darby Murray had managed to retain their farms by 1825. The additional information given in the 1828 Census shows that Dubliner Darby Murray had become quite a substantial landholder owning over eight hundred acres of land of which fifty acres were used for cultivation and he also owned two hundred cattle. He was married to Eleanor Burke also from Dublin who came out on the Tellicherry but they, apparently, had no family. Pat Murnane from Limerick had a holding of fifty acres with ninety five cattle, Daniel Kelly of Co. Dublin also had fifty acres with thirty eight cattle, with fourteen acres cultivated; his wife Margaret had come out on the Broxbornbury and they had a family of two sons. Edmund Burke of Co. Limerick, who was still only forty years of age, had cleared all of his fifty acre farm but had only four cattle and six acres in cultivation. His wife Esther, then aged twenty four, was born in the colony and they had three young children. Nicholas Lacey from Kilkenny also

Sarah Byrne – the wife of Hugh Vesty Byrne, photographed in old age about 1860.

owned land as did Patrick Gore of Kildare while his fellow Kildare man, Philip Ennis, held fifty acres at Airds, twenty five acres of which was cultivated. Barnaby Butler of Kilkenny, who was described as a farmer, held only four acres, all of which was in cultivation. Lawrence Fenlon who, with Hughie 'The Brander' Byrne and John Fitzpatrick were described in 1805 to Governor King by Marsden as dangerous criminals, was in 1825 described as working for the Government but, sadly, in 1828 he had apparently blotted his copybook once more and was confined to the Prison Barracks in Liverpool. Many of the surviving men were now reaching the ages of between sixty and seventy but Thomas Cuffe at seventy eight was still working as a labourer while John Kearney, at the age of seventy, was working as a gardener. Owen Clarke of Dublin, at the age of sixty nine, was now an invalid, but had been taken in by Martin Burke who was looking after him. Thomas Shaughnessy of Co. Dublin who was working as a carpenter in 1814 had now progressed to the more lucrative trade of cabinet maker at his premises in Hunter St., Sydney. His wife had been transported on the Experiment in 1804 and they had a family of four young children. Patrick Maher from Tipperary was working as a tailor and his two teenage sons were already tenant farmers.

The Tellicherry women also had somewhat mixed fortunes in the intervening years: Margaret Hayes, who in 1814 had been married to a man called Parsons, was by 1825 in the Benevolent Asylum, Sydney; Ann Mathews who was formerly married to Constable Tutty, was working as a dairymaid in 1828 while Mary Lamb who was described as the wife of Francis Wild, Sydney, both in 1814 and 1825, is listed three years later as his housekeeper! Marriages which had endured over the period however include those of Eleanor Burke who had married Darby Murray, Mary Smith who had married Thomas Brown, a labourer, and Anastasia Shanley who had married William Cook, a bricklayer in Parramatta who was almost thirty years older than her.

Catherine McLaughlin who had been living in the Female Factory, Parramatta, with four children in 1814 was now married to Thomas Gorman who had come out from Ireland on the Rolla in 1802 and was now a prosperous farmer, but Mary Rice who had been living with Hugh Mulhall in 1814 was a patient in the Lunatic Asylum, Liverpool. Mary Golledge was still married with four children while Eleanor Tyrrell, who now had two grown-up sons and a younger son who was, seemingly, in the Orphan School in Sydney, was still married to Michael Grant, a shopkeeper in Sydney. Mary Kelly, who was formerly an upholsterer in Dublin, was now making a living as a fruiterer in Parramatta while Abigail Kelly was listed as a householder also in Parramatta. Finally Catherine Hinchy, who in 1825 was listed as the wife of James Lennox, had by 1828 become a laundress working for Jer Leonard in Cumberland St., Sydney.

Behind these cold statistics for the Tellicherry men and women there were undoubtedly many forgotten tales of poverty, cruelty, hardship and lonely deaths especially among those who remained single, but they all contributed in their own small anonymous way to the development of the colony mainly through the dent of sheer physical labour. But a far greater contribution was to come from their descendants and from the children and in particular from the descendants of Michael and Mary Dwyer, John Mernagh and Mary Johnson, Hugh and Sarah Byrne and Arthur and Priscilla Devlin. In 1831 Arthur Devlin's eldest son James married Ann Hartigan and following her early death he then married Susannah Hughes of Richmond, the eldest daughter of the County Down schoolteacher Mathew Hughes. James Devlin, who had two children by his first wife and a further eleven by his second, became a very wealthy man, accumulating vast properties ranging from Wagga to Ganmain and his house at Ashfield has been preserved and is on the National Trust list of historic Australian homes. His younger brother Arthur Charles Devlin became a sea captain, explored the east coast of Australia and was the first colonist to sail up the Clarence River. Arthur

Devlin had named one of his daughters Anne and she married Michael Byrne who was a twin brother of William Byrne who had married Hugh Byrne's daughter Anne the only marriage connection between the five Wicklow families in the colony.

In the 1830s and 1840s the remainder of the large family of Hugh and Sarah Byrne married into the emerging merchant classes of the colony: Mary Byrne to John Hurley, a businessman who later represented Narellan as a Member of Parliament; Sarah Byrne to Charles Merritt of Cooma; James Byrne, who became a publican at Taralga, married Jane Partridge; Sylvester Byrne married Mary Ann Vardy and became one of the first 'overlanders' who travelled to Adelaide; Winifred Mary Byrne married Dr Isadore Blake who had a practice at Yass; Elizabeth Mary Byrne married John Henry Eccleston of Cottage Creek, Cooma; Bridget Byrne married Samuel Bowler, a race horse breeder and trainer from Liverpool and the youngest of the family, Rose Byrne married Joseph Tucker, a wine and spirits merchant from Sydney.

Hugh and Sarah Byrne continued to live at their farm in Airds and a further hundred acres was granted to them in 1835. Hugh Byrne died there aged about seventy in 1842 but Sarah Byrne lived on for another thirty years and her death in 1872 was reported in the local Freeman's Journal under the heading "Death Of A Very Old Colonist":

"On the 2nd instant a very old and respected resident of Campbelltown departed this life in her 98th year. Mrs. Sarah Byrne who emigrated to this colony with her husband Mr. Hugh Byrne in the year 1802, during the administration of Governor King; being at that time twenty eight years of age and a mother of four children, born in Ireland. Mrs. Byrne, it will be manifest, was not behind hand in obeying the Divine injunction, for she succeeded in rearing a large family consisting of five sons and nine daughters, the latter of whom were well and respectably married. The old lady had the satisfaction of seeing her grand children of the fourth generation before she exchanged a terrestrial for a more perfect and spiritual existence. Her great great grand children are eight in number. The writer of this notice had been for many years a near neighbour of Mrs. Byrne, and therefore had numerous opportunities of conversing with her on various subjects, but more particularly on those eventful and exciting incidents that occurred during the period antecedent to her departure from her native land. Up to a short time previous to her death her faculties were in full vigour; her memory remarkably tenacious, relating remote events which came within her own experience while in Ireland with a freshness and accuracy as to names and dates wonderful in a person of her advanced period of life. The wrongs of Ireland were her chief and most absorbing theme. Though passionately and deeply sympathising with her country people, her mind was entirely free from, and uncontaminated by, any unreasonable feeling of animosity towards Englishmen. She led a pious, useful life. Some time before her death, she received the full rights of her church. Her mortal remains were interred in the family vault at St. John's Church Campbelltown, and her funeral, which was a very large one, comprised persons of various denominations."

John Mernagh lived on until the age of eighty on the farm of his daughter Elizabeth, son in law Daniel Canvin and his ten grandchildren at Burland near Braidwood and died there in 1859.

The fortunes of the Dwyer family also became linked with the southern part of New South Wales as new land areas were rapidly opened up there in the 1830s. Mary Ann Dwyer married for a second time to a Wicklow man, Patrick Grace, who had arrived on the Countess of Harcourt in 1822 and they moved to Goulbourn where their four children were born. In 1837 Bridget Dwyer married John O'Sullivan, a native of Millcove, Berehaven, Co. Cork, who had come out on the Marquis of Huntley with her two brothers and became the first bank manager in the area of Goulbourn, and he also took on the frustrating task of looking after the tangled financial affairs of Fr Therry.

In 1838 John and Peter Dwyer, both of whom had married some years before, moved from Sydney to the area of Bungendore south of Goulbourn where a new settlement had been set up two thousand feet above sea level in the highlands of the Brindabella range close to the recently discovered Lake George. With them came their sister Esther who had married Owen Byrne, the son of another Wicklow man Andrew Byrne, and they set up the Harp Inn which was strategically situated outside the main Bungendore settlement in an area which led to a mountain pass and was also beside the local barracks. Unlike their father, they were hard-nosed business people and the inn flourished. By 1841, out of the forty one people living in Bungendore, twenty four were credited to be living in the Harp Inn. In 1840 John Dwyer had become a poundkeeper and with John O'Neill received a license also to run a Post Office. The Harp Inn later transferred to new premises in the village of Bungendore and eventually became the Lake George Hotel. Owen and Esther Byrne also set up their own establishment which was called Byrne's Inn and which provided them also with a good living. Richard Brooks, who was one of the magistrates who presided over the Liverpool Courthouse inquiry which led to the dismissal of Michael Dwyer as Chief Constable in 1820, had moved down to Bungendore in 1825 and held four thousand acres near the southern end of Lake George. His estate was later divided into two parts when his two daughters married Nathaniel Powell and a Captain Zouch. The Zouch half of the estate was called Ashby after Captain Zouch's birthplace, Ashby de la Zouch in England and when it was offered for sale in 1855 the thousand acre property was bought by John Dwyer whose original Harp Inn was on the edge of the property.

James Dwyer, who had been put in charge of the ill-fated Harrow Inn at the age of fifteen before owning his own premises, married Jane Perry from Co. Cavan at the age of forty one and they moved to the area of Lachlan where they reared a family of five children. Peter Bodicene, the husband of Eliza

Dwyer, died in the 1830s and she then married George Butler and reared a second family of two sons.

When Fr Therry moved to Hobart Mary Dwyer went to live with her daughter Bridget and son in law John O'Sullivan in Goulbourn and she also spent some time with the rest of her family in the region of Bungendore. She was aged about eighty when she died on June 12 1860. There is something of a mystery about her death as the address stated on her death certificate is Castlereagh St., Sydney. She seems to have been living on her own at the time and, with none of her immediate family present, the person who informed the authorities of her death was John Sheehy from Crown Street who is described as a friend. It is not clear if this proud independent-minded woman had decided to spend her last days in Sydney, and the funeral service in St. Mary's Cathedral on June 15th 1860 was, no doubt, conducted by her grandson Fr Michael Joseph Dwyer, a son of John Dwyer who had joined the Benedictine order and who had been ordained a year before, having adopted the religious name of John. Fr Dwyer was also one of the principal clergymen who received the remains of Fr Joseph Therry at St Mary's Church in Sydney in May 1864 when it was brought there from Balmain where he had spent his last years. The remains of Mary Dwyer were buried in Devonshire Cemetery in Sydney and, eighteen years later, in 1878, Fr Dwyer had the remains of Michael and Mary Dwyer transferred to a vault in the cemetery. Fr Dwyer had, by then, become Dean Dwyer and was one of the most prominent clerics in the area of Sydney, being the compiler of the Catholic Directory, a leading figure in the St. Joseph's Investment and Building Society and was also a member of the boards of Sydney Hospital, the Benevolent Hospital and Randwick Orphanage.

In 1868 there was a political sensation in New South Wales when Prince Alfred, Australia's first royal visitor, was shot in the back by a deranged Irishman, Henry James O'Farrell. Prince Alfred recovered quickly from his wound but O'Farrell was sentenced to be hanged. Fr Dwyer was chaplain in

Darlinghurst Jail at the time, attended to O'Farrell at the time of his execution and also thwarted the efforts of Henry Parkes, the colonial secretary, to stir up sectarian feelings by claiming that the attack was a Fenian plot to murder the prince. Fr Dwyer smuggled out of the jail a duplicate confession made by O'Farrell in which he denied any complicity with the Fenian movement and Fr Dwyer, for his troubles, was dismissed from his post as chaplain. Fr John Dwyer died, at the comparatively early age of fifty two, in 1884.

John Dwyer's only daughter Mary Ann became a Benedictine nun in the Subiaco convent in Parramatta as did Rose Dwyer the daughter of Peter Dwyer, while Ellen Dwyer, another daughter of Peter, became a nun in the order of the Sisters of Charity.

Following her marriage to Patrick Grace, Mary Ann Dwyer and her young son William Hughes Jnr moved to the area of Lachlan River where they ran a sheep farm and, later still, with their own three children they purchased a farm at Sheaoak Log in South Australia where Mary Ann Dwyer died in 1869.

John Dwyer, the owner of Ashby in Bungendore, divided his property into farms and allotments and sold out in 1872, just two years before his death, as two of his children were in religious orders and a third son, John Elicius Benedict who married Isabel Carrington, seems to have lost contact with his family. The house at Ashby and the largest segment of the divided estate was, however, bought by Patrick Doyle who was a grandnephew of Mary Dwyer (nee Doyle) who had come out to New South Wales from Wicklow in 1858 and his sons subsequently became well known farmers in the area. The Doyles retained possession of Ashby until the 1930s and, for many years, a life-size portrait of Michael Dwyer hung in the lounge of the house but is now believed to have been lost in a subsequent fire on the property.

A view of the Dwyer monument in Waverley Cemetery,
Sydney featuring the names of various Irish patriots.

11

As the nineteenth century progressed in Ireland the fame of
Michael Dwyer as a rebel leader and a peasant folk hero
grew in almost direct proportion to the increase in Irish
nationalism. The stories of his exploits during his five year span
as a fugitive in the Wicklow mountains became part of the oral
tradition, not only of his native county but in the rest of the country too, and although a certain re-evaluation of his patriotic
orthodoxy was engaged upon in the Wicklow mountains when
news filtered back that he had become a constable in New South
Wales, these reservations became almost a guarded secret to be
whispered around firesides at night, and were totally swallowed
up in the tide of nationalistic deification which occurred especially after the publication of T.D. Sullivan's poem, in the latter part
of the nineteenth century, which related, in stirring fashion,
Dwyer's escape from the cottage at Derrynamuck and which was
simply called 'Michael Dwyer':

"At length brave Michael Dwyer and his
undaunted men
Were scented o'er the mountains and tracked
into the glen;
The stealthy soldiers followed, with ready
blade and ball,

And swore to trap the outlaw that night in
   wild Imaal.
They prowled around the valley, and towards
   the dawn of day
Discovered where the faithful and fearless
   heroes lay;
Around the little cottage they formed in a ring,
And called out: "Michael Dwyer! Surrender to
   the King!"
Thus answered Michael Dwyer - "Into this
   house we came
Unasked by those who own; they cannot be to
   blame;
Then let those guiltless people, unquestioned,
   pass you through,
And when they've passed in safety, I'll tell you
   what we'll do."
'Twas done, "And now," said Dwyer, "your
   work you may begin;
You are a hundred outside - we're only four
   within;
We've heard your haughty summons, and this
   is our reply -
We're true United Irishmen - we'll fight until
   we die."

This poem was later complemented by a haunting ballad
set to music composed by Norman Reddin which became
equally popular and called The Three Flowers in which the
name of Michael Dwyer is linked with Wolfe Tone and
Robert Emmet:

"She took and kissed the first flower once
And sweetly said to me:
This flower came from the Wicklow hills,
Dew wet and pure, said she.

Its name is Michael Dwyer
The strongest flower of all;
But I'll keep it fresh beside my breast
Though all the world might fall."

The sentiments expressed in these verses with regard to Michael Dwyer were kept alive in Australia too by thousands of Irish emigrants who continued yearly to emigrate there and plans to commemorate the centenary of the 1798 Rising coincided with the announcement in Sydney in 1898 that the remains of those who had been buried in the Devonshire Street cemetery in Sydney were to be reinterred because of the fact that the Central Railway Station was to be built on that site. An appeal was then made by a committee headed by Dr Charles McCarthy to Irish people all over Australasia "to commemorate the honour and memory of the Wicklow chieftain, Michael Dwyer and all other insurgents whose remains lie here". A large sum of money was donated and the erection of the imposing monument at Waverley Cemetery began. On May 22nd 1898 the remains of Michael and Mary Dwyer were taken first to St Mary's Cathedral where a service was held and an oration was given by Cardinal Moran. After Mass the remains were taken around the aisles of the Cathedral on the shoulders of ten Irishmen and the subsequent funeral procession to Waverley Cemetery was of massive proportions.

The first carriages contained the grandchildren, great grandchildren and great great grandchildren of Michael and Mary Dwyer who had come to Sydney from all parts of Australia and these were followed by the Australian Holy Catholic Guilds, the band of the first regiment of the Hibernians and the Irish National Foresters. The hearse itself was drawn by six black horses wearing favours of blue and white on their headgear and green cloths with Irish emblems in gold at their sides. The glass sides of the hearse were taken out and the top converted into a canopy, topped by a Celtic Cross. The cross was capped with a laurel wreath and from its base ran garlands which capped the drapery of Irish flags and blue and white silk, representing the colours of both Ireland and Australia.

Over four hundred carriages and four thousand men marched in the procession and an estimated number of one hundred thousand people lined the funeral route. At Waverley Cemetery Dr Charles McCarthy gave the graveside oration in a manner which fitted the emotions of the occasion: "Of all that noble band of patriots who rose in dark and evil days to right their native land there is no one whose relics we could be more honoured and blest in possessing and reverencing than those of the central figure amongst the exiles here - the brave insurgent Chief of the Wicklow Mountains - Michael Dwyer". It was an extraordinary day for the Irish, for in addition to honouring the memory of Michael and Mary Dwyer, they were paying homage to the land of their forefathers and at the same time adverting to their own growing power, prosperity and influence in Australia. The imposing monument at Waverley Cemetery, which was completed two years later, is of white marble, bronze and mosaic and is also intended as a memorial to the memory of all Irish patriots. On the back wall are engraved the names of a great number of those connected with the struggle for Irish independence since 1798 but, sadly, there is no place for the names of John Mernagh, Hugh Byrne, Arthur Devlin or Martin Burke.

In Ireland monuments have been erected also in honour of Michael Dwyer and his 1798 comrades in the towns of Wicklow and Baltinglass while, at the roadside in Glenmalure, a simple granite monument bears both the names written in Irish of Michael Dwyer and Fiach McHugh O'Byrne, the famous sixteenth century chieftain. In 1948 the cottage at Derrynamuck, where Sam McAllister died and from which Dwyer managed to escape, was restored and declared a national monument by the President of Ireland Sean T. O'Ceallaigh, while in the same year Taoiseach Eamonn De Valera, during a visit to Australia, paid a visit to the Waverley Monument, as did President Patrick Hillery in 1985.

No folk hero like Michael Dwyer could ever live up to the heroic image and the sanitised reputation which an emerging nation bestowed posthumously on him. Dwyer himself had no unique political philosophy, he won no major battles, his ambitions always remained modest, but they were central to the aspirations of the generations of peasant farmers in Ireland who continued to struggle, throughout the nineteenth century, to win for themselves the basic right to own their own land holdings, to live in peace and to be able to provide a decent standard of living for themselves and their families. Many having failed were forced, following eviction, to emigrate to Australia where their lifelong ambitions were fulfilled. The legacy of Dwyer and his comrades are twofold: in Ireland, by holding out, against all odds, for five years in the Wicklow mountains, they gave a pride and a sense of self respect to those whose own hopes had been cruelly denied. In Australia, their major contribution has come in the shape of the generations of their families and descendants who have helped to shape their country and to create an individualistic nation which has always been acutely aware of the fundamental right of human freedom.

ACKNOWLEDGEMENTS

In the process of gathering research material for this book I received valuable and generous help from a great number of people:

Billy Byrne of Bolenaskea, Glenmalure, Co. Wicklow, was a living example of the oral tradition of history at its best. In Wicklow also I was helped by genealogist Paul Gorry from Baltinglass and Joan Kavanagh of the Wicklow Heritage Centre.

In Dublin I received every co-operation from Ann Neary of the State Paper's Office, Dublin Castle; from Martin Ryan of the National Library in Kildare Street and also from the staff of Trinity College, Dublin Castle State Apartments and Kilmainham Jail.

In London I received assistance from the staff of the British Library, the Public Record Office in Kew, the National Portrait Gallery and the Herefordshire Public Record Office.

Anne Maree Whitaker undertook much of the research work in Sydney and in particular helped to tease out the Dwyer bankruptcy details and located many of the Australian illustrations. My thanks also to the staff of the Mitchell Library and in particular to Jim Andrighetti, and to the staffs of the New South Wales Archives and the Land Titles Office. I received valuable information also from local historians Angela Young of Mossvale, Fr Brian Maher of Bungendore and Harry Quince and Bert Sheedy of Canberra who allowed me to read a typescript of the unpublished memoirs of James Sheedy; also to direct descendants of Michael Dwyer including Fr Gregory Beath of Canberra and Pat and Brian Donlan of Sydney. I received additional information also from Dr Clement Christesen of Melbourne University, a direct descendant of Hugh and Sarah Byrne, and from Dr Barry O'Dwyer of Macquarie University, Sydney. I would also like to acknowledge the pioneering genealogical work of George Cargeeg of Perth, another descendant of Michael Dwyer.

The illustrations in the book are published with the permission of the Office of Public Works, the National Library of Ireland, the Mitchell Library, Sydney, and the National Portrait Gallery, London. The photograph of Sarah Byrne was discovered by Dr Clement Christesen among family papers.

In RTE I received continuing support and advice from former RTE Chief Librarian Diarmaid Breathnach and from Mary Murphy, the Reference Librarian. I must also thank Billy Wall, Brian Mac Aongusa and Mike Murphy for their encouragement; John Cogan of Corporate Design supervised the layout and designed the cover, Mary Bracken took the photographs in Wicklow and Dublin, and Brian O'Higgins of KeySpeed dealt patiently and efficiently with the typed manuscript.

Finally I would like to thank my wife Terry for coping patiently with the 'long haul' to publication and who now claims to know a great deal more about the subject than I do.

SELECT BIBLIOGRAPHY

PART ONE

Annual Register 1804, 1805.

Cloney, Thomas:
A Personal Narrative of Wexford 1798; (Dublin 1833).
Devlin, Anne:
The Anne Devlin Jail Journal written by Luke Cullen,
Ed. J.J. Finnegan; (Cork 1968).
Dickson, Charles:
The Life of Michael Dwyer; (Dublin 1943).
Cullen, Luke:
Insurgent Wicklow; Ed. Myles V. Ronan; (Dublin 1948).
'98 in Wicklow; Ed. Myles V. Ronan; (Wexford 1938).
Landrett, Helen:
The Pursuit of Robert Emmett; (Dublin 1949).
McDonagh, Michael:
The Viceroy's Post Bag.
Madden, R.R.:
Ireland in '98.
Whitelaw, Rev. James:
Essay on the Population of Dublin; 1798.
West, William:
Directory and Picture of Cork; 1810.

Pamphlets:

Mason, St. John:
To Pedro Zendono - Inquisitor of Kilmainham; 1807.
Pedro Revividus - Prison Abuses in Ireland; 1810.
Tandy, James:
(1) An Appeal To The Public
(2) An accurate and impartial report of the action
brought against Brabazon Morris; (Dublin 1807).

Trevor, Edward:
  Dr Trevor's Statement - a vindication of himself;
  (Dublin 1809c).
Fitzpatrick, James:
  Thoughts On A Penitentiary; 1790.

Newspapers:

Freemans Journal, Dublin Journal, Dublin Evening Post, Belfast
  Newsletter, London Times, Cork Mercantile Chronicle,
  Waterford Mirror, Ennis and Clare Advertiser, New Cork
  Evening Post, Limerick Chronicle.

Documents and Letters:

State Paper Office, Dublin; Public Record Office, Kew
  Gardens; Herefordshire Public Records Office - papers
  of William Wickham.

PART TWO

Bateson, Charles:
  The Convict Ships (1787-1868); Sydney 1974.
Birch, A, and Macmillan, D.:
  The Sydney Scene (1788-1960).
Clarke, C.M.H.:
  History of Australia, Vol. 1. From the Earliest Times
  To The Age of Macquarie; Melbourne 1962.
Clune, Frank:
  The Norfolk Island Story; Sydney 1967.
Costello, Con:
  Botany Bay; Dublin & Cork 1987.
Cunningham, Peter:
  Two Years In New South Wales; 2 Vols; London 1827.
Ellis, M.M.:
  Lachlan Macquarie; Sydney 1947.

Giblin, R.W.:
The Early Years in Tasmania, 2 Vols; London 1838.
Harris, Alexander:
Settlers And Convicts; London 1847.
Kiernan, Colm:
Ireland and Australia; Dublin 1984.
Kiernan, T.J.:
Transportation From Ireland to Sydney 1791-1816;
Canberra 1954.
Mackaness, C.J.:
Life of Vice-Admiral Bligh, 2 Vols.; London 1931.
Macquarie, Lachlan:
Journal of A Tour of New South Wales 1810;
Ed. Shepherd and Newman.
O'Brien, Eris:
The Life and Letters of Archpriest J.J. Therry; Sydney
1922.
The Dawn of Catholicism in Australia, Volume One;
Sydney 1928.
O'Farrell, Patrick:
The Irish in Australia; Sydney 1986.
Shaw, A.G.L.:
Convicts and Colonies; London 1966.
Wentworth, W.C.:
A statistical, historical and political description of the
colony of New South Wales; London 1819.

Publications:

Chords From The Harp, by Fr Brian Maher.
Ripe For The Harvest, by Angela Young.

Newspapers:

Sydney Gazette (Microfilm - Mitchell Library, Sydney).

Census:

General Muster of New South Wales 1814, published by A.B.G.R. - Australian Biographical and Genealogical Records; Sydney 1987.
General Muster 1825; Public Record Office, London.
Census 1828; Ed. Sainty, M. and Johnson, K.; Sydney 1980, (copy in State Papers Office, Dublin).

Reports:
The proceedings of the 1807 Trial; Microfilm - City Archives, Sydney.
1821 Liverpool Enquiry; Microfilm, City Archives, Sydney.
Wentworth Papers; Mitchell Library, Sydney.
New South Wales Historical Records, Vols. I-VII; 1787-1811.
Proceedings of A General Court Martial of Lieut. Col. George Johnston on a charge of mutiny. Reported by M. Bartnum; London 1811.
Report of the Select Committee of Transportation; 1812.
The Inquiry into the Affairs of New South Wales, by Mr J.T. Bigge, 1819-1822.

APPENDIX ONE

Ships Indent - Tellicherry, August 1805

MALE PRISONERS

Antrim (1): Joseph Kelso (March 1803 - 7 years).
Armagh (1): Joseph Carlahan (April 1805 - 7 years).
Carlow (7): Richard Doyle (1803 - Life), Myles Dolan (1803 - 7 years), John Ryan (1803 - Life), Pat Mulhall (1803 - 7 years), John Fitzpatrick, Hugh Byrne, Laurence Fenlon (1804 - Life).
Clare (4): Maurice Flahavan, Jer Griffin or Griffith (1803 - 7 years), Pat O'Meara (1803 - Life), James Sheedy (or McNamara) (1804 - Life).
City of Cork (1): Richard Dooley (Spring 1805 - 7 years).
Co. Cork (1): Darby Donovan (Spring 1805 - Life).
Down (1): Michael Maguire (October 1803 - Life).
Co. Dublin (24): Thomas Price (June 1804 - 7 years), William Lawler (August 1802 - Life), Daniel Kelly and Darby Murray (Feb 1803 - Life), John Kearney (Feb 1803 - Life), John Nowlan (July 1803 - 7 years), Thomas Shaughnessy and John Hughes (July 1803 - Life), John McCabe and Pat McMahon (July 1804 - Life), Henry Kelly (November 1804 - Life), Lawrence Townsend (June 1804 - 7 years), Arthur Doyle (July 1803 - 7 years), James Griffin (October 1802 - Life), Robert Fox (December 1803 - Life), Pat Tiernan (July 1803 - 7 years), Owen Clarke (November 1804 - Life), Edward Doyle (July 1803 - 7 years), Peter White (July 1803 - Life), Roger Keogh (May 1803 - 7 years), James Williams (December 1803 - 7 years), Thomas Cuff (July 1805 - 7 years), Tim Murphy (July 1805 - Life), James Magrath (June 1805 - 7 years).
City of Dublin (22): Lawrence Bailey and Walter Clare (Sept 1803 - Life), Bartholomew Tiernan (January 1804 - Life), Laurence Harman (July 1803 - Life), John Connolly (February 1805 - 7 years), Henry Austen (April 1805 - 7 years), John Reynolds (June 1805 - 7 years), Lawrence Magee (July 1802 - Life),

Bernard Brennan (July 1803 - Life), John Reilly (May 1804 - 7 years), William Ward (August 1804 - 7 years), Michael Kenna (January 1805 - 7 years), Daniel Leary (March 1803 - 7 years), Daniel Sleaven (November 1804 - 7 years), John O'Neill (July 1804 - 7 years), John Mooney, Thomas Holden, John Shannon, Hugh Woods, Francis Darby, Daniel Rowson and Michael Coughlan (June 1805 - 7 years).

Kildare (14): John Cogan (Summer 1802 - Life), Michael Magrath, Patrick Gore, Pat Farrell (Spring 1803 - 7 years), Stephen Hyland (Spring 1803 - Life), Martin Dogherty (Summer 1803 - Life), Philip Ennis (Spring 1804 - 7 years), Pat Masterson and Denis Farrell (Spring 1804 - 7 years), Edward Francis (Spring 1805 - Life), Hugh Conlan (Spring 1805 - 7 years), Lawrence Fox (Spring 1803 - 7 years), James Behan (Summer 1802 - 7 years), Christopher Gallagher (Lent 1803 - 7 years).

Kilkenny (7): John Flin (Flynn) (1802 - 7 years), Nicholas Lacey (1803 - 7 years), Denis Ryan and Pat Harris (1803 - Life), James Johnson and Pat Heneran or Kirwan (1804 - 7 years), Barnaby Butler (1804 - Life).

Kings Co. (Laois) (1): James Hutchinson (1805 - Life).

City of Limerick (5): James Malone and James Henchy (1802 - 7 years), Michael Fitzgerald and John Redmond (1803 - 7 years), Pat Murnane (1804 - Life).

Co. Limerick (6): Pat Keough (1802 - 7 years), John Mortill (1803 - 7 years), Pat Hogan and Pat Sweeney (1803 - Life), Edmund Burke and Malachy Ryan (1804 - Life).

Londonderry (1): Edward Jones (Spring 1803 - 7 years).

Longford (2): William Scott (Spring 1804 - 7 years), John Murphy (Spring 1805 - 7 years).

Mayo (6): Thomas Gibbins (1803 - Life), Laughlin Monaghan (1805 - Life), John Jones (1803 - 7 years), Pat Keenan (1804 - 7 years), John Dent (1804 - 7 years), Thomas Tighe (1805 - 7 years).

Roscommon (1): Bryan Gannon (Spring 1803 - Life).

Tipperary (13): Pierce Condon (1803 - Life), Pat Dawson and Thomas Meagher (1803 - Life), Arthur Halfpenny (1803 - Life),

Thomas Hughes, Denis Sullivan, John Quinn and Pat Kenna (1804 - 7 years), Edmund White, William Halfpenny, James Halfpenny and Pat Meagher (1804 - Life), Pat Cleary (1805 - 7 years).
Waterford (1): Charles McMahon (1804 - 7 years).
Westmeath (1): Pat Cox (Spring 1805 - 7 years).
Wicklow (7): John Bryan (Spring 1803 - 7 years), John Reynolds (Spring 1803 - Life), Michael Dwyer, John Merna, Arthur Develin, Hugh Byrne and Martin Burke (Note: in the ship's indent they are listed as Co. Dublin and as being prisoners for life, June 1805).

FEMALE PRISONERS

Armagh (1): Bridget McMahon (July 1804 - 7 years).
Clare (2): Margaret Hayes and Elizabeth Kennedy (1803 - 7 years).
City of Dublin (21): Mary Barry and Catherine McLaughlin (January 1803), Mary Rice (Jan 1803 - 7 years), Mary Bradshaw (September 1802 - 7 years), Catherine Brady (June 1803 - 7 years), Mary McNulty (June 1805 - 7 years), Sarah Cooksey (October 1803 - 7 years), Anastasia Shanley (October 1803 - 7 years), Mary Kennedy, Catherine Hill and Margaret O'Brien (January 1804 - 7 years), Mary Smith (Jan 1804 - 7 years), Mary Gough (May 1804 - 7 years), Mary Byrne (March 1804 - 7 years), Ann Mathews (May 1804 - 7 years), Eleanor Burke (January 1804 - 7 years), Eliza Cooper (August 1804 - 7 years), Mary Lamb (September 1804 - 7 years), Mary Shannon (December 1804 - 7 years), Bridget Johnson (Feb 1805 - 7 years), Mary Kelly and Catherine Finnis (Fynnes) (October 1803).
Kerry (1): Mary Grady (1804 - Life).
City of Limerick (5): Catherine Hinchy (1802 - 7 years), Honora Mollowny (Moloney) (1803 - 7 years), Bridget Shea (1803 - 7 years), Catherine Leeson (1803 - 7 years), Eleanor Leonard (1803 - 7 years).

Meath (2): Mary Johnson and Eleanor Tyrrell (Spring 1805 - 7 years).

Monaghan (1): Mary Begley (Spring 1804 - 7 years).

Londonderry (1): Ann Forbes (Spring 1803).

Westmeath (1): Mary Fagan or Nagle (Spring 1805 - 7 years).

APPENDIX TWO

Tellicherry transportees listed in the 1825 General Muster for New South Wales

MALE

Carlow (4): Myles (Michael) Dolan - Landholder Liverpool. Lawrence Fenlon - married, living in Parramatta - Government Employee. Pat Mulhall, Cowkeeper, Sydney. Sons, William 17, George 15, Patrick 12, Thomas 9, John 7, Michael 5. John Ryan, Labourer.

Clare (3): Jeremiah Griffin - Employee of Michael Hogan. Pat O'Meara - Government Employee. James Sheedy - Landholder, Liverpool.

Co. Dublin (4): Arthur Doyle - Employee William Klensendorlffe, Camden. Daniel Kelly, Landholder Wilberforce; two sons, Thomas 11, Charles 9. William Lawler - Benevolent Asylum, Sydney. Lawrence Townsend - Labourer, Windsor.

City of Dublin (4): Darby Murray - Landholder, Campbellstown. Daniel Rowson - Labourer, Campbellstown. John Mooney - Labourer, Richmond. Henry Austen - Publican, Sydney.

Kildare (4): John Cogan - Landholder, Bringelly. Denis Farrell - Labourer, Parramatta. Patrick Gore - Landholder. 2 sons 1 daughter. Michael Magrath - employed by Mr Trotter, Appin.

Kilkenny (1): Nicholas Lacey - Landowner, N. Boundary.

City of Limerick (2): James Malone - Labourer, Sydney. Michael Fitzgerald - Government Employee, Sydney. 1 son, 1 daughter, Michael and Ellen age 15.

Co. Limerick (2): Edmund Burke - Landholder, Campbellstown. Wife Esther born in colony. 1 son 2 daughters.

FEMALE

Clare (2): Margaret Hayes - Benevolent Asylum, Sydney. Elizabeth Kennedy - Government Employee, Port Macquarie.

City of Dublin (5): Anastasia Shanley - wife of William Cook,

Parramatta. Catherine McLaughlin - wife of Thomas Gorman. Mary Lamb - wife of Francis Wild, Sydney. Catherine Fynnes - wife of Nicholas Garrigan, Windsor.

City of Limerick (2): Bridget Shea - wife of William (Michael) Fitzgerald, Sydney. Charlotte (Catherine) Henchy - wife of James Lennox.

Meath (2): Mary Johnson - Resident, Liverpool (with John Mernagh). Eleanor Tyrrell - 3 sons, George Tyrrell - carpenter, Sydney, William Tyrrell, carpenter, Sydney, Thomas Tyrrell age 12, Orphan School, Sydney.

Monaghan (1): - Mary Begley - wife of Mc Teague, Argyle.

Westmeath (1): - Mary Neil (Nagle) - wife of Pinkerton, Liverpool. *Also listed* Mary Donnelly - Female Factory, Parramatta. Elizabeth Fitzgerald - wife of John Power, Mary Gillespie - Campbellstown, wife of Thomas Kelly, Parramatta, 2 daughters Catherine 9, Mary 4. Pat (?) Hogan, servant to Mr Johnson (?), Minto.

Londonderry (1): Edward Jones - Blacksmith.

Longford (2): William Scott - Labourer, Parramatta. John Murphy - Landholder, Mt. Evan.

Mayo (1): Patrick Keena (Kenna) - Labourer, Windsor.

Tipperary (3): Patrick Maher - Labourer, Sydney. Thomas Maher - Labourer, Sydney. Patrick Cleary - Stonemason, Wilberforce.

Westmeath (1): Pat Cox - Employee of Mr Beckford, Sydney.

Wicklow (4): John Bryan - Employee of Mr King, Melville. Hugh Byrne - Landholder, Campbellstown. Sarah Byrne and family. Martin Burke - Landholder, Sydney (?). John Mernagh - Landholder, Liverpool. Michael and Mrs Dwyer and James 20, Bridget 16, Eliza 12 - Landholder. John Reynolds - Settler, Liverpool. There were two John Reynolds on board the Tellicherry from Wicklow and Dublin and there are also Tellicherry listings for Richard Webb - a discharged soldier, Thomas Cargill - a labourer in Parramatta, Hugh Brown, a landholder in Campbellstown and Daniel Brown, who was killed by aborigines 1824. These were probably crew members or members of the military guard.

APPENDIX THREE

1828 Census: List of surviving Tellicherry transportees

MALE

Carlow (2): Lawrence Fenlon (Finlay), Prisoners Barracks, Liverpool. Patrick Mulhall - married to Rachael Mulhall. John Ryan age 60 - Labourer to Thomas Gunn - Pitt Town.
Clare (2): Jeremiah Griffin age 50 - Carpenter to Michael Ryan - Botany Bay. James Sheedy age 47, Landholder - Cabramatta, married to Jane Sheedy (nee Black) age 40. Holding: 14 acres, 10 cleared, 10 cultivated.
City of Dublin (2): Edward Doyle age 40 - lives with Patrick Martin, Airds. John Reilly (Riley) age 67, Labourer - U. Richmond.
Co. Dublin (7): Daniel Kelly age 48, Landholder, Wilberforce, married to Margaret Kelly (came out on the Broxbonbury). 2 sons - Thomas and Charles. Holding 50 acres, 30 acres cleared, 14 acres cultivated, 2 horses, 38 cattle. Thomas Cuffe: age 78. Labourer. John Kearney: age 70 - Gardener to Thomas Bray. Owen (John) Clarke age 69, invalid, lives with Martin Burke. Thomas Shaughnessy age 49, Cabinet Maker, Hunter St., Sydney (wife came out on the Experiment 1804), 4 children, Jane 7, Ann 5, Charles 3, Theresa 1. Darby Murray - Settler - Airds, age 50, married to Eleanor Murray (nee Burke) age 48. Holding: 806 acres, 110 acres cleared, 50 acres cultivated - 5 horses - 200 cattle.
Kildare (2): Patrick Gore age 52 - Settler Castle Hill - 2 horses (no further details given). Philip Ennis - Settler, Airds. Holding: 40 acres, 36 acres cleared, 25 cultivated, 12 sheep.
Kilkenny (2): Nicholas Lacey, age 51. Settler, Field of Mars. Married to Ann Lacey (age 34). (Earl Cornwallis - no children listed). Barnaby Butler, age 56. Farmer. Holding: 4 acres, 4 acres cleared, 4 acres cultivated.
City of Limerick (2): James Malone, age 60. Labourer to John

Connell, Holdsworthy. Pat Murnane, age 53 - Farmer, N. Richmond. Holding 50 acres - 16 cleared - 6 cultivated - 2 horses - 95 cattle.

Co. Limerick (1): Edmund Burke, age 40. Farmer, Illawarra. Holding: 50 acres, 50 acres cleared, 6 acres cultivated - 4 cattle. Wife Esther age 24 - born in colony, 3 children, Eleanor 7, Margaret 5, John 2.

Longford (1): William Scott, age 52 - Labourer, Parramatta.

Mayo (2): Patrick Kenna (Keenan) Labourer with Pat Murnane, N. Richmond. Lawrence (Laughlin) Monaghan, age 75, Landholder, Cabramatta, married to Ann Monaghan (F.S. Friends) age 60, no children listed.

Tipperary (1): Patrick Maher (Meagher), age 53, Tailor - 2 sons Thomas 18, John 15, both tenant farmers of Sol Levy.

Westmeath (1): Pat Cox, age 42 - Port Macquarie.

Wicklow (4): John Bryan, age 70, Labourer with Ann Curtis. Hugh Byrne, age 50, Campbellstown, and family. Holding 210 acres - 163 cleared, 66 cultivated - 6 horses - 236 cattle. Martin Burke - tenant - Pitt. John Mariner (Mernagh), age 60 (?) - shoemaker, lives with James Sheedy.

There are no less than three John Reynolds listed with Tellicherry connections: John Reynolds, age 70, Lodger, with Thomas Ward, Princes St. Sydney. John Reynolds, age 59, Householder - Sussex St., Sydney. John Reynolds, age 50, Butcher - Cabramatta. (It is possible that the first named was an ex-member of the Tellichery crew). Patrick Hagan, ex-Tellicherry guard, is listed as living at Hyde Pk Barracks, Sydney.

Also listed are Henry Ashebey, servant to Rev Samuel Marsden, Richard Webb, age 68 and Douglas McKellar, both labourers at Windsor and John Mercener age 75, shearer to Mr Jameson. These were, presumably, ex-crew members or members of the military guard on board the Tellicherry.

There is a listing also for an Andrew Mathews age 40 who with Ann Mathews worked for John Lacey but at a different farm in Camden. John Lacey lived in Cumberland St. Sydney.

FEMALE

City of Dublin (7): Ann Brown (nee Mary Smith) age 56, married to Thomas Brown labourer - Windsor (no children listed). Ann Mathews, age 40, formerly married to Constable E. Tutty, a dairymaid to John Lacey, Bemblow. Anastasia Cooke (nee Shanley) age 38, married to William Cook age 66, Bricklayer, Parramatta (no children listed). Eleanor Burke, age 48, married to Darby Murray, settler, Airds. Mary Lamb - housekeeper to Frank Wilde, Philip St. Sydney. Catherine Gorman, age 45 - (nee McLaughlin) wife of Thomas Gorman age 52 (Rolla 1802), Landholder. Holding: 100 acres, 64 acres cleared, 39 acres cultivated, 24 cattle. Three children, Ann 22, Thomas Jnr. 8, Jane 5. Mary Kelly - age 43 - Fruiterer in Parramatta.

City of Limerick (2): Mary Rice (living in 1814 with Hugh Mulhall) - patient, Lunatic Asylum, Liverpool. Catherine Hinchy (Inch), age 48, Laundress to Jer. Leonard, Cumberland St., Sydney.

Meath(1): Eleanor Grant (nee Tyrrell) married to Michael Grant (Portland 1807) - shopkeeper Georges St. Sydney.

Other Tellicherry listings: Mary Golledge age 46 - married to Thomas Golledge, Constable, Windsor (1790 Neptune) - four children, George, Gemima, Thomas and Isaac. Bridget Fitzgerald (?) age 68 - Hunters Hill. Mary Donnelly age 41 - Female Factory, Parramatta. Abigail Kelly age 50 (not listed on ships indent) - Householder, Parramatta. Mary Mc Donnell age 51 - Benevolent Asylum, Sydney. Elizabeth Power (nee Fitzgerald) age 30 - married to John Power age 38 (Three Bees 1814), Labourer, Hunters Hill. Four daughters - Mary 10, Catherine 8, Elizabeth 5 and Eleanor 1. (Note: If she did come on the Tellicherry she would have been seven years old. She was, possibly, a daughter of Bridget O'Shea who married Michael Fitzgerald (Tellicherry) and was credited with having three children in the 1814 Census). Catherine Kelly age 23, Housemaid to Jesse Reans, Philip St. Sydney. If her age is correct she was born in 1805, the same year that the Tellicherry left Ireland. She may have been the daughter of Abigail Kelly.

APPENDIX FOUR

The Family of Michael and Mary Dwyer (nee Doyle)

1. Mary Ann - born 1799, Wicklow. Married (1) Patrick Hughes, Dublin, c1826 - 1 son; (2) Patrick Grace, New South Wales - 2 sons, 1 daughter. Died 1869.
2. John - born 2-1-1801, Wicklow, married Ann Kennedy 1832, 2 sons, 1 daughter. Died 1882.
3. Peter - born 1801 Wicklow, married Mary White (c1835), New South Wales, 10 sons, 1 daughter. Died 1876.
4. Esther - born 1804 Wicklow, married Owen Byrne 1833, 1 son, 3 daughters. Died 1874.
5. James - born 1807, New South Wales, married Jane Perry 1847, 1 son, 4 daughters. Died 1874.
6. Bridget - born 1808, Van Diemens Land, married John O'Sullivan 1837, 1 son, 3 daughters. Died 1878.
7. Eliza - born c1812 New South Wales, married (1) Peter Bodicene 1827, 1 son, 1 daughter; (2) George Butler 1837, 2 sons. Died 1888.

APPENDIX FIVE

The Family of Hugh and Sarah Byrne (nee Dwyer)

1. Philip - born c1798, Wicklow, reared by Sarah Byrne's parents, Dublin. Remained in Ireland.
2. Michael - born 1800, Wicklow, married Jane Warby, Campbellstown, 1829, 6 sons, 4 daughters. Died 1879.
3. Rose - born 1803, Wicklow, married William Craft, Campbellstown, 1 son, 1 daughter. Died 15-3-1825.
4. Anne - born 1807 c.Jan, aboard the Tellicherry, married (1) William Byrne, Campbellstown, 2 sons, 4 daughters; (2) Joseph Byrne, 2 sons; (3) Patrick McKeogh, Yass, 1855, no family. Died 1864.
5. Catherine Agnes - born 1807, Liverpool, New South Wales, married John Keighran, Campbellstown, 1825, 5 sons, 10 daughters. Died 1859.
6. Charles - born 1809, Liverpool, married Elizabeth McCarthy 1833, 1 son. Died 1873.
7. Bridget - born 1811, Liverpool, married Samuel Bowler 1829, Liverpool, N.S.W., 3 sons. Died 1859.
8. Mary - born 1813, Liverpool, married John Hurley, M.P., Narellan, 3 sons, 3 daughters. Died 1859.
9. Sarah - born 1816, Liverpool, married Henry Charles Merritt, Cooma, 1 son, 2 daughters. Died 1850.
10. James - born 1818, Airds, married Jane Partridge, 1 son. Died 1852.
11. Sylvester - born 1820, Airds. Married Mary Ann Vardy 1842, Cambellstown, 2 sons, 6 daughters. (Died?)
12. Winifred Mary - born 1822, Airds, married Dr. Isadore Blake, Yass, 1843, 6 sons, 4 daughters. Died 1892.
13. Elizabeth Mary - born 1824, Airds, married Henry John Eccleston, Cooma, 3 sons, 3 daughters. Died 1893.
14. Rose (2nd) - born 1826, Airds, married Joseph Tucker 1853, 2 sons, 3 daughters. Died 1864.

INDEX

Sheehy John, 253
Sheridan Brinsley Richard, 122
Short, Captain, 158
Simmons James, Lieut., 169
Simpson (Jailer), 97, 99
Sirr Henry, Major, 21, 27, 71, 103
Slater Edward Dr., 226, 227
Sligo Marquis of, 40
Small Thomas, 248
Smith Mary, 219, 251
Somerville Marcus, Sir, 85, 86
Sorrell William, 253
Squires James, 163, 170, 171, 187, 207
Stacey Denis, 177, 178, 189
Stewart, Surgeon General, 97
Stockdale John, 122
Stroud William Hawkes Sgt., 177,
183, 186, 220, 238
Stroud Ann, 238, 239, 244-246
Sullivan, T.D, 257

Tandy James, 84,-87, 96, 97, 105, 121
Tandy Napper, 81, 85
Tennison, Captain, 47
Therry Joseph, Fr., 226, 228, 236, 244,
254, 256
Thompson Andrew, 161, 170, 178
Tolan Michael, 220
Tone Wolfe, 81, 260
Trevor Edward, 35, 58, 59, 64, 68, 73,
80, 83, 85, 88, 90-108, 114, 118, 119,
122, 123, 202
Trotler Sergeant, 214
Troy, Dr., 34, 226
Tucker Joseph, 249
Tutty, Constable, 219, 251
Tyrrell Eleanor, 136, 219, 252

Vardy Mary Ann, 249
Vassan Colonel, 22
Vensiggort Nicholas, 106

Warby Jane, 247
Wentworth D'Aray, 208, 235, 236
Wentworth Willian Charles, 218

White Andrew, 232, 233
White Edward, 98
White Luke, 96
Wholloham John, 193
Wickham William, 14, 27, 28, 32, 34,
35, 44, 45, 50, 60-63, 67, 74-77, 83, 86,
102, 122, 123
Wild Francis, 246
Williams Henry 220
Wilson James, 78
Windham William, 41, 169, 190, 195
Wolfe Elizabeth, 25, 26
Wolfe Richard, Rev., 25
Wrotlesley John, Sir, 79

Yorke Charles Philip (see Earl of
Hardwicke)
Yorke Charles 36, 40, 42

Zonek, Captain, 255